MW00582564

George Washington's Religion

George Washington's Religion

The Faith of the First President

Stephen J. Vicchio

Foreword by Thomas L. Benson

WIPF & STOCK · Eugene, Oregon

GEORGE WASHINGTON'S RELIGION
The Faith of the First President

Wipf & Stock
An Imprint of Wipf and Stock Publishers
199 W. 8th Ave., Suite 3
Eugene, OR 97401

www.wipfandstock.com

PAPERBACK ISBN: 978-1-5326-8839-3
HARDCOVER ISBN: 978-1-5326-8840-9
EBOOK ISBN: 978-1-5326-8841-6

Manufactured in the U.S.A.   AUGUST 9, 2019

To Bootsie, who gave me life and so much more.

Contents

Foreword

NO MAJOR FIGURE IN American history has enjoyed greater measures of reverence, even awe, than George Washington. The less-than-abundant historical materials relating to his early life, his relatively light literary output, and his famously taciturn style have left later generations ample opportunity to fill in the blanks with imaginative hagiography. Mythology and hyperbole notwithstanding, there can be little doubt that Washington deserves to be called the "father of his country" and a place of honor as one of the noblest and most accomplished of the nation's founders.

The notion that character is destiny pertains not just to individual lives but to the fate of nations and empires as well. The remarkable career of the United States owes in large measure to men and women of exemplary character who have played crucial roles at decisive points in our history. It is both fascinating and important for us to examine the lives of these leaders and to learn what we can about the sources of their self-understanding and the principles that guided their lives.

While the concepts of moral character and religious devotion are often associated, they are independent notions. A person may have little religious conviction, but nevertheless manifest outstanding moral character, and, correspondingly, if somewhat less often, a person may have deep religious convictions, but exhibit less-than-sterling character. Professor Vicchio's important study of Washington's religious beliefs and practices establishes that there was a very close relationship between his moral character and his religious life. George Washington's religious convictions shaped both how he understood the world and his sense of vocation, in private life and as the nation's leader in war and peace.

The formation of Washington's mature religious views was a complex process, encompassing both the religious instruction in his childhood, the influence of his mother, his personal study of the Bible, the Anglican churches in Virginia that he attended, his interaction with the philosophical ideas of the late Enlightenment—the somewhat-thin and borrowed zeitgeist that shaped the views of a number of his close associates, including Jefferson, Madison, and Franklin—and his exceptionally rich and varied life in military combat and revolutionary struggle. Professor Vicchio pays close attention to each of these elements, drawing on the best and latest scholarly work on Washington and his times.

As if anticipating the questions of an especially perceptive reader, Professor Vicchio reviews and summarizes Washington's ideas concerning the nature and existence of God, the role of the Bible and prayer in everyday life, and how to make sense of suffering and evil in the light of a benevolent divine providence. Vicchio's treatment of these issues is almost certainly unprecedented in depth and detail. Beyond these large, foundational questions, there are the equally important questions concerning what Washington's beliefs led him to think and do about the urgent and complicated moral problems he faced: war, religious bigotry, slavery, and the responsibilities of leadership. Here again, Professor Vicchio proves to be a thorough and judicious guide, helping the reader make sense of the complex dilemmas Washington faced and the difficult, not-always-perfect decisions he made.

Washington understood himself to be a Christian, and his ambition was clearly to be true and honorable in his religious life. At the same time, as Professor Vicchio notes, Washington practiced tolerance toward other religious traditions that were being practiced in the country of his time, including Judaism and Islam. He was equally tolerant with respect to the substantial divisions among contemporary Christians, and he attempted to foster peaceful relations between Roman Catholics and the diverse Protestant strands within late-eighteenth and early-nineteenth-century Protestantism. In these views, as in many others, Washington was considerably ahead of his time, setting a high standard for interfaith understanding that subsequent generations of Americans would (and still) struggle to match.

In this highly informative and unique portrait of Washington and his religious values, Professor Vicchio provides useful insights into the wellsprings of our first president's character and record of service. Careful and useful historical scholarship should strive to meet at least three important standards. The work should be clear, comprehensive, and compelling. Professor Vicchio's study of Washington and his religious roots meets all three of these standards. Veteran academics and amateur students of American history will find the writing lucid and the arguments accessible. As for comprehensiveness, few clues to Washington's religious background and its significance in his life are left unexamined. For example, until Professor Vicchio raised the issue, it seemed certain that no other scholar has attempted to understand how Washington reconciled his religious convictions with his all-too close and personal experiences with suffering and evil. As for the third standard, if the question to be answered is "Were George Washington's religious background and convictions the decisive factors in shaping his truly remarkable career as both a military and a political leader?," Professor Vicchio has provided a powerful and convincing case in the affirmative.

—THOMAS L. BENSON, PHD

Acknowledgements

THIS BOOK COMES AFTER countless discussions with my students, colleagues, friends, and family members. I must acknowledge the help and assistance from Dr. Tom Benson, my undergraduate mentor at the University of Maryland, who wrote the foreword. For my friend at Saint Mary's Seminar, Father Paul Maillet; Father Brown, the rector and president at Saint Mary's; the gang at Sab's; Vince, Lisa, Phil, Larry, Pietro, Rocco, Scoop, Lynn, and Lauren; my friends at Troia's Cafe, Carol, Lisa, Joe; mi amiga linda Irene; and my friendship with, and encouragement from, my dear friend Marguerite Villa Santa, I am deeply thankful. I am grateful for the friendships of the library staff at St. Mary's, Tom and Suzi, the dedication and care of Matthew Wimer and Caleb Shupe at Wipf and Stock Publishers, and my friend, Linda Canestraro. But, most of all, I must thank my family, Myra "Bootsie" Vicchio, to whom this book is dedicated; my wife Sandra and son Jack, my major intellectual companions these days; and my in-laws, Tom and Mary Lee Parsons, who always have encouraged my scholarly and writing life.

Introduction

IN THIS STUDY, WE hope to explore the religious life of the first President of the United States, George Washington. We will begin this exploration by making some observations about Washington's earliest blushes with religion, mostly with the American Anglican Church. As we shall see in Section I of this work, Washington's parents, Augustine and Mary, were devout Anglicans; in fact, Augustine served on the vestry of their church on Pohick Creek, in Northern Virginia.[1]

After describing the early life of the Washington in Virginia, we shall concentrate in Section I on Augustine and his family. In that regard, we will examine George Washington's early schooling, his penchant for copying poetry, and his fondness of mathematics that, later on, aided him in his surveying career, beginning at age sixteen. We also will describe and discuss the two Anglican churches that the Washington family attended in George's youth, and later, as we shall see, he too served as a vestryman in the same Pohick church, as did his father.[2] The other Anglican church Washington attended as a child was Saint George's Parish in Fredericksburg, Virginia, across the Rappahannock River. Indeed, later in life, Mary Ball Washington lived just a few blocks from that church.

As part of Section I, we also will explore the "Thirty-Nine Articles of Faith" to which adherents of the Anglican Church were pledged to believe in Washington's youth.[3] Additionally, in Section I, we will make some observations about a book called *The Rules of Civility*, by which George Washington learned the interworking of the Virginia gentry.[4] We also will show other books owned by Washington's mother that she appears to have employed in the early religious education of her children and grandchildren—books like those by Matthew Hale, Thomas Comber, John Scott, and James Hervey, as we shall see, were all used by Mary Ball Washington to educate her children.

Finally, we will show that Washington's brother Lawrence married into the Fairfax family, and that Lord Fairfax was a mentor of sorts to the first

President, particularly in regard to the life of a Virginia gentleman, as well as a sponsor for George's early career as a surveyor, beginning around 1748.[5]

In Section II of this study, we shall describe and discuss what George Washington had to say about God. We make eleven separate claims about what George Washington believed about the Divine, or what he usually called "Good Providence."[6] We also will show that Washington used more than a hundred synonyms for the Divine, and that the first President assented to the ideas that God is all-good, all-knowing, and all-powerful. We also will show in Section II of this essay that Washington believed that God created the universe *ex nihilo*, that is, out of nothing; and that Washington, unlike the deists of his time, believed that God acts in history.

In Section III of this work, we shall explore George Washington's uses of, and relations to, the Bible. There we will show nearly four dozen examples where the first President appears to have directly quoted from Holy Scripture, as well as a variety of Biblical images, idioms, and metaphors Washington regularly employed from the biblical text.[7] Additionally, we will show that the expression "vine and the fig tree," in the book of Micah, was his favorite Old Testament passage, while the narrative of the widow's mite in Mark 12:41–44 and Luke 21:1–4 was the New Testament passage of which he was most fond.[8] We also will show a number of particular Bibles that played roles in the life of George Washington. Among those Bibles were a three-volume set his father, Augustine Washington, purchased as the family Bible. Another was the Lewis family Bible that Washington's mother brought into the marriage and read from to her children and grandchildren; and a third Bible the first President borrowed from the Masonic Lodge in New York, which was used when Washington appeared at his first inauguration in 1796 without one.[9]

Washington's belief in, and attitudes toward, religious toleration will be the subject matter of Section IV of this essay. There, we will show that Washington believed that the founding documents of this country should be the foundation of religious toleration in America, as well as what his many Founding Father colleagues had to say about the issue.[10] As we shall see, one of the many primary sources for understanding George Washington's views on religious toleration was English philosopher John Locke's *Letter on Toleration*, published in Latin in 1698. We also will show that the best way to understand the first President's attitudes toward religious toleration is to examine the many letters that Washington wrote to various religious congregations during his presidency, where the President responded to occasional concerns of minority religious groups that they were discriminated against.

As we shall see, Washington believed these letters were often a way of ameliorating the worries of religious minorities so that they would not be able to exercise their religious rights. Among these letters, Washington wrote to the Virginia Baptists, to the Swedenborgians in Baltimore, to the Presbyterians, the Catholics, and to two congregations of Jews, in regard to ensuring them that their rights to worship when and where they chose would be guaranteed by the US government in Washington's administration.

Ethics and virtue shall be the focus of Section V of this work. In that section, we shall explore what the first President had to say about the moral good and the practice of virtue, particularly stoic virtue, about which he was very fond. At the close of this section, we provide a summary of George Washington's major beliefs about ethics, morality, and virtue, as well as Washington's ten most important leadership qualities, both as a general and as a president.[11] 11

In Section VI of this study on George Washington's religion, our major focus shall be what the first President had to say in his public speeches, as well as private writings, about the concept of, and uses for, prayer. There, we will show when Washington tended to pray, and what he generally asked for when he did. In that regard, Washington appears to have prayed, both publicly and privately, more than any other president, over the full length of his public life.

In Section VII of this work, we shall attempt to answer two simple questions: "Was George Washington a Christian?" and "Was America founded as a Christian Nation?" We will show that, in regard to the former question, if the standards by which this question is asked is that of contemporary Evangelical Christians, then the answer to our question is "no." But if the standard we use is Washington's own time, the late eighteenth century in Britain and America, among the believers of the Anglican Church, then the response to our question is a resounding "yes!"

Virginian Anglicans in Washington's time were staid and conservative, with more emphasis on dogma and ritual than the Baptists and Methodists of the Great Awakening, and their religion centered on religious experience, Conversion experiences, altar calls, and movements of the Holy Spirit, as we shall see in Section VII of this essay, were at the center of the faiths of the Baptists and the Methodists.

In regard to the query about whether America was founded as a Christian Nation, the available evidence is mixed. On the one hand, Justice Brewer and several modern American presidents, as we shall see, believed the answer to our second question is "yes." But, on the other hand, Supreme Court decisions in the twentieth century generally suggest that the answer to the second query is "no."

The subject matter of Section VIII of this essay will be the classical philosophical conundrum known as the "problem of evil."[12] In this section, we will attempt to uncover how George Washington answered the question "If God is all-good, all-knowing, and all-powerful, then why is there so much evil and suffering in the world?" As we shall see in Section VIII, George Washington's overall theory to explain, or in response to, evil and suffering is what we have labeled the "divine plan theory." The adherents to this divine plan theory, of which the first President appears to have been one, argues that all evil and suffering in the world will someday, perhaps at the end of time, be seen as part of a divine plan in which all will work out for the good.[13]

Additionally, in Section VIII of this study, we will maintain that the first President also employed, or made references to, five other traditional responses to the problem of evil. These will be called, as we shall see, "retributive justice," the "moral qualities approach," the "test view," the "influences of demonic forces" answer," and what we shall call the "practical approach to suffering."[14]

This latter view appears to be favored, as we shall see in Section VIII, by the Jesus of the Gospels. None of these responses, however, are nearly as important when it came to Washington's overall view on evil and suffering—the divine plan theory.[15] Since the eighteenth century, the problem of evil in the West is sometimes called the issue of "theodicy." The word was coined by German philosopher G. W. Leibniz in a book called *Theodicy*. The word comes from two Greek words, *theos* and *dike*, the former meaning "God" and the latter being "Justice." Thus, the idea of theodicy is the process of showing God's justice. Other Western philosophers like Immanuel Kant, for example, also employed the name "theodicy."[16]

Finally, Section IX of this essay is an attempt at providing the major conclusions we have made in the other eight sections of this work. We shall now turn to the phenomenon of religion in George Washington's early life.

Endnotes to the Introduction

1. Slaughter, *History of Truro Parish*, 10–11.

2. See the official website of Pohick Church at http://www.pohick.org/index.html. See also Slaughter, *History of Truro Parish*, 42–48.

3. Bray, *Faith We Profess*.

4. Towles, *Rules of Civility*.

5. Chernow, *Washington*, 56–57.

6. Thompson, *In the Hands*.

7. Thompson, *In the Hands*, 16–18, 148–49.

8. See the King James Version of Mic 4:4; 1 Kings 4:25; and Zech 3:10 for examples.

9. "George Washington Inaugural Bible."

10. We have in mind here the US Constitution, particularly its First Amendment and several of the Federalist Papers.

11. For more on the nature of the moral good, see Trainer, *Nature of Morality*.

12. Vicchio, *Voice from the Whirlwind*.

13. Vicchio, *Voice from the Whirlwind*, 1–3.

14. Vicchio, *Voice from the Whirlwind*, 85–160.

15. Vicchio, *Voice from the Whirlwind*, 85–160.

16. Leibniz, *Theodicy*; Kant, *Groundwork for the Metaphysics of Morals*.

I

Religion in Washington's Early Life

George Washington is the greatetost man on Earth simply because he
disbanded his Army and chose to be a Servant to his Nation.

—KING GEORGE III OF ENGLAND

BY THE TIME GEORGE Washington was born on February 22, 1732,
the Washington family had been in North America for four generations.
John Washington, the president's great-grandfather (1631–77), was granted
land in England by King Henry VIII. Much of the family's fortune, however, was lost during the Puritan Revolution, and in 1657, George's grandfather, Lawrence Washington (1659–98), migrated to the Virginia colony.
Very little is known about the Washington family—besides the fact that
John Washington's father was an Anglican minister—until George's father,
Augustine Washington (1694–1743), was born in the colony.

Augustine Washington was an ambitious colonist who acquired land
and slaves, built mills, and grew tobacco. He also had an interest in an iron
mine. Augustine Washington married his first wife, Jane Butler, and they
had three children. In 1729, Jane Washington (1699–1729) died at the
age of thirty, and Augustine married Mary Ball in 1731. The couple had
six children, of whom George was the oldest. The Washington family lived
on Pope's Creek in Westmorland County, Virginia. They were moderately
prosperous members of Virginia's "middling class," roughly equivalent to
America's contemporary upper-middle class.

For the most part, Augustine Washington made his living as a tobacco farmer. He held a number of properties throughout Virginia. He belonged to the moderately prosperous middle-class, landed gentry.

In 1735, Augustine Washington moved his family to Little Hunting Creek Plantation, later to be known as Mount Vernon; the family then moved again in 1738, this time to Ferry Farm on the Rappahannock River—just opposite Fredericksburg, Virginia. It was on Ferry Farm where George Washington spent most of his childhood years. Of all that is known about the life of George Washington, very little is known about his early years, which fostered many of the tales and fables that sprung up about the first president's boyhood, beginning shortly after his death.

Among these fables were that George threw a silver dollar across the Potomac River, and that after chopping down his father's prized cherry tree, he openly confessed to the crime, for he "could not tell a lie."[1] Very little is actually known about George Washington's early life. It is likely that he was homeschooled from the age of seven until fifteen. Some evidence suggests his schoolmasters may have been a tenant on one of Augustine's farms, by the name of Hobbey or Hobbes; then by a local church sexton, a man named the Rev. James Marye, the rector of St. George's Parish in Fredericksburg; and possibly a third teacher who taught the boy practical math, a smattering of Latin, and some rudiments of the British literary classics.[2] Or it may have been that the Rev. Marye instructed the young George Washington in these subjects, as well.

Although Washington did not formally study Latin for very long, he did know a few Latin phrases, including the one that forms the motto of his family's coat of arms, *Exitus acta probat,* or "The event justifies the deeds." The same motto also may be rendered into English as eighteenth-century British lexicographer Robert Ainsworth did: "All is well that ends well."[3] Colonel William Ball, George Washington's maternal grandfather, also employed a Latin motto on his coat of arms. To wit, "*Coelumque tueri.*" This Latin expression is shorthand for a longer passage from Ovid's *Metamorphoses* that describes how God created Adam. Joseph Davidson translated this Latin line into English as follows:

> He gave to man a lofty Countenance, commanded him to lift his
> Face to Heaven, and behold with erected Eyes and Stars.[4]

At any rate, just how much Latin George Washington actually knew and understood remains a mystery for scholars of the first president. Even if Washington knew little Latin beyond these key phrases, he could have read the English translations of Ovid and other classics. He also owned an

English translation of Aesop's *Fables*, for example. In fact, in his adult life, he sometimes made some references to particular fables.

On one occasion, for example, Washington made a reference to the fable of the "Fox and the Grapes," which he had recalled from years earlier. A certain fox stood beneath a grapevine with a succulent bunch of grapes overhead. The fox jumped up several times with no success in securing the grapes. Gradually, the fox comes to realize that the grapes are unattainable, and by then that "the grapes are as sour as crabs." Washington took to heart what he saw was the lesson to be learned from the tale—that one cannot always extend one capabilities.[5]

Saint George's Church, completed in 1741, was across the Rappahannock River in Fredericksburg. Saint George's was one of the two Anglican churches that George Washington's family attended when he was a child, the other being the church at Pohick Creek. The Creek is in the South-central portion of Virginia. The body of water is named after the Pohick Native American tribe.

Some of George Washington's school exercise books are extant. There is a set of school papers from the years 1743 until 1748, when he was eleven to sixteen years of age. Other evidence shows that he continued his studies beyond the most recent entries in the extant manuscripts; but these school exercises reveal both his literary interest and his fondness for mathematics, as well as the genesis of his career as a surveyor.[6]

At the age of seventeen, mostly through the influence of Lord Fairfax, in July of 1749, Washington secured an appointment as county surveyor for the newly created Culpepper County. He served in this capacity until November of 1750. He then worked in the Northern Neck of Virginia for the Fairfax family from 1750 until 1752, when Washington was eighteen to twenty years old. At the time, the salary of county surveyors were only exceeded by the finest attorneys in the colony.

Altogether, just shy of two hundred surveys are attributed to George Washington. Of the 199, fewer than seventy-five are extant today. All of Washington's survey reports are finely finished and stylized, with a symmetrical appearance. The geography and map division of the Library of Congress owns several of Washington's surveys, including a November 17, 1750 survey of a plat for John Lindsay of 460 acres along the Great Cacapon River. In the corner of this document, Washington put the initials "S.C.C.," to stand for "Survey of Culpepper County."[7]

The few surviving school exercises of George Washington's also indicate that Washington studied inside, as well as outside, the classroom. They show his mastering of various subjects, learning what he needed to become a gentleman among the Virginia gentry. Friend and fellow patriot George

Mason (1725–92) was one of Washington's schoolmates. In one of his letters to Washington, Mason mentions another schoolmate named David Piper, who also turned to the surveying of roads in Fairfax County after their school years.[8]

Mr. Piper also appears to have been a bit of a bad young man. He was later repeatedly brought to court on various civil, and even criminal, matters.[9] Washington and Piper may have been classmates at the Lower Church of Washington Parish of Westmorland County, where Mattox Creek enters the Potomac River, but we cannot know this for sure. The exact extent of Washington's early education is still very shrouded in mystery.

We do know, however, that George Washington excelled in penmanship, and as an adolescent he developed an interest in writing, or the copying of poetry. One of his extant copied poems is entitled "On Christmas Day."[10] It is filled with happy shepherds, barnyard animals, and hymn-singing angels, all watching over a newborn Savior. The narrator of the poem is female. She closes the poem by reminding herself to always remember Christmas.

In the bottom corner of the page containing the poem, the final two lines are obscured. Among the other lines of this poem, we see in Washington's adolescent hand:

> Oh never let my Soul this day forget, but pay in graitfull[sic] praise her Annual Debt to him, whom 'tis my Trust, I shall [adore] when Time, and Sin, and Death, shall be no more.[11]

Commenting on this poem, Kevin Hayes observes:

> The picture of young Washington that emerges from his copy of the poem is that of a boy confident in his religious beliefs but pleased to have another confirm them.[12]

The young Washington did not record the poet's name from whom he copied the poem. We know now that it came from the February 1743 issue of *Gentleman's Magazine*. The published poem is signed by one "Orinthia," a pseudonym used by English poet Elizabeth Taft of Lincolnshire. In the magazine, the editor capitalized the beginning of each line of the poem, but Washington left out the capital letters in his copy.[13]

Another copied poem from George Washington's school days also survives in manuscript form. It is entitled "True Happiness." This poem also originally appeared in *Gentleman's Magazine*, but in a much later issue. The *Gentleman's Magazine* had been established in London in January of 1731 by Edward Cave. The *Magazine* was published, without interruption, until 1922. It was the first English periodical to use the name "magazine." Samuel Johnson's first job as a writer was with this periodical. The original title of the publication was *The Gentleman's Magazine: A Trader's Monthly Intelli-gencer.* The *Magazine* appealed to readers throughout Colonial America, and it included everything from commodity prices to Latin poetry. Mary Washington appears to have received a copy in the mail to aid in the education of her children and her grandchildren.

It was common that the children of Virginia gentry were taught at home by private tutors or in local private schools. Boys generally began their formal education around the age of seven with lessons in reading, writing, and arithmetic. Later, they were taught Latin and Greek, as well as practical subjects like geometry, book-keeping, and surveying. The wealthiest Virginia planters often sent their sons to England for finishing school. This was done for Washington's older half-brothers, Lawrence and Augustine Jr., who both attended the Appleby School in England, as had their father before them.

The Appleby Grammar School, now called the Appleby Academy, was founded by the mayor of the town of Appleby in Northwest England, at the heart of the Eden Valley, in 1452. Today the school is coeducational, but in the days of George Washington's older half-brothers, it was for boys ages eleven to seventeen before they went off to University.

The death of Washington's father, Augustine Sr., made the possibility of schooling abroad for George to be an impossibility. It appears as though George Washington attended school in Fredericksburg, in Stafford County, or in Westmorland County. Some evidence suggests he excelled in geometry and there learned the rudiments of surveying. There is no evidence that he learned any Greek, but as mentioned before, he did have a basic knowledge of Latin.

If the Rev. Marye (1692–1768) did in fact instruct George Washington, it was at the former's school at St. George's Anglican Church, established in 1721.[14] It was common at the time for Anglican Church rectors to supplement their salaries by administering schools.

The Rev. Marye was a French Jesuit priest who converted to Anglicanism when he moved to England. Marye also enlarged the church in Fredericksburg with a thirty-two-foot addition, and erected a gallery at the West end of the church in 1759. The cemetery at the church was also walled-in during the Rev. Marye's time there. Marye's son, the Rev. James Marye Jr. (1731–80), followed his father into the ministry after graduating from William & Mary College, as did Thomas Jefferson and other Founding Fathers.

If George Washington was a student at the senior Rev. Marye's school, he was responsible for the copy of the *Rules of Civility*, from which Washington copied the maxims we will discuss below in this section. Parson Marye Sr. also may have been responsible for the first training that Washington received as a surveyor. At the time, a surveyor had a professional status akin to a lawyer or a doctor in Tidewater, Virginia. Washington inherited surveying tools from his father. He likely received training in the profession at the hands of George Hume (1698–1760), a prominent, local surveyor, sometimes employed by Lord Fairfax.

In fact, George Washington is mentioned in surviving records of surveys of the Tidewater counties of Virginia made by Mr. Hume. Some of these are signed by "George Hume, Surveyor," with a second signature of "George Washington, Assistant Surveyor." We know that George Hume was fifty-two years old when the first president was given his first surveyor job at seventeen. Hume was a crown surveyor, having been commissioned by King George II, when Culpepper County was separated from Orange County, Virginia, in 1749.

George Hume moved to the newly formed Culpepper County in the early 1750s, and he appears to have resided there until his death in 1760. Hume is buried in a family plot in a graveyard near the Rapidan River, in Northwest Central Virginia. The Rapidan River is the largest tributary to the Rappahannock River.

While president, it was clear that George Washington had no knowledge of foreign languages like French, Spanish, or German, unlike Thomas Jefferson, who was fluent in Greek, Latin, and French, as well as his native tongue of English; in fact, there are reports that when Jefferson was the Ambassador to France, between 1784 and 1789, he spoke no English for months at a time; but unlike Jefferson, who also attended William & Mary College, Washington did not attend a college or a university, though he was embarrassed by this fact for the remainder of his life.

George Washington's father died when he was eleven years old. George became the ward of his half-brother, Lawrence, who was fourteen years George's senior. Lawrence Washington had inherited the family's Little Hunting Creek Plantation, and he married the daughter of Colonel William Fairfax, Ann. Under the tutorage of Lord Fairfax, the young George Washington was schooled in the finer points of Virginian colonial culture.

Washington became a part of the extended family of the Fairfax family. He was a frequent companion to Colonel Fairfax in his fox-hunting adventures. In fact, many people report that Washington was an excellent horseman—some say the best of his day. In 1748, Washington accompanied the colonel's eldest son, George William Fairfax, on a surveying expedition across the Blue Ridge Mountains to the Fairfax family's property in the Shenandoah Valley, of Virginia.

This trek to the Shenandoah Valley was important to the life of Washington for three reasons. First, it was Washington's first experience in surveying. Secondly, his experiences in the Western lands of Virginia gave him much experience for his early military assignments. And finally, Washington's associations with the Fairfax family gave him invaluable instruction concerning how to live the life of the Virginia gentleman in the mid-eighteent century.

With Augustine's death, Lawrence inherited the 2,500 acres of Little Hunting Creek, which he renamed "Mount Vernon," in honor of British Vice-Admiral Edward Vernon (1684–1759), under whom Lawrence had served in the British Navy. Admiral Vernon had been the head of the British Navy's East Indies Station and Admiral of the White Squadron of the British fleet.

The marriage between Ann Fairfax and Lawrence was a social coup for the Washington family, as the Fairfax family was one of the most powerful families in Colonial Virginia. The Fairfaxes lived at what was known as the Belvoir Estate, four miles down the Potomac River. During the Revolutionary War, Fort Belvoir became a U.S. Army installation, as well as the site of the earliest U.S. Census. Since the war, Fort Belvoir has remained the property of the U.S. Army to the present day. It is now the Arlington National Cemetery.

The Fairfax family controlled what was known as the "Fairfax Grant," a tract of 5,282,000 acres in the Northern Neck of Virginia, between the Rappahannock and the Potomac rivers. Thomas Fairfax, the absentee proprietor of the Northern Neck, visited the colony from England in 1746, and he moved there to stay in 1747. Originally, he stayed at the Belvoir Plantation, but in 1752, Lord Fairfax, a lifelong bachelor, established his residence at Greenway Court, near White Post in Clarke County, Virginia. Lord Fairfax died there in 1781.

Thomas Fairfax Jr. (1693–1781), the sixth Lord Fairfax, was a Scottish peer and son of Thomas Fairfax Sr., the fifth Lord Fairfax, who had a great influence on the early adult life of George Washington. Fairfax, a lifelong bachelor, acted as a mentor, neighbor (and for a while, employer), and friend of the first president. The relationship between Lord Fairfax and Washington began in the latter's teenage years, between 1750 and 1752, and continued until the Fairfax's death.

In 1751, Washington sailed with his half-brother Lawrence to Barbados. Lawrence was suffering from tuberculosis, and he was advised by his doctor to spend the winter in the tropics. His wife, Ann, could not go with him. The couple already had lost three infants in early life, and they could not afford to risk the life of their only surviving daughter, Sarah. So, as a consequence, George sailed with his brother. The brothers sailed on a small sloop known as the *Success*. The voyage took a full seven weeks. They left in mid-September, and the crew sighted the coast of Barbados on November 2, 1751. The trip was not successful, for Lawrence died the following year of the disease. This is the only time that George Washington travelled outside the colonies/United States in his entire life.

Lawrence Washington held the post of adjutant general, with the rank of major of the Virginia militia. When he died of a lung ailment in 1752, Lieutenant Governor Robert Dinwiddie and the Virginia House of Burgesses decided to divide Lawrence's post into four separate parcels. George Washington immediately lobbied for the Northern District, which included Mount Vernon and Belvoir Plantation. Instead, he was given the Southern District, with the rank of major in the Virginia Militia. But when the Northern District became vacant, George again lobbied for the post, and in November of 1753, he received the job. He appears to have received the post because of his deep knowledge of the Western edges of the Fairfax Grant because he had surveyed those lands. During his stint as major in the Western regions of the Fairfax Grant, Washington was described as "a youth of great sobriety, diligence, and fidelity."[15]

To return to George Washington's early religious life, we can be certain that George Washington was baptized by sprinkling as an infant on April 5, 1732, about eight weeks after his birth.[16] It is also likely that George attended church services at the local Anglican church as a child, at both Saint George's in Fredericksburg and at the church on Pohick Creek. There is also sufficient evidence that the Washington family owned a King James Bible Version of the Scriptures, purchased by Augustine Washington in 1819, and that Mary Washington, the future President's mother, read the Scriptures to her children in the family home, either from this family Bible or one brought into the marriage by Mary from her first husband's family. This was the Custis Family Bible, later known as "Martha's Bible."

As indicated earlier, many of Washington's letters in his later life reveal that the president, like Abraham Lincoln, was sensitive about the lack of his formal education. One can only say that both Presidents compensated by studying in the "School of Hard Knocks," as the first president's experience on the Western frontier and in the Continental Army clearly testified. In Lincoln's case, we may cite the experience that he got as a clerk and while traveling on the legal circuit. These experiences fostered Washington's leadership skills, and they offset his lack of a formal education.

Another source for discussing the early years of George Washington's life is a handbook called the *Rules of Civility*, a guide to gentlemanly behavior in polite society that the president copied as a boy.[17] The book, which contains 110 rules, was a combination etiquette manual and moral code, designed to show a young gentleman how to behave with his sometimes-powerful and influential friends and neighbors.

Washington's copy of the *Rules of Civility* was found in the final ten pages of a book on personal notes by the president. They were a series of moral maxims and social rules that the young Washington likely copied as an exercise to improve his penmanship. These rules were originally composed by French Jesuits in the 1590s, designed to assist French noblemen in the arts of etiquette and proper behavior for a gentleman in Paris and other urban areas, and were translated into English by Francis Hawkins in London around 1640, most likely brought from England by the Rev. Marye.

In Washington's boyhood, he schooled himself, then, in the gentlemanly arts by copying the 110 maxims of the *Rules of Civility*. Many of these rules, like those about spitting, scratching, and nail-biting (numbers nine, eleven, and ninety, respectively), were about proper personal habits. These also included not killing fleas and ticks in the sight of others (number thirteen) and not passing gas in company (number sixteen).[18] The young Washington most likely began his copying of these rules between the ages of twelve and fourteen.

Other of the *Rules of Civility* were clearly much more moral in content. Rule number one suggests that "Every action done in Company ought to be with some sign of Respect to those that are present." Rule eighty-two tells the youth to "keep his promises." Rule eighty-nine suggests one not "speak evil of the absent, for it would be unjust."[19] Rule 108 speaks of what to do when speaking of the Divine. It says:

> When you speak of God or His attributes, let it be seriously and with reverence. Honor and obey your natural parents, although they may be poor.[20]

Other of the rules tell the student not to "puff your cheeks" (number 16); not to laugh "too loudly" (number 24); not to turn your back on others (number fourteen.); not to "take your clothes off in the presence of others," nor to "leave your chamber half-dressed (number seven); "don't sing alone, nor hum, nor drum your fingers (number four); and not to put one's hands to "parts of the body not usually discovered" (number two).[21]

The 109th of the rules advises the young man to let his "recreations be Manful, and not Sinful."[22] The 110th and final maxim of the *Rules of Civility*, tells the young man to "Keep alive in your breast that little spark of Celestial fire called Conscience."[23] This suggests that Washington had a view of conscience quite like that of both Thomas Jefferson and Abraham Lincoln, who both believed that God placed an identical conscience into the heart of every human being. Indeed, Jeremiah 17:1 was among Washington's favorite Biblical passages. That verse, in the King James Version, tells us:

> The sin of Judah is written with a pen of iron, and with the point of a diamond: It is graven upon the table of the heart, and upon the horns of your altar.[24]

This notion of God writing conscience into the hearts of men is employed by Old Testament writers in Deuteronomy 6:6, Jeremiah 4:4, Ezekiel 11:19–20, and in the New Testament in Hebrews 8:10, 2 Corinthians 2:11–12, and 3:7–11.

In an address in 1789, Washington again tied conscience to freedom and morality. He wrote:

> I have often expressed my sentiments that every man, conducting himself as a good citizen, and being accountable to God alone for his religious opinions, ought to be protected in worshiping the Deity according to the dictates of his own Conscience.[25]

More will be said on ethics and conscience in section V of this essay. The copy of the *Rules of Civility* from which Washington did his copying was Francis Hawkins's text, published in London in 1668.[26] Other of the rules advised, "Take no salt or bread with a greasy knife" (number ninety-two); "shake not your head, feet, nor legs, and roll not your eyes" (number twelve); and "don't lift one of your eyebrows higher than the other" (number thirteen).[27]

Washington's *Rules of Civility* originally were published, along with various others of the first president's youthful writings, in the mid-nineteenth century. They have been continually reprinted since that time in various American newspapers. They were published in book form for the first time in 1888, with many subsequent editions following. The original copy is owned by Mount Vernon.[28]

As indicated earlier, when George Washington was sixteen years old, in 1748, he traveled with a surveying party plotting land in what was then Virginia's Western territory. The following year, aided by Lord Fairfax, Washington received an appointment as the official surveyor of Culpeper County. For the next two years, from sixteen to eighteen years old, the young George surveyed lands in Culpeper, Frederick, and Augusta Counties in Virginia alongside his surveying mentor, George Hume. These experiences taught him how to be resourceful, and it toughened both his body and his soul.

Two other books that Mary Washington brought to her marriage and family life were John Scott's *Christian Life* and James Hervey's *Meditations and Contemplations*. Scott (1639–95) was an English clergyman. His volume provides "directions for private devotions," which Mary most likely employed with her children and grandchildren. James Hervey (1714–58) was also an English Anglican priest and writer. His "devotions," as he calls them, were modeled on Robert Boyle's *Occasional Reflections*, published in 1665, another standard religious devotional text in the eighteen century. Robert Boyle (1627–91) was one of the great English scientific thinkers of the seventeenth century.[29] In fact, many credit Boyle to be the father of modern chemistry.

Although Washington attended church as a child, from 1748 until 1759, it appears that George Washington rarely attended church as a surveyor, and then as a young soldier in the French and Indian War from 1753 until 1755. After his marriage and settling into Mount Vernon, he and Martha were regular church attendees. Indeed, he was elected vestryman in the two parishes of Truro and Fairfax, and from those elections he became intimately involved in the affairs of both Saint George's in Fredericksburg and the small Anglican church on Pohick Creek.

Lawrence Washington died of tuberculosis in July of 1752, when George was twenty years old. This made George the heir apparent of the Washington lands. Lawrence's only surviving child, a girl named Sarah, died two months later, and George became the head of one of Virginia's most prominent estates, Mount Vernon.[30] Washington was now twenty years old. Throughout his adult life, Washington held farming to be a noble profession. He gradually increased his land holding until it included over eight thousand acres.

When Washington was a child, he attended services at what came to be called the Pohick Church, so-named because of its proximity to Pohick Creek. It was an Anglican parish founded in 1695. It was originally called the Occoquan Church, and it was attended by several generations of the Washington family. The original church had been built sometime prior to the year 1724. In 1732, the Virginia General Assembly had established the Truro Parish, defining its lands in the colony as "everything above the Occoquan River, extending all the way to the Western Front."[31]

Colonists living within the parish soon elected twelve men to serve on the governing board known as the vestry. One of those vestrymen was Augustine Washington. He was elected on November 18, 1735. He also sponsored the nomination of Dr. Charles Green to serve as the Parish's first permanent minister, or rector, of the church. The Pohick Church vestry book is still extant. The first entry in the book is dated from 1732, when Truro Parish was formed from Hamilton Parish at that time.

The church at Pohick Creek also had an adjoining cemetery that holds the remains of a number of prominent early Virginia citizens, including

Colonel John Dandridge, Washington's father-in-law; William Paul Jones, the brother of John Paul Jones; the Rev. Edward McGuire; Archibald McPherson; and Fielding Lewis.

The vestry book records all of the parish's activities during George Washington's childhood.[32] The Rev. Green was elected rector by the church vestry in 1735, when Washington was three years old, and he was confirmed the following year. One of the interesting things about the Pohick Church is that the Rev. Green was a medical doctor, not a doctor of divinity or of the ministry.

Since there were no Anglican bishops in Virginia at the time, Dr. Green had to receive his orders from His Grace, the Bishop of London, which he did by letter in 1737. According to Helen Coughlin in her 1908 book *Colonial Churches in the Original Colony of Virginia*, she describes Dr. Green, the first rector, as being "A man of high character, faithful to his duties, enjoying the friendship and esteem of George Mason, George Washington, and other prominent members of the Vestry and community. He remained in charge of the Parish until his death, in 1765."[33]

By the early 1750s, the French had begun extending their control in North American lands to areas that are now Pennsylvania. On October 31, 1753, Virginia's lieutenant governor, Robert Dinwiddie, sent Washington to Fort LeBoeuf, now Waterford, Pennsylvania. Washington's job was to get the French to leave, for the lands were owned by the British Crown. When the French refused, Washington returned to Williamsburg, the capital of Virginia. On hearing the news of Washington's failed attempt, Dinwiddie sent Washington back to Pennsylvania with a number of troops. He was to establish a post at Great Meadows, in present-day Fayette County, Pennsylvania.

Once Washington reached his destination, he found that French had driven away colonial traders, and they began constructing a fort on May 28, 1754. Washington's troops attacked the fort, killing ten Frenchman, including their commander, Coulon de Jumonville.[34] The remaining French troops were taken prisoners. This was the beginning of George Washington's military career.

To return to Washington's early religious life, George Washington became the trustee of the Rev. Charles Green's Estate upon his death in 1765. At that time, the Green Estate comprised three thousand acres of land, about two thousand of which was at Goose Creek, in what was then Fairfax County, but now is Loudoun County. The other thousand acres was a parcel of land known as Green's Leislip, which had been given to the rector by Lord Fairfax. The *Diaries of George Washington*, published by the University of Virginia Press in 1976, includes copious mentions of Rector Green.[35] The

Rev. Green served as rector from 1732 until 1765, and was succeeded by the Rev. Lee Massey.

From the year 1760 until 1765, there was but one minister in all of Fairfax County, the Rev. Green, and he was an old man in failing health. After the death of Rev. Green at the end of 1765, this created the need for a new minister for the Pohick Church. Mr. Lee Massey submitted his case to pursue ordination to take the place of the Rev. Green. Washington, Mason, Fairfax, and McCarty, as well as other vestrymen of the parish, signed letters to the governor of Virginia and the Bishop of London to recommend Mr. Massey entering Holy Orders to become rector of the church on Pohick Creek.

Mr. Massey sailed off to England in order to read for ordination under the auspices of the Bishop of London in 1766. He returned to Virginia ten months later, his letter of ordination being accepted by the governor and the vestry. A short time later, the Rev. Lee Massey was made rector of the two churches of Truro Parish. The same month that he became rector, the vestrymen decided to build a new Pohick Church of brick and stone to replace the original wood structure, which they did shortly afterwards in 1769.

During the Colonial period, most marriages, baptisms, and funeral services of the new Pohick Church were not celebrated at the church. Rather, they were performed, for the most part, in private homes. The George Mason Family Bible, for example, records the Rev. Lee Massey to have baptized the Masons last four children (Elizabeth, Thomas, Richard, and James) at the family home at Gunston Hall, from 1768 until 1773.[36] It is not at all clear, however, how much influences either the Rev. Green or the Rev. Massey had on the early religious life of George Washington.

Gunston House, the Mason Family home, was located in the center of a five thousand, five hundred acre farm, not all that far from Mount Vernon. Construction of Gunston House began in 1755, and it was completed in 1759. The interior of the house was mostly the work of William Buckland, a carpenter, joiner, and indentured servant from England. Buckland went on to design several other significant buildings in the Colonial Chesapeake Region.

At the time of Washington's childhood, the American Anglican Church accepted the practices of three sacraments—baptism, communion, and marriage. There is some debate about how often the adult Washington took part in communion, even though he was a regular church attendee. More will be said about this question later in this essay. It is enough now to say, however, that Washington received communion before the war, but very rarely afterwards.

After the Revolutionary War, Washington would often leave the Sunday service *before* the administering of Communion, leaving Mrs. Washington behind to participate in the sacrament without her husband. There is even evidence that Washington was once rebuked by an assistant rector of Christ Church, the Rev. James Abercrombie, in Philadelphia, for leaving the Sunday service before the administering of communion. Later, interestingly enough, Washington commended the cleric for doing so.[37]

Although the Church of England in America was hierarchical, there were no bishops nor cathedrals in Colonial America. For the most part, priests were trained and ordained in England, as was the Rev. Massey. Many of these young priests who came to the colonies were deeply influenced by the rationalism and empiricism of the Enlightenment. Some of these ideas may have been presented at Sunday services, and even at the services on Holy Days.

The only artifact that survives from this early period of Pohick Church is a baptismal font. Experts at the Ashmolean Museum at Oxford University suggest that the large marble font is most likely a medieval mortar from the eleventh or twelfth century. Most likely it was taken from the kitchen of an English medieval monastery during the Reformation period.[38]

The site of the Pohick Church is now the Cranford Methodist Church, where the Baptismal font is still employed for that purpose. The font has "A.D. 1773" etched on its side—most likely the year it was shipped to America.[39]

As mentioned above, in 1769, a new church was built on the Pohick Church site. It was funded in part by money raised by George Washington. By the late nineteenth century, however, the Pohick Church fell into disrepair. This was due in part to the separation from the Anglican Church after the Revolutionary War, and partly to the establishment of the Episcopal Church in North America. In adulthood, Washington purchased two family pews at the Pohick Episcopal Church of Truro Parish in Lorton, Virginia: pews number 28 and 29. Washington also served on the vestry of Truro Parish, from October 25, 1762 until February 23, 1784. One of the responsibilities of late-eighteenth-century vestrymen was to oversee the needs of the poor. This remained an interest of George Washington's for the rest of his life.

Lord Fairfax also served as a vestryman for the Pohick Church. In fact, there is an entry in the vestry book where the baron paid sixteen pounds, seventeen shillings to purchase surplices and books for the church. It is not clear how long Lord Fairfax served on the vestry, but George Washington resigned from that body on February 23, 1784.[40]

One other important fact in regard to the Pohick Church is that the Rev. Mason Locke Weems, the author of the "Life of Washington," served as rector of the Pohick congregation in the final years of the eighteenth and the beginning of the nineteenth centuries. This, of course, adds gravitas to the Rev. Weems's account of the life of the first president.

George Washington surveyed the land where the Pohick Church was built. According to the *Historical Background of Fairfax County's Pohick Church Overlay District Design Guidelines*:

> The builder of Pohick Church, Daniel French, began construc-
> tion of the Church in 1769 and may have based his design on
> work by the architect, James Wren. The brick Church was typi-
> cal of the Colonial Anglican churches of the time—rectangular,
> plain, and finely crafted. George Washington and George Ma-
> son, were both Church Vestrymen, and played prominent roles
> in the location and building of Pohick Church.[41]

Both as a child and as an adult, George Washington attended the church on Pohick Creek. It is likely that Washington was taught, and as-sented to, the major theological beliefs of the Anglicans in early America, including the Thirty-Nine Articles of the Anglican Church. In fact, when Washington was a young man, the Rev. Massey wrote:

> I never knew so constant an attendance at church as Washing-
> ton. And his behavior in the house of God was ever so deeply
> reverential that it produced the happiest effect on my congrega-
> tion, and greatly assisted me in my pulpit labors. No company
> ever withheld him from Church. I have been at Mount Vernon
> on Sabbath morning when his breakfast table was filled with
> guests; but to him they furnished no pretext for neglecting his
> God and losing the satisfaction of setting a good example. For
> instead of staying at home, out of false complaisance to them, he
> used constantly to invite them to accompany him.[42]

By the year 1837, the bishop of Virginia, Bishop William Meade (1789–1862), exclaimed in a pathetic apostrophe, upon visiting the Pohick Church, "Is this the House of God built by the Washingtons, the Masons, the McCartys, the Grahams, the Lewises, and the Fairfaxes? . . . The House in which they used to worship the God of our Fathers according to the ven-erable forms of the Episcopal Church, and some whose names are still to be seen on those who have deserted these pews?"[43]

When the Washington family did not attend services at the Pohick Church, they went instead to St. George's Episcopal Church in Freder-icksburg, Virginia, across the Rappahannock River. An area of land was designated for the church as early as 1720, but construction of the church did not begin until 1732. The structure had a wooden frame. It was completed in 1741. George Washington's mother, Mary Ball Washington, attended this Old Saint George's Church. The congregation joined the Protestant Episcopal Church of the United States in 1789. The old church was replaced with a brick structure in 1815.

The first rector of St. George's was the Rev. Richard Charlton (1700–1779), who was sent from England to be the first minister of the Fredericksburg congregation. The Rev. Charlton came to Virginia in 1732, and the Washington family began attending St. George's in 1738, when George was six years old. Very little information is available concerning the relationship of Rector Charlton and George Washington, if there was one. It's likely that George heard the rector preach, and that Mary Washington, George's mother, most likely discussed issues at home that may have arisen at the service.

The first rector of the New Saint George's Church was the Rev. Edward McGuire (1793–1858), who was rector from 1813, when he took over at the age of twenty, until 1858, when he died. The Rev. McGuire served in all three of the church buildings of Saint George's, supervising the building of two of them. When he died, the *Fredericksburg News*, on October 12, 1858, wrote about the Rev. McGuire:

> Under his faithful leadership, his Congregation greatly multiplied in numbers and flourished in all of its highest spiritual interests.[44]

The *Weekly Adviser*, at the same time, noted that he had, "baptized a whole generation in his communion and increased the Church from a mere handful to hundreds." Indeed, from a small number of parishioners when the Rev. McGuire first arrived, by his death the number had grown close to three hundred. On a plaque dedicated to his memory at the church, the Rev. McGuire is noted as being "amiable in character, prudent in action, sound judgment and consistent conduct characterized both his work as a builder and an Evangelical."[45]

The theological beliefs to which colonial Anglicans were bound was the Thirty-Nine Articles. This document had developed from Reformation Archbishop Thomas Cranmer in 1553 as a way of distinguishing the Anglican Church from Roman Catholicism. Up until the nineteenth century, Anglican and Episcopal priests in America took an oath to follow the provisions of the Thirty-Nine Articles. Peter A. Lillback, in his *George Washington's Sacred Fire*, tells us this about Washington's earliest religious beliefs:

Basically, what we see Washington as is a creedal Christian from the Reformation Era. He held to the 39 articles of the Anglican Church, he was a Vestryman, he was a Warden, he was a Parishioner, he held a pew in two different Churches, and he was on the building committee of these Churches.[46]

The Thirty-Nine Articles were divided into four sections. Articles one to seven were about "Faith." Issues such as the Trinity, the dual natures of Jesus, the nature of the Holy Spirit, the concept of resurrection, the divine inspiration of the Old Testament, and the idea of Sola Scriptura, or by "Scripture alone," were the subjects of this first section.[47]

Articles nine to eighteen dealt with "Personal Religion." This section included mentions of original sin, free will, justification by faith, the importance of good works, predestination, and the obtaining of salvation only through Jesus Christ; these were the theological issues covered in section II of the Thirty-Nine Articles.[48]

"Corporate Religion" was the subject matter of articles nineteen to thirty-one, or section III. These articles deal with the nature of the church and its authority, general councils, the idea of purgatory (rejected by the Anglican Church), ministers in the congregation, the nature of the sacraments, the importance of Jesus's death on the cross, and the fact that services should be conducted in the vernacular language.[49]

The final section of the Thirty-Nine Articles, numbers thirty-two to thirty-nine, were referred to as "Miscellaneous." Subjects included marriages of priests, excommunication, the consecration of bishops, and other theological issues.[50] Since there is so little extant information about President Washington's early life, we cannot be certain about how reverent the young George was in his faith, nor to which of these theological beliefs outlined above Washington and his family regularly assented. The Thirty-Nine Articles of Faith were established by the Anglican bishops, clergy, and laity of the Protestant Episcopal Church of the United States on September 12, 1801.[51]

Anglicans of Washington's day were also bound by the Book of Common Prayer, which was originally devised in 1549. It was developed during the reign of King Edward VI, and it was a product of the English Reformation. The 1549 version was soon succeeded by a more Reformed version in 1552, under the leadership of Thomas Cranmer, the archbishop of Canterbury. In 1559, under the reign of Queen Elizabeth I, a more permanent version was published, mostly because of the many churches who strayed from their use of the 1552 version. The 1559 version is the source of the contemporary Book of Common Prayer for the Church of England, as well as the Contemporary Episcopal Church.

Nevertheless, if Peter Lillback is correct, then George Washington grew up in a religious environment connected to Anglican Virginia gentry in the first half of the eighteenth century. Few other conclusions can be made about the earliest years of Mr. Washington's religious education.

The family of Augustine Washington during George's childhood attended the Anglican Churches, first at Pohick Creek, and then at Saint George's Church across the river in Fredericksburg. Very little is known about George's earliest church attendance, nor what he thought of the ideas and beliefs about which he heard in the sermons preached in those two churches.

From the materials presented in section I of this essay on George Washington's religion, the most important aspects of Washington's earliest upbringing appear to be three in number. First, the religious and pious bent of his mother, Mary Washington: she clearly influenced her oldest son's religious education by taking him to church, reading to him from the family Bibles, and educating his moral sense with other supplemental reading.

Secondly, there is the influence of his brother Lawrence, after the death of their father, when George was eleven years old. Lawrence saw to it that his brother George was good on a horse and knew about firearms, as well as received instruction in the other arts of the Virginia gentry.

And finally, there is George's early association with the Fairfax family, with whom he learned more about the ways of the Virginia gentry, including their dedication to the American Anglican Church. The Fairfax family was also instrumental in young George Washington's career as a surveyor. Like George Washington and George Mason, Lord Fairfax served as a vestryman of St. George's Episcopal Church.

As we have shown, other significant sources for the early religious life of George Washington include the Rev. James Marye, and possibly the Revs. Massey, Charlton, and McGuire, as well as his other early Christian teachers, including the Fairfax family.

We shall now turn to the president's understanding of God.

II

Washington on God

George Washington was first in war, first in peace,
and first in the hearts of his Countrymen.

—GENERAL HENRY LEE

IN THIS SECOND SECTION of this study on George Washington's religion, our main aim is to say something about what the first president believed about God and his relationships to America, and to Washington's private and personal life, as well. Altogether, in this section we shall make eleven major conclusions in regard to what Washington thought about the divine. The first of these is the fact that George Washington seems very rarely to have used the word "God."

In its stead, the first president often used as a substitute for the divine a number of synonyms that many have pointed out had "deistic tendencies." In an appendix to their book, *Washington's God*, Michael and Jana Novak provide a list of over one hundred terms the first president employed to speak of the divine. Among these synonyms for God he used were the following, among many others: "Providence," "the Architect of the World," "the Great Author of Every Public and Private Good," "the Invisible Hand," "the Almighty," "the Lord and Ruler of Nations," "the Most Gracious Lord," "the Most Mighty and Merciful Father," "the Divine Majesty," "the All Powerful Dispensation of Providence," "the Hand of Providence," "the Great Creator," "the Great Director of Events," "the Great Power Above," "the Great Governor of the Universe," "the Giver of Victory," "the Giver of Life," "the Eye of Omnipotence," "the Father of All Mercies," "Supreme Ruler of Nations," "the Great Director of Events," "Supreme Disposer," "Supreme Ruler of the Universe," "the Great Searcher of Human Hearts," "and the Supreme Being"—among many others.[52]

From these many substitutes that George Washington used to refer to the divine, one might also adduce what the first president believed about the attributes of God. It is clear from his speeches and his personal letters that George Washington thought that God was all-good, all-knowing, all-powerful, Creator of the universe out of nothing, and that God regularly acts in history. This latter attribute Washington believed occurs in miracles, in the answering of prayers, and in the favoring of sides in military matters.

This practice of using multiple names for God in early America was not limited just to George Washington. There is evidence, for example, that Thomas Jefferson employed at least twenty-six different terms for designating the divine.[53] For example, Thomas Jefferson used "Preserver and Regulator," "Fabricator," "Supreme Ruler," "Intelligent and Powerful Agent," "Nature's God," and the "Common Father."[54] Because of his use of these deistic references to signify God, Thomas Jefferson was often accused of being a deist, as well. In fact, in 1800, Timothy Dwight, the president of what was then Yale College, said the 1800 election was a choice between "God and a religious President, or Jefferson and no God."[55]

Eighteenth-century British nobleman Lord Bolingbroke used "Nature's God," to stand for God, as did the *Declaration of Independence*; and Alexander Pope, in his "Essay on Man," refers to God as the "Ruling Mind," a name that Washington also employed for the divine.[56] Benjamin Franklin, in a letter to Ezra Stiles, the president of Yale from March 9, 1790, called God "the Creator of the Universe" and "Providence."[57]

In a speech at the Constitutional Convention on June 28, 1787, "Franklin referred to the Divine as "the God Who Governs the Affairs of Men."[58] Samuel Adams, in his essay "The Rights of Colonists," completed in 1772, called God "the Great Law Giver," "the Head of the Christian Religion," "the Almighty," and "the Almighty Being."[59] And Alexander Hamilton, while dying in a duel on June 12, 1804, spoke of the divine as the "Mercy of the Almighty."[60]

In America, Thomas Paine, Ethan Allen, and Benjamin Franklin in his youth, referred to themselves as deists. Indeed, Franklin called himself a "thorough deist." He said, "In my youth, I began to suspect that their doctrines may be true and useful."[61] At the age of twenty, Franklin wrote a pamphlet entitled "Articles of Belief and Acts of Religion" that, at the time, expressed deistic tendencies.[62]

Thomas Paine, in his *Age of Reason*, carefully sketched out his belief in deism. It was there that he wrote:

The religion that approaches the nearest of all others to true Deism, in the moral and benign part thereof, is that of the Quakers.[63]

In another section of the *Age of Reason*, Thomas Paine remarked:

How different is Christianity to the pure and simple Deism! The true Deist had but one deity, and his religion consists of contemplating the power, wisdom, and benignity of the Deity in his works, and endeavoring to imitate him in everything moral, scientific, and mechanical.[64]

By far, the term that President Washington used the most often to refer to the divine was the word "Providence." The first president employed this term continuously from his first Inaugural Address on April 30, 1789, until his Farewell Address, delivered in 1796. In the former, Washington related:

It would be peculiarly improper to omit, in this first official act, my fervent supplications to that Almighty Being who rules over the universe , who presides over the Council of Nations, and whose Providential aid can supply each human defect.[65]

In his Farewell Address, as well, from September 19, 1796, Washington speaks of the "Eternal Father" and his Providence through "His Son and Holy Spirit of Light."[66] Between these two events of the Inaugural Address and the Farewell Address, George Washington constantly returned to the idea of divine Providence.

On October 3, 1789, for example, Washington uses Providence in thanking God for the Constitution. Washington said:

Whereas it is the duty of all nations to acknowledge the Providence of Almighty God . . . I do recommend . . . rendering unto Him our sincere and humble thanks, for . . . the favorable interpositions of His we have experienced in the course and conclusion of the late war . . . for the good and rational manner we have been enabled to establish our Government.[67]

In a letter to Colonel Barakiel Bassett on April 25, 1773, George Washington again speaks about divine Providence. The general observed:

The ways of Providence being inscrutable, and the justice of it not to be scanned by the shallow eye of humanity, nor to be counteracted by the utmost efforts of human power or wisdom, resignation, and as far as the strength of our reason and our Religion can carry us, a cheerful acquiescence to the Divine Will, is what we are to aim.[68]

In a letter to John Augustine Washington from July 18, 1755, President Washington began in this way: "By the All-Powerful Dispensations of Providence." He added, "The miraculous care of Providence . . . protected me beyond all human expectation."[69] The first president deeply believed in divine Providence and employed that term about three hundred times in his writings and speeches. Washington clearly believed that God is all-good, all-knowing, and all-powerful, and that he regularly acts in the affairs of men. This is one of the major arguments against the belief that President Washington was a deist, an issue to which we now shall turn.

The first thing to say about deism is that it was not a religion in the seventeenth and eighteenth centuries. Rather, it was a religious philosophy. It advanced the theory that there is a God, that he created the universe and the rules by which it runs, but he does not intervene in the affairs of humankind. The deistic movement emerged during the Enlightenment from the mid-seventeenth century, initially in England, then later in France and other European countries, as well as America.

Deism, as we shall see, was consistent with the foremost scientific theories of the day, particularly Sir Isaac Newton's physics and metaphysics. Deists generally placed their confidence in reason, and they disdained revelation, as well as the specific teachings of many churches. Some elements of deism have survived in the Unitarians. Washington, Franklin, Jefferson, and Thomas Paine all were labeled deists at one time or another. Benjamin Franklin, in his "Articles of Belief and Acts of Religion," which he wrote when he was twenty-two years old in 1728, summarized much of what deists of the day believed. Franklin wrote:

> For I believe that Man is not the most perfect being but One. Rather that as there are many Degrees of Beings his Inferiors, so there are many Degrees of Being that are superior to him. Also, when I stretch my imagination beyond our system of planets, beyond the visible fixed stars, into that space that is every way Infinite, and conceived it filled with Suns like ours, each with a Chorus of worlds forever moving around, then this little Ball on which we move, seems, even in my narrow imagination, to be almost Nothing, and myself less than nothing, and of no sort of Consequence.[70]

Franklin seems to imagine here the possibility of many universes and, perhaps by implication, many gods. Nevertheless, he continues this way:

> When I think thus, I imagine a great Vanity in me to suppose that the Supremely Perfect, does in the least regard such an inconsiderable Nothing as Man. More especially, since it is impossible

for me to have any positive or clear idea of that which is infinite and incomprehensible, I cannot conceive otherwise that He, the Infinite Father, expects or requires no Worship or Praise from us, that He is even Infinitely above it.[71]

Here Benjamin Franklin seems much closer to traditional deism. There is a God in this view, but he seems not to require worship or praise from human beings. In Enlightenment-era deism, this seems consistent with historical deists like Voltaire and Ethan Allen, for examples. In fact, Allen wrote about how many considered him to be a deist, when he said:

I have generally been denominated a Deist, the reality of which I never disputed. Being conscious that I am no Christian, except mere infant baptism makes me one; And as to being a Deist, I know not, strictly speaking, whether I am one or not. For, I have never read their writings; mine will therefore determine the matter. For I have not in the least disguised my sentiments, but have written freely without any conscious knowledge of prejudice for or against any man, sectary or party whatever; but I wish that good sense, truth, and virtue may be promoted and flourish in the world, to the detection of delusion, superstition, and false religion; and therefore, my errors in the succeeding treatise, which may be rationally pointed out, will be readily rescinded.[72]

There is some confusion about the origin of the philosophical term "deism." In the English-speaking world, the term first appears in Robert Burton's *The Anatomy of Melancholy*, published in 1621.[73] Others suggest that Lord Herbert of Cherbury (1583–1648) is generally considered the "Father of Deism," and his book *De Veritate*, "On Truth," where the term may be found.[74] David L. Holmes, the author of *The Faiths of the Founding Fathers*, also attributes the beginning of deism to Lord Herbert.[75] By the time of Samuel Johnson's (1709–84) 1755 *Dictionary*, he defines "deism" in sixteen words. He says:

The opinion of those who only acknowledge one God, without the reception of any revealed Religion.[76]

Dr. Johnson seems to have seen deism as a movement that believes in a Creator God and the rules that the world works by, but then that God takes no part in what happens in that world after its creation. A homilist from 1670 points out that, for many people of that time, "We have a generation among us, Deists, which is nothing but a new court word for Atheism."[77] This would indicate that at least some seventeenth-century thinkers thought a "deist" was equivalent to an "atheist." At any rate, as a cultural movement, deism was strongest from roughly the mid-seventeenth-century until the close of the nineteenth-century, in both Britain and America, as well as in France.

Besides George Washington, many other colonial-era patriots also were accused of being deists. These include Thomas Jefferson, John Adams, Thomas Paine, Ethan Allen, and James Madison, among many others.

For our purposes, the idea of deism is best understood as the notion of a philosophical concept that arose in the seventeenth century after the publication of Sir Isaac Newton's *Principia Mathematica* in 1687.[78] At the end of that work, the English scientist suggested a metaphor by which one can understand the relationship of God to the world. Newton said the relationship of God to the world is like that of a watchmaker to his watch.[79]

In the eighteenth-century, four separate philosophical responses developed for interpreting this metaphor. The theists believed that the watchmaker was the omni-attributed God of traditional Christianity, who created the universe and continually acts in history by performing miracles, answering prayers, and choosing sides in military skirmishes. G. W. Leibniz (1646–1716) and Alexander Pope (1688–1744), are fine examples of this view.[80]

The Manicheans, or the dualistic view, our second position, held that there are two gods, one good and one evil, and they take turns ruling the universe. Pierre Bayle (1647–1706) is a representative example of this view.[81] This view was very popular in the Roman Empire in the fourth and fifth centuries. In fact, Saint Augustine of Hippo joined the Manicheans for nearly a decade in the 370s, and the Manichean Movement had a revival in the seventeenth and eighteenth centuries, during Pierre Bayle's time.

The third view, atheism, completely rejected the watch analogy because they believed the watchmaker did not exist. The Baron d'Holbach (1723–89) is a representative example of this position.[82] Denis Diderot is another eighteenth-century example. Both of these European men were among the outwardly professed atheists during the Enlightenment Era.

The fourth eighteenth-century view, the one we are analyzing here, grew out of the Latin expression *Deus absconditis*, or "A God who absconds" or "goes away." In this fourth view, proponents in the eighteenth-century believed that God created the universe, and the rules it works by, and then withdrew from acting in it. In this fourth position, God does not perform miracles, does not answer prayers, does not choose sides in battle, and otherwise does not act in history.[83]

Peter Byrne, in his book *Natural Religion and the Nature of Religion*, suggests that the principle difference between deism and traditional theism is "a distinction between a supposed act of divine truths specially

communicated by God in history and a real system of truth available to all
by the use of unaided reason."[84] Russell Kirk provides a definition of deism
in his book, *The Roots of American Order*. Kirk says:

> Deism was neither a Christian schism nor a systematic Philoso-
> phy, but rather a way of looking at the human condition ... The
> Deist professed a belief in a single, Supreme Being, but rejected
> a large part of Christian doctrine. ... For the Deist, the Supreme
> Being was indeed the Creator of the Universe, but He did not
> interfere with the functioning of His creation.[85]

However, in the eighteenth century, the deist did believe that God
created the universe as a watchmaker, but that the watch was entirely self-
winding, operating on its own after its creation. In the deist view, then, God
does not answer prayers, perform miracles, or act in history in general.
The French writer Voltaire (1694–1778) is a representative example of this
view.[86]

At any rate, by the close of the eighteenth century, the religious associations of Enlightenment and their responses to Newton's watch and
watchmaker analogy, philosophers looked like this:

Figure II.1.

	Newton		
I. Theism	IV. Deism	II. Dualism	III. Atheism
G.W. Leibniz	Voltaire	Bayle.	D'Holbach.

Among contemporary scholars, a significant number of them believe that
George Washington, along with many of the other Founding Fathers of this
nation, were deists (position number four) and not theists (position number
one). Michael and Jana Novak, for example, in their book *Washington's God*,
devote an entire chapter to why they believe that Washington was not a
deist. They call this chapter "What's a Deist? The Deist Tendency."[87] Their
conclusion is that George Washington was no deist, principally because the
first president thought that God acts in history, performs miracles, answers
prayers, and plays a role in the victors of military battles.

David L. Holmes, in his book *The Faiths of the Founding Fathers*, cat-
egorized Washington as a "Christian Deist."[88] This was also a designation
used by a number of British thinkers in the eighteenth century, including
Thomas Chubb (1679–1746) and Thomas Morgan (1695–1743.) In France,
Pierre Viret (1511–71), a Swiss Reformed thinker who also may have coined

the word "deist," and Pierre Annet (1693–1769), in his *Deism Fairly Stated*, published in 1744, also referred to themselves as "Christian Deists."[89]

Another Washington biographer, Barry Schwartz, suggests that Washington's "practice of Christianity was limited . . . because he was not himself a Christian." He adds, "In the Enlightenment tradition of his day, he was a devout Deist—just as many of the clergymen who knew him had suspected."[90]

In a 2012 book, historian Gregg Frazer argued against the view that Washington was a deist. Instead, he calls the first president a "theistic rationalist." Frazer also says this view rejected core Christian beliefs like the divinity of Jesus, the Trinity, and the doctrine of original sin. Frazer seems to suggest that George Washington was a deist, as well.[91] Indeed, there appears to be very little difference between theistic rationalism and deism.

Even in his own time, many of Washington's contemporaries believed he was a deist. In his book *George Washington and Religion*, Paul F. Boller Jr. quotes a New-Jersey-born Presbyterian minister Ashbel Green (1762–1848), who knew Washington. The Rev. Green said that the first president "often said in my hearing that while the President was very deferential to religion and its ceremonies, he was not a Christian, but a Deist."[92]

The Rev. James Abercrombie, an assistant rector at Christ Church in Philadelphia, indicated that "Sir Washington was a Deist!"[93] This judgment came as a consequence of a chastisement of the first president because Washington left the service before communion was administered. Abercrombie followed up his comment about deism by saying, about Washington:

> I cannot consider any man as a real Christian who uniformly disregards an ordinance so solemnly enjoined by the Divine Author of our holy religion.[94]

Apparently, it was the view of the Rev. Abercrombie that Washington must have been a deist because he did not receive the sacrament of the Holy Eucharist. But why would one who is a deist want to conform to any of the myths, symbols, and rituals of the Anglican church in Virginia? The fact that Washington did not receive communion says more that he was not a good, or a devout, Christian than that he was a deist.

In contemporary Western scholarship, four major arguments are made by scholars to conclude that the first president was a deist. First, Washington did not take communion at Sunday services of the Anglican/Episcopal churches, as indicated in the above analysis. Second, he refused to make public statements about his personal religious beliefs. Third, he rarely used the word "Jesus" in both his private letters and his public announcements. Finally, while he believed in some sort of God and saw Providence as acting in his life and the life of the nation, it seems more like a Greco-Roman understanding of fate than confidence in traditional monotheism. More will be said about Washington's views on fate, stoicism, and virtue in a later section of this essay (section V).

There are also at least six responses to the above views, arguing that Washington was a Christian. First, he religiously observed the Sabbath as a day of rest and often attended services on that day. Second, many around him reported that the first president reserved time for private prayer in his everyday life. More also will be said about Washington's views on prayer, as well, in a later section (section VI). Third, Washington saved many of the dozens of sermons and homilies he had been sent by clergymen over the years—and he read many of them aloud to his wife, Martha.

Fourth, Washington supervised the hanging of two paintings in the dining room at Mount Vernon. One was of the Virgin Mary, and the other of Saint John the Evangelist, so it is unlikely that Washington was not a devout Christian. Fifth, many of the chaplains who served under him during the war believed him to be a practicing Christian. And finally, unlike Thomas Jefferson, he was never accused of not being a Christian.

It is also worth noting that Washington agreed to be a godfather for at least eight different children, while Jefferson refused to take on the job because he had doubts about many of the theological beliefs that lay behind the practice.[95] This can be seen in Jefferson's appending of the Gospels.[96]

Timothy Dwight, the president of Yale College, wrote a poem drawing the historical parallel between Joshua and Washington, and Canaan and America. The poem is called *The Conquest of Canaan*, and he dedicates it to George Washington. Dwight tells the story of Joshua, a powerful military hero who leads the chosen people to victory. The unspoken parallel has numerous ties, in Dwight's mind, to American history.[97] The portrayal of New England as the "new Canaan" had been an important part of Puritan Literature since the early seventeenth-century. In Dwight's poem, Joshua resembles Washington, both in terms of his leadership and his military prowess.[98]

In his footnotes to the poem, Dwight made the analogy between the Biblical story and American history explicit, with references to heroes of the Revolutionary War. The poem also embodies a number of key concepts that already had become part of the American Ethos. In one portion of the poem, Dwight writes:

> In that dead hour, beneath auspicious skies
> To nobler bliss your world shall rise.[99]

In the footnote to this couplet, Dwight explains that he was referring to "Freedom and glory of the North American States."[100] Clearly Timothy

Dwight was one of those thinkers who saw America as the "New Jerusalem," and George Washington as the "New Joshua."

In the chapter on deism in the Novaks' book, the major argument that they make against the idea that George Washington was a deist are the many examples where they show that the first president clearly believed that God acts in history, performs miracles, and takes sides in military actions. Indeed, this brings us to our second conclusion concerning George Washington's view of God—that God protected the new American nation with a special form of grace, not unlike Moses leading the chosen people out of Egypt in the Old Testament narrative and wandering for forty years in the desert, or Joshua leading the Jews after Moses' death.

It is also clear that George Washington believed that America was a "new Jerusalem," a nation that is protected in a special way by the hand of Providence. In one of his letters, the first president tied the Hebrew people to the new independent nation when he wrote:

> Since the delivering of the Hebrews from their Egyptian Op-
> pressors and planted them in the Promised Land—and Whose
> Providential Agency has lately been conspicuously in establish-
> ing these United States as an independent Nation—still con-
> tinue to water them with the dews of Heaven and to make the
> inhabitants of every denomination participate in the temporal
> and spiritual blessings of that people whose God is Jehovah.[101]

Here Washington clearly likened the American separation from the tyrant Britain to be like that of Moses leading the Hebrew people out of their captivity in Egypt. In this regard, it was common in the late eighteenth-century to compare Washington to Moses, or Joshua, and the American colonists to the chosen people of Israel, or a "new Jerusalem," as well as Pharaoh to King George III.

In another instance, Washington expresses this idea of the new American nation having a special status when he wrote:

> . . . And it is my earnest prayer that we may soon conduct our-
> selves as to merit a continuance of those blessings with which
> we have hitherto been favored.[102]

It is also clear that Washington believed that God was behind his military defeats, as well. After the 1777 American defeat at Germantown, for example, the first president remarked:

> We must endeavor to deserve better of Providence, and, I am
> persuaded, she will smile on us.[103]

It appears that, at times, General Washington believed that the Providence of God was in favor of the American enemies. Additionally, the first president also believed that his particular life and actions were especially protected by the hand of God. Indeed, Washington often attributed changes in the wind, or particular victories in the war, to be nothing more than the product of Providence.

One example of this phenomenon is the Battle of Boston on March 5, 1776. The night before, the American soldiers had dug trenches for the forthcoming battle. The British were surprised the following morning by how much progress Washington's army had made; but just as the battle commenced, it was suddenly interrupted. The weather had dramatically shifted from clear skies to stormy by noon. As the day turned to evening, the weather changed to hail and sleet, "and the wind blew almost to a hurricane."[104]

As a result of the storm, the British Commander, General Howe, decided not to attack, and eventually ordered a retreat from Boston. Like many other people, particularly Americans, Washington attributed the storm of March the 5th, 1776, to the intervening "hand of God." In a letter to Joseph Reed at the time, Washington attributed the retreat to the Providence of God providing a special blessing to the colonists.[105]

The Battle of Boston also was seen as crucial to a number of other early colonial leaders. John Adams said of the battle, "On that night the formation of American independence was laid." Daniel Webster said of the fight at Boston, "From that moment, we date our severance with the British Empire."[106]

The Rev. John Witherspoon, one of the signers of the Declaration of Independence, was another of the many Founding Fathers that recognized the imposition of the divine at the Battle of Boston. He observes, as Washington also did, that it was God who was behind that victory.[107]

At a later battle at New York Harbor, a fleet of British ships began to attack the Continental Army there; but the ships suddenly became paralyzed when the wind shifted against them. Before the Battle of Trenton, to cite another example, where Washington crossed the Delaware, the Hessian commander in charge of the fort did not receive a note about Washington's movements until it was far too late.[108]

To some, these random events appeared to have been coincidences or just good luck, but to George Washington and to many others, they were nothing less than the very fingerprints of God on the behalf of the colonists.

George Washington also saw the hand of Providence in the Battle of Long Island in 1776. Washington and his men were trapped on Brooklyn Heights, Long Island. The British were poised to crush Washington's army the next day, which may have brought an end to the rebellion. However,

Washington made a bold move by evacuating his troops under the cover of darkness. He did this by using every available fishing vessel, rowboat, and other small, local craft; but there was not enough time to complete the task.[109]

When the morning came, the fog of the night remained for a while, and the British could see the last American boat crossing the East River, beyond the reach of the British guns. Michael Novak, in his book *On Two Wings: Humble Faith and Common Sense at the American Founding*, gives a compelling description of the battle.[110] Novak says that Washington clearly understood that the victory at the Battle of Long Island was nothing more than an act of Providence.

That the feeling of being aided by the hand of God was held by George Washington in regard to his own, personal life, also can be seen in a July 18th, 1755 letter to John Augustine Washington. The President wrote:

> By the All-Powerful Dispensations of Providence, I have been protected beyond all human probability and expectation; for I had four bullets through my coat, and two horses shot from under me; yet, I escaped unhurt, although death was leveling my companions on every side.[111]

In his first inaugural address, George Washington made it clear that he believed that the United States was seen as a New Jerusalem, a new chosen people. The President remarked:

> No people can be bound to acknowledge and adore the Invisible Hand, which conducts the Affairs of men more than the people of the United States. Every step, by which they have advanced to the character of an independent nation, seems to have been distinguished by some token of Providential Agency.[112]

The expression "Invisible Hand," used here by President Washington, was also employed by Adam Smith in his *Theory of Moral Sentiments*, written in 1759. Smith also used the same term in his more famous *Wealth of Nations*, published the same year as the American independence, in 1776. Both Smith and Washington employed the expression to speak of the silent workings of God on the world as an invisible hand.[113] Washington also used the term in a letter to the Hebrew congregation of Savannah, Georgia, on June 14, 1790.[114]

In another private letter on August 20, 1778, Washington called himself a "Preacher of Providence." He relates, "The Hand of Providence has been so conspicuous in all this, that he must be worse than an Infidel that lacks faith, and more than wicked, that has not gratitude enough for me to turn Preacher."[115] The first president adds, "When my present appointment ceases, and therefore I shall add nothing more to the Doctrine of Providence."[116]

Another conclusion that can be made about Washington's views of God is that he believed that all nations have duties to God. He characterizes these duties in terms of obedience, gratefulness, and humility. On October 3, 1789, in New York City, for example, the first president proclaimed a day of thanksgiving reiterating these three duties. Washington observed:

> Whereas it is the duty of all nations to acknowledge the Providence of Almighty God, to obey His Will, to be grateful for His benefits, and humbly to implore His Protection and favor.[117]

Among the many "General Orders" of the Continental Army, there is this one, in which General Washington again refers to the duty of gratitude for God's blessings. The general wrote:

> The Commander-in-Chief is confident, the Army under his immediate direction, will show their gratitude to Providence, for thus favoring the cause of Freedom in America; and by their thankfulness to God, their zeal and perseverance in this righteous Cause, continue to deserve His future blessings.[118]

Michael and Jana Novak comment on this Washington passage. They write:

> In other words, Washington believed that prayer without self-reform would be hypocritical. His men must make themselves worthy of Divine favor.[119]

The Novaks go on to point out: "In fact, completely contrary to any purported Deist tendency, he never hesitated to be explicit about his belief and a reliance on 'Providence,' and its much needed 'interpositions' in the War."[120] Indeed, in a later "General Order," after the War had progressed a great deal, the commander-in-chief tells us that:

> Another appeal to Heaven, with the blessings of Providence, it becomes the duty of every officer and soldier to humbly supplicate, so that we shall prove successful.[121]

And in another "General Order," the general urged his troops to recognize and be thankful of the "reiterated and astonishing interpositions that Providence has demanded of us."[122] In a letter to his wife Martha, President Washington again speaks of Providence and gratitude when he writes: "I shall rely, therefore, confidently on that Providence, which has heretofore preserved and has been bountiful to me, not doubting that I shall return safe to you in the Fall.[123]

Washington again makes reference here to his belief that God has granted a special grace and protection in regard to his personal life. The first president, despite the fact that he was in the middle of a war, had "no doubt" that he would return to his wife, Martha.

One final judgment that we can make about George Washington's understanding of God is that he firmly believed that God is the sole judge of human hearts. He made this clear in a letter to Benedict Arnold on September 14, 1775, before he became out of favor in Washington's eyes. Washington wrote:

> While we are contending for our Liberty, we should be very cautious not to violate the rights of Conscience in others, considering that God alone is the Judge of the hearts of men, and to him only in this case they are answerable.[124]

From all that we have said in the second section of this essay on George Washington's religion, we have made the following eleven conclusions from our analysis. First, although Washington regularly used the word "God" in his public life, he also employed more than a hundred synonyms for the divine. Second, President Washington's most-used term for God was the "Providence of God" and its many derivatives. Third, the first president thought that all nations, and especially America, have duties to God, and among those are obedience, gratitude, and humility.

A fourth conclusion to be made about George Washington's view of God is that he firmly believed that the Unites States was a "new Jerusalem," or a "new promised land," and was given appropriate grace in regard to that status. Fifth, the first president believed that America was given a special protection by Providence. Sixth, Washington saw himself as a "Instrument of the Hand of Providence," in regard to conducting the affairs of the new nation. Seventh, although the first president clearly was a man of the Enlightenment, he does not appear to have been a deist, primarily because Washington thought that God acted in history, answered prayers, took part in military skirmishes, and performed miracles.

An eighth conclusion we have made in this section in regard to Washington's view of God is his conclusion that because he was never injured in combat—despite the fact that two horses were shot beneath him, and on one occasion he left a battle with four bullet holes in his coat—Washington also saw himself as having a special protection by the hand of Providence. He interpreted that protection as a sign of the "footprints of the Divine."

Ninth, while believing in God and that he has sometimes a profound influence in his personal life, Washington also seems to have been influenced by Greco-Roman views of fate, as well as Roman stoicism.

Tenth, as Michael and Jana Novak have pointed out:

> It is not at all unusual for public men in a pluralistic American life to maintain a notable reserve about their private convictions. They do not burden the public with declarations of their deepest beliefs, whose general force they trust their actions will sufficiently reveal. In the public forum, they happily give to Caesar what is Caesar's, and in the private forum, to God what is God's.[125]

And finally, George Washington firmly believed that God alone is the judge of human hearts. Indeed, he was a clear advocate that the divine both punishes and rewards human beings, in this life and in this next.

It is abundantly clear from the public life of George Washington that the first president appears to have kept his religious cards pressed closely to his vest; but that he seems to have been very private in his religious life does not make him much different from many of his contemporary thinkers, like Adams and Jefferson, for example.

From these eleven conclusions regarding Washington's views on God, we may imply at least three others. These conclusions are related to the first president's views on ethics, the problem of evil, and the nature and belief in Jesus. In relationship to the first of these, Washington sometimes referred to God as the "Author or Arbiter of every Public and Private Good." This seems to suggest that God is the sole author of the moral good. This view is sometimes called "Divine Command Theory" in the history of Western philosophy.[126]

We will say a great deal more about the divine plan response to the problem of evil in section VIII of this essay, as well as a number of other responses to that problem, some of which are mentioned in the above analysis.

The advocates of divine command theory believe that whatever command God makes about the moral nature of an action, that, in itself, makes the action morally good. In many places in his public and in his private lives, it seems that George Washington was a believer in this theory. Philosophical problems associated with divine command theory were first raised by Plato in a dialogue known as the "Euthyphro." According to Plato, the crux of what is known as the "Euthyphro Dilemma" is whether God is all-good, or if goodness is good simply because God says so.[127] Again, more will be said about Washington's views on ethics and virtue in a later section of this essay, section V.

In one of his private diaries, George Washington made periodic comments about the issues of Theodicy and the Problem of Evil. In one of these entries, Washington prays:

> Help all in affliction or adversity. Give them patience and a sanctified use of their affliction, and in Thy good time, deliverance from them; forgive my enemies, take me unto Thy protection this day, keep me in perfect peace, which I ask in Thy name for the sake of Jesus. Amen.[128]

From this comment in his private diary, Washington appears to have believed in three traditional responses to the problem of evil. The first is called the test view. It says that God uses evil and suffering to test the characters of people. The second view, which is called the "Moral Qualities View," says that the divine employs evil and suffering in the lives of humans to make them better people, morally. In Washington's view, patience and perseverance are by-products of withstanding evil and suffering.[129]

Finally, Washington's use of the expressions "the sanctified use of their affliction" and "deliverance from them" seems to imply that God has "sanctified" reasons for bringing evil and suffering to human beings. This suggests that George Washington was a believer in what is sometimes called the "divine plan" point of view. Proponents of this theory maintain that God sometimes brings evil and suffering to people and to nations, but in the long run, that evil and suffering will someday be seen as part of a larger divine plan for the good.[130] This may occur in this life or the next. More will be said about Washington's views on the problem of evil in a subsequent section of this essay, section VIII.

In this same diary from May 14, 1787, to May 18 of that same year, George Washington mentions the person of Jesus Christ a dozen times, and in all of them, it is with an attitude of solemnity, respect, and devotion. It is true that George Washington did not mention Jesus very often in his public life, but his private life was another matter. Much more will be said about George Washington's views on Jesus Christ, as we shall see, in section VII of this essay.

One final aspect of George Washington's views on God is what the first president had to say about the relationship between religion, specifically belief in God, and reason. In one of his speeches, Washington made the claim that "Religion is as necessary to reason, as reason is to religion. The one cannot exist without the other. A reasoning being would lose his reason in attempting to account for the great phenomena of nature, had he not have a Supreme Being to refer to."[131]

On another occasion, the first president returned to the same theme:

> It is impossible to account for the creation of the universe, without the agency of a Supreme Being. It is impossible to govern the universe without the aid of a Supreme Being. It is impossible to reason without the aid of a Supreme Being.[132]

In a November 22, 1798, letter to Alexander Spotswood, President Washington again wrote about religion and reason. He said, "To give opinions unsupported by reasons might appear to be dogmatical."[133] From these letters, it is clear that the first president believed that there was an intimate connection between reason and belief in God; but that belief might just as well be the God of deism, as that of traditional theism.

With this final point, we now have eleven major conclusions we can make in regards to George Washington's views on God. These may be summarized in the following way:

1. George Washington rarely used the word "God."

2. In its stead, he substituted over one hundred different synonyms for the divine.

3. His favorite term for the divine was Providence.

4. All nations, and not simply America, have duties to God.

5. Providence acts in special ways in regard to America.

6. America is a new Jerusalem, and Washington is a new Moses, or a new Joshua.

7. Providence brought special blessings and graces to the life of Washington.

8. Washington believed in divine command theory.

9. Washington was not a deist.

10. Washington was influenced by Stoic virtue theory.

11. And finally, Washington believed there is an intimate connection between reason and religious belief.

This now brings us to the third section on the first president's relationship to, and uses of, the Bible.[134]

III

Washington on the Bible

It is but natural to begin with George Washington,
for with him begins that which is truly clear of America.

—CALVIN COOLIDGE, "SPEECH AT MOUNT RUSHMORE," AUGUST 10, 1927

GEORGE WASHINGTON'S KNOWLEDGE OF the Bible ranged from Genesis to the book of Revelation. He makes more than two hundred Biblical allusions or citations in his letters, and in his private and public speeches, these include references to Christianity, to God, Heaven, to Jesus, the Golden Rule, and to the Ten Commandments.

There can be little doubt that Mary Ball Washington read from the Bible to her children, including George, when they were young. There is also an undated entry in one of Washington's memorandum books that he kept in his teen years, where he says that he had been studying the Bible of late, now that he began to make his living as a surveyor.[135] There is very little other evidence, however, that suggests that Washington was a regular reader of Holy Scripture until late in his life.

In this third section of this study on Washington's religion, we will explore the many uses that George Washington employed for the Holy Bible. We will begin by taking a look at many of the president's favorite Bible passages, among his many quotations of Holy Writ, though Washington, like other Virginia gentry at his time, rarely employed quotation marks in his writings.

This will be followed by an examination of a number of particular Bibles that served roles in the life of the first president. We move, then, to a

36

number of Washington's favorite Old Testament passages. As we shall see, Washington's favorite Old Testament expression was the "vine and the fig tree," from the Prophet Micah.

George Washington often incorporated familiar Biblical idioms and phrases into his every-day vocabulary. Among those idioms and phrases are "the forbidden fruit," of the third chapter of Genesis; Genesis 45:18's reference to the "fat of the land"; "Seven times seven" of Leviticus 25:8; the "thorn in the side" found at Numbers 33:55 and Judges 2:3; the idea of the "firstfruits" in Deuteronomy 26:2; and the notion of "sleeping with one's fathers" at Deuteronomy 31:16, 2 Samuel 7:12, and 1 Kings 1:21. Washington also employed Psalm 121:4 and Isaiah 5:27's "neither sleep nor slumber"; Psalm 23:6's "all the days of your life"; and "like sheep to the slaughter" found at Psalm 44:22.

Michael and Jana Novak, in their book *Washington's God*, tell us that:

> Before the War of Independence, Washington had purchased from London a beautifully printed Book of Psalms to carry in his coat pocket, and many of its descriptions of a Creator and Divine Architect seeped into his imagery.[136]

This copy of the Psalms purchased by Washington is now owned by the Freer Collection in Detroit, Michigan. It is designated as GK Ms. II. It is a hardback text. The Palala Press has recently issued a facsimile of *Washington's Psalms*, complete with black and white illustrations, in 2016.[137]

In a number of places in their book, the Novaks stressed the fact that Washington's God "seems very much like the Lord God described in the Hebrew Torah, the historical books and the Psalms, who in furthering His own designs interposes himself in history."[138] A little later on in their book, the father and daughter Novak team says of Washington and the gods of the Old and New Testaments:

> To be sure these older Christian terms with a decidedly Hebrew cast, expressed in a preference for the language of the Psalms and Micah and the other Prophets more often than in the tender terms of attachment for Jesus Christ.[139]

Washington seemed much more comfortable with the God of the Old Testament than that of the New Testament. It also is true that George Washington rarely mentioned Jesus in his public discourse. It is clear that President George Washington, in the writing of his "Thanksgiving Proclamation" of 1795, for example, used as his model the entirety of Psalm 67. The King James Version of these verses tell us:

God be merciful unto us, and bless us; and cause His face to
shine upon us; Selah. That thy way may be known upon earth,
thy saving health among all nations. Let the people praise thee,
O God; let all the people praise thee. O let the nations be glad
and sing for joy: for thou shalt judge the people righteously, and
govern the nations upon earth. Selah. Let the people praise thee,
O God; let all the people praise thee. Then shall the earth yield
her increase; and God, even our own God, shall bless us. God
shall bless us, and all the ends of the Earth shall fear Him.[140]

In his "Thanksgiving Proclamation" of 1795, Washington centers his
remarks on the themes of mercy, praise, the increase of abundance, and
above all, the fear of the Lord, in offering thanksgiving. The proclamation
was signed by Washington in the city of Philadelphia, on the first of January
of 1795.

Another Biblical image that was employed regularly by President
Washington was his use of "swords to plowshares" that can be found at
Isaiah 2:4, Joel 3:10, and Micah 4:3. The first president used this Old Testament image in a letter to Congress on December 20, 1776.[141] The image of
"sowing and reaping," borrowed from 1 Kings 4:25 and 2 Kings 18:3, also
was used many times by George Washington.[142] This latter image also can be
found at Galatians 6:7, Luke 6:38, and 2 Corinthians 9:6.

In a letter to Robert Morris on May 28, 1778, Washington employed
the idiom "reaping the fruit of our toil and labor." This biblical image can
be found in the Old Testament at Psalm 128:2 and in the New Testament at
Philippians 1:22.[143] The phrase "Unable to pay to the utmost farthing," of
Matthew 5:26, also was used by Washington in a letter to his mother, Mary
Ball Washington, on February 15, 1787.[144] Washington employed the image
of "seven times seven" from Leviticus 25:8 in a letter to his wife, Martha, on
June 18, 1775. The phrase is also employed in Matthew 18:22.[145]

George Washington also regularly referred to the idiom of "thorn
in the side." In a letter to Samuel Purviance, for example, from March 10,
1786, and in another correspondence to James Madison, on the morning
of March 31, 1787, he also used that same image. The same idiom may be
found at Numbers 33:55 and Judges 2:3.[146] Washington also employed the
image in Deuteronomy 26:2 of firstfruits, on numerous occasions, mostly
in his letters. In one letter to General Thomas Nelson Jr., from February 8,
1778, for example, the image may be found.[147]

The same "firstfruits" image also can be found in a correspondence
from the first president to Daniel Bowers, from May 28, 1779;[148] and Washington employed the image a number of other times in his letters, such as
a June 28, 1786 letter to Richard Sprigg, Maryland attorney,[149] as well as

a correspondence from Washington to Francois Barbe-Marbois on July 9, 1783.[150] Mister Barbe-Marbois (1745–1837) was a French politician and acquaintance of Washington's.

At times in his letters and speeches George Washington mentioned particular Old Testament figures in the course of his everyday activities. In one note to himself, for example, he wrote, "If you can't find it in the Book of Ezekiel, look for it in Israel."[151] In a letter to his brother-in-law, in the context of the health of his tobacco crop, he said his crop was "being assailed by every villainous worm that had an existence since the days of Noah."[152] In the context of being worried about profiteers, Washington said, "They should be hanged upon a gallows five times as high as the one prepared for Haman."[153]

The Old Testament figure of Haman, of course, is the villainous character in the book of Esther. He was an advisor to the Persian king, and plotted to have the Jews destroyed by hanging their leaders, when he ended up being hanged on the same gallows he had prepared for the Jews' execution. Those gallows were reported to be "fifty cubits high."[154]

At times, Washington made an analogy to the ancient Hebrews and the idea that the outcome of a struggle would be determined by the moral characters of those involved in the conflict. When things were going badly in the war, Washington would quote Old Testament passages like Genesis 15:16, that "The measures on iniquity not yet had been fulfilled."[155] In the "Circular Letter" to the governor of the states, to give another example, Washington closes the letter with a prayer that God would:

> Most graciously be pleased to dispose us all, to do justice and to love mercy.[156]

This is nearly a direct quotation from Micah 6:8, that in the King James Version tells us, "He hath shewed thee, O man, what is good; and what doth the Lord require of thee, but to do justly, and to love mercy, and to walk humbly with thy God?"[157]

By far, however, the most popular ancient Hebrew phrase of the Old Testament employed by the first president is found at Micah 4:4, 1 Kings 4:25, Zechariah 3:10, 2 Kings 18, Isaiah 36, and 1 Maccabees 14:12. This latter passage in the King James Version tells us, "For every man sat under his vine and his fig tree, and there was none to fray him."[158] This notion of "under his vine and under his fig tree" was employed by General-President Washington over fifty times in the second half of his life.

John Avlon, in his book *Washington's Farewell*, describes Washington's use of this image on the vine and the fig tree. He observes:

This reference to the "vine and fig tree" was Washington's favorite Old Testament citation. From the Book of Micah, it flowed from the story of a poor farmer freed from military oppression, living free from fear on his own land in a state of contented self-sufficiency. Washington referred to the "vine and fig tree" almost fifty times in his correspondence, often mentioning it in relation to his own hopes of retirement at Mount Vernon. And it appropriately appears one last time in his Farewell Address.[159]

Beginning as early as November 19, 1776, the first president used the image of "the vine and the fig tree" in a letter to John Augustine Washington.[160] He again employed the phrase in a January 22, 1784 correspondence to Charles Thomson (1729–1824.).[161] Between 1796 and 1790, Washington's letters are peppered with the use of the phrase, including Washington to Landon Carter (1710–78) in a correspondence from October 17, 1796;[162] to John Quincy Adams on June 25, 1797;[163] and to Oliver Wolcott (1726–97) on May 15, 1797.[164]

Additionally, Washington employed the "vine and the fig tree" in a June 24, 1797 correspondence to Charles C. Pinckney (1757–1824)[165] and in a letter to his friend Sarah Cary Fairfax on May 16, 1798.[166] Sarah Cary Fairfax, called "Sally" (1730–1811), was the wife of George William Fairfax and the mistress of the Belvoir Plantation.

Washington employed the "vine and the fig tree" as well as in his 1790 correspondence to the Hebrew congregation of Newport, Rhode Island, to whom he ensured that: "Everyone shall sit in safety under his own vine and fig tree, and there shall be none to make them afraid."[167]

Clearly, Washington wished to capture the agrarian ideals of simplicity, contentment, and self-sufficiency. Above all, it is also a confirmation of the idea of private property as a Biblical idea, and a prohibition against land-grabbing. Mr. Washington was also fond of a number of Biblical proverbs and aphorisms. In his "Circular Letter" from January of 1782, for example, the first president wrote that "The race is not always to the swift, or the battle to the strong," an obvious reference to Ecclesiastes 3:1 and 17.

On many other occasions, Washington also turned to the employment of idea of the Biblical term *hevel*, or "vanity," found at Ecclesiastes 1:14; 2:11, 17, 26; 4:4, 16; and 6:9, among other places. Indeed, he used the expression "It may be vanity and vexation of spirit" in a number of places.[168] Two examples of this phenomenon can be found in Washington's letter to Willian Vans Murray (1763–1803) from December 3, 1797, and in his "Circular Letter to the Northern States," written on January 31, 1782.[169]

The first president also employed the idea of "The rising of the Sun to the setting of the same." This is an Old Testament phrase found at Psalm 50:1 and 113:3, as well as Malachi 1:11, that tells us:

> From the rising of the Sun even to the going down of the same, my name shall be great among the Gentiles, and in every place where incense may be.[170]

At times, President Washington even employed Old Testament ideas in conducting his political affairs. In the final sentence of his June 8, 1783 "Circular Letter," for example, he paraphrased Micah 6:8 in expressing how citizens were to treat each other. He reveals:

> We should humbly imitate the Characteristics of the Divine Author of our blessed religion, for the political purpose of America "becoming a happy nation."[171]

Washington was also fond of several other Old Testament passages, including Genesis 1:22 and 28, Leviticus 26:9, Deuteronomy 15:11 and 24:14, and Psalm 35:10. He employed the first pair of these passages so that Americans would "increase and multiply." The final three were used by Washington to describe our duties "to the poor and to the oppressed of the Earth."[172]

George Washington also was a regular user of Psalm 29:2, that tells us in the King James Version, "When the righteous are in authority, the people rejoice. But when a wicked man rules, the people groan."[173] Washington employed this image to refer to King George III and the British Empire, as well as America as a righteous nation. Washington also employed Psalm 14:34, for similar purposes. The verse in question in the King James Version tells us:

> Righteousness exalts a nation, but sin is a reproach to any nation.[174]

George Washington also was fond of 1 Timothy 2:2, because it asks for prayers for kings and other rulers "who are in authority that we may live a quiet and peaceable life in all Godliness and reverence."[175] Needless to say, he had himself in mind when he often employed this New Testament passage.

The first president regularly employed Old Testament passages to establish the claim that America is a new Jerusalem or a new promised land, "filled with milk and honey," as Joshua 5:6 tells us. Washington also used Deuteronomy 11:9; 26:9, 15; 27:3; and 31:20, for similar purposes.

The theme of God's controlling Providence directing the affairs of human beings also runs through the Old Testament and the works of George Washington. Washington was fond of the King James Version of Zechariah 4:6, and its "Not by might, nor by power, but by the Spirit, saith the Lord of Hosts."[176] He also used Proverbs 16:19, "A man's heart deviseth his way, but the Lord directeth his steps."[177] In many of his letters, the first president quotes Proverbs 16:33, "The lot is cast into the lap; but the whole disposing thereof is of the Lord."[178]

In a letter to his friend and fellow Virginian, David Stuart (1753–1814), from June 15, 1790, Washington speaks of illness and death. After telling Stuart he had been sick twice recently, Washington went on to say, "I already had within less than a year, two severe attacks—the last worse than the first—a third, more than probable will put me to sleep with my fathers."[179] The metaphor to "sleep with one's fathers" is a reference to waiting for the resurrection of the body after death, at the end of time, as exemplified in Daniel 12:1–3.

The idiom of "sleeping with one's fathers" is used throughout the Torah, particularly at places like Deuteronomy 31:16; 1 Kings 2:10; 11:43; 16:6; 22:50; 2 Samuel 7:12; and 2 Kings 14:16; 15:7; and 16:20. This Hebraic point of view, of course, is distinct from the Greek view of immortality of the soul, in which the soul separates from the body to go off to be judged.

Many of these uses of these Old Testament idioms and phrases are a good argument against the view that George Washington was a deist, as we have seen in section II of this essay. Washington also often employed New Testament idioms and phrases in his everyday speeches and writings. It is to the New Testament to which we now turn.

George Washington quoted the New Testament not nearly as much as he cited the Old Testament. In his "Circular Letter" from June of 1783, for example, Washington said:

> The pure and benign light of Divine Revelation, have had an ameliorating influence on mankind and increased the blessings of Society.[180]

By the "Light of Revelation," of course, the first president meant the Holy Scriptures, counting as one of the contributing foundations of the confluences that produced the American nation. Among the New Testament idioms and Greek phrases to which he often turned were the following: Washington had a fondness of the "sheep to slaughter" metaphor at Romans 8:39; he frequently quoted the "separation of the wheat from the tares," from Matthew 13:1–13; the image of a "millstone hung around the neck" that appears at Matthew 18:6, Mark 9:42, and Luke 17:2, and was also quoted by President Washington over a dozen times in his collected works.

Washington employed the letter of Hebrews' reference to the "Throne of Grace," at Hebrews 4:16, in an April 20, 1789 correspondence to the German Lutherans of Philadelphia. At the end of the letter, Washington wrote, "I hope to hold the same place in your affections, which your friendly declarations induce me to believe I possess at present; and, amidst all the vicissitudes, that may await me in this mutable existence, I shall earnestly desire the continuation of an interest in your intercession at the Throne of Grace."[181]

Washington also quoted Matthew 24:6 and Mark 13:7 about "wars and rumors of wars." He speaks of Jesus' penchant for saying "My good and faithful Servant" in Matthew 25:21–23, and he employs Jesus words while healing at Mark 2:9 and John 5:8–12, when he commanded, "Take up thy bed and walk." The first president also refers to the "widow's mite" of Mark 12:42 and Luke 21:2, 3 on many occasions, and he uses Acts of the Apostles 9:18 when speaking of "scales dropping from the eyes."

Washington employs the image of Hebrews 4:16 that says in the King James Version:

> Let us therefore come boldly unto the throne of grace, that we may obtain mercy and find grace to help in time of need.[182]

In a letter to his friend, the Marquis de Lafayette, President Washington employed a variety of New Testament images and idioms, including his comment that "I wished to see the sons and daughters of the world in Peace, and busily employed in the most agreeable amusement of fulfilling the first and the second great commandments," an allusion to:

> This is the first and great commandment. And the second is like unto it, Thou shalt love thy neighbor as thyself. On these two commandments hang all the law and the prophets.[183]

Indeed, in this one letter to Lafayette, from July 25, 1785, Washington borrowed from Genesis 1:22–28 to be "fruitful and multiply"; he uses the two commandments of Matthew 22:38; and to the "concern for the downtrodden and the poor" from Deuteronomy 15:11; and all of this in the space of three paragraphs of the 1785 letter to his French friend.

Washington also employed Matthew 6:19–20's "Lay not up for yourselves treasures upon the earth, where moth and rust doth corrupt, and where thieves break through and steal" to argue against the idea of stealing land.[184] He regularly quotes from, or paraphrases, the Golden Rule, in regard to thieves poaching on Washington's deer,[185] and in a letter to his step-grandson, in which he urges the lad to spend more times with his books and less with girls. Washington observes, "Recollect again the saying of the wise man, 'There is a time for all things,'" an obvious reference to chapter 3 of the book of Ecclesiastes.[186] Washington, like many people of his time, believed that Ecclesiastes was written by King Solomon.

The King James Version translation of Ecclesiastes 3:1-2 tells us, "To every thing there is a season, and a time to every purpose under the heaven: A time to be born, and a time to die; a time to plant, and a time to pluck up that which is planted."[187]

On many occasions, George Washington employed the image of a "widow's mite," when discussing charity and giving to the poor. These are clear references to a story at Mark 12:41-44 and Luke 21:1-4, where an elderly widow in the temple at Jerusalem gives more than she could afford to the poor.[188] In fact, she gave all she had.

Washington appears to have been very fond of this tale and often quoted it in his own dealings with the poor.[189] For example, in a letter to his nephew, Bushrod Washington, from January 15, 1783, he tells him, "Remember always the estimation of the Widow's Mite."[190] In a letter to Landon Carter on October 27, 1777, Washington appears to borrow some phrases from Romans 8:28 that are revealed in the King James Version:

> And we know that all things work together for good to them who love God, to them who are called according to his purpose.[191]

Washington was fond of this passage for a number of reasons, but the primary one is that it was one of the foundations of the first president's principal view on the philosophical problem of evil, as we shall see in section VIII of this essay. Similarly, Washington also quoted Ephesians 6:18, particularly when addressing his troops, for it urges us to "Keep alert with all perseverance." Indeed, in one order to his troops from October 17, 1779, Washington said:

> The troops should manifest a patience, perseverance, and valor that do them the highest honor.[192]

Mary V. Thompson suggests that Washington "internalized certain principles expounded in the Bible," including "To trust altogether the justice of our cause, without our own utmost exertions, would be tempting Providence."[193] This is an allusion to the King James Version's James 1:2-3, which reveals:

> My brethren, count it all joy when ye fall into divers temptations; Knowing this, that the trying of your faith worketh patience.[194]

Ms. Thompson also suggests that the above passage is related to "Thou shalt not tempt the Lord, Thy God," an employment that mimics the Old Testament's Deuteronomy 6:16, and the New Testament's Matthew 4:7.[195] The latter verse in the King James Version tells us: "Jesus said unto him, 'It is written again, Thou shalt not tempt the Lord, Thy God,'" while the former says, "Ye shall not tempt the Lord thy God."[196]

By far, the story of the widow's mite at Mark 12 and Luke 21 appears to be George Washington's favorite New Testament tale, particularly for what he sees as the moral merits of the story, and its emphasis on philanthropy. Contemporary exegete Byron Carrier, in his essay "The Widow's Mite and the Widow's Might," gives this summary of the narrative in question:

> I'm not one to prove a point by quoting scripture, as if it puts the wisdom in us, but the Widow's Mite story says so much about the reality of our country's economic relations I just have to use it. Luke 21 tells of Jesus observing the collection bowl at the temple. A rich Pharisee makes a big show of putting in a relatively large amount. A widow merely puts in a mere mite. "See," Jesus says to his followers, "She gave *more*, for she gave *everything* she had, while he gave only a *bit* of what he had left over."[197]

The Rev. Carrier continues his commentary:

> Jesus didn't have it backwards. Though the Pharisee gave the equivalent of hundreds of dollars, while she gave only a dollar, he calls her gift "more."[198]

Altogether, George Washington employed the tale of the widow's mite nearly two dozen times, most of them in his letters, like the afore-mentioned letter to his nephew, Bushrod Washington: "Never let a person ask, without receiving something, if you have the means, always recollecting in what light the Widow's Mite was viewed."[199] This tells us a great deal about what the first president believed about the nature and applications of justice, as well as the uses of philanthropy. Bushrod Washington (1762–1829) was a Virginia attorney, and later served on the U.S. Supreme Court as an associate justice.

In addition to these varieties of quoting both the Old and New Testament passages, George Washington also employed the Holy Scriptures in a variety of other contexts. When he delivered his oath of office on the balcony of Federal Hall in New York City, for example, Washington's left hand was upon the Bible, opened to chapter 28 of the book of Deuteronomy.[200] In his other oath of office, the Bible was open at Genesis 49:13, which tells us:

> Zebulun shall dwell at the haven of the Sea; and He shall be as a haven for ships; and his border shall be unto Zidon.[201]

Many critics have noted this odd verse upon which George Washington took his oath. Apparently, the Bible was opened at random that day. Since that day, no other presidents have chosen that particular verse as their model; but several presidents—Harding, Eisenhower, and George H. W. Bush—have picked the Washington Bible for their oaths of office. Both Jimmy Carter and Dwight Eisenhower actually employed two Bibles—the Washington Bible and a family Bible. George W. Bush intended to use the Washington Bible in his 2001 inauguration, but the weather was too poor to expose the volume to the elements.

As noted earlier, in a letter to the Jews of Newport, Rhode Island, Washington wrote, "Every one shall sit safely under his own vine and fig tree, and there shall be none to make him afraid, another reference to Washington's favorite Old Testament expression from the Hebrew Bible."[202] The same letter continues:

> For happily the government of the United States gives to bigotry no sanction, to persecution no assistance, and requires only that those who live under its protection should demean themselves as good citizens, in giving it on all occasions their effectual support.[203]

More will be said about this letter to the Jews of Newport in a later section of this essay (section IV). It is enough to say now, however, that the first president was tolerant of all Christian denominations, and of Judaism and Islam, as well. In fact, there is some evidence that George Washington owned several Muslim slaves.

Further evidence of Washington's commitment to the Bible can be seen in the cemetery at Mount Vernon. Inside the Washington Burial Vault, on the back wall, is an inscription that quotes some of Jesus' words from the Gospel of John. The quotation comes from John 11:25–26, where Jesus tries to reassure Lazarus's family that his earthly death was not the end.

The verses in question tell us:

> Jesus said unto her, I am the resurrection, and the life: he that believeth in me, though he were dead, yet shall he live: And whosoever liveth and believeth in me shall never die.

The inclusion of John 11:25–26 unmistakably associates the Washington couple with the promise of the resurrection of the dead, certainly the most important link of the Christian Chain of Faith. In one of General Washington's general orders to his troops, from November 27, 1779, he says:

> Whereas it becomes us humbly to approach the Throne of Almighty God, with gratitude and praise for the wonders which His goodness has wrought in conducting our forefathers to this western world . . . and above all, that he hath diffused the glorious light of the Gospel, where by, through the merits of our Gracious Redeemer, we may become the heirs of his eternal glory.[204]

The "Throne of God" is an image borrowed from 2 Chronicles 18:18 and Matthew 5:34. The former in the KJV tells us, "Therefore, hear the word of the Lord; I saw the Lord sitting upon His throne," while the latter says, "But I say unto you, Swear not at all; neither by heaven, for it is God's throne."[205] Indeed, on many occasions, sometimes in his general orders to his troops, he mentions the issue of swearing. On one general order issued on the fourth of July, General Washington ordered:

> The foolish and wicked practice of cursing and swearing is a vice so mean and low that every person of sense and character detests and despises it.[206]

On another occasion, Washington wrote:

> When it was reported to General Washington that the army was frequently indulging in swearing, he immediately sent out the following Order: "The General is sorry to be informed that the foolish and wicked practice of profane cursing and swearing—a vice little known heretofore in the American Army—is growing into fashion. Let the men and officers reflect 'that we cannot hope for the blessing of Heaven on our Army if we insult it by our impiety and folly.'"[207]

On a third occasion, the general returned to the same subject when he ordered:

> The General most earnestly requires, and expects, a due observance of those articles of war, established for the government of the Army which forbids profane cursing, swearing and drunkenness; and in like manner, requires and expects, of all officers, and soldiers, not engaged in actual duty, a punctual attendance on Divine service, to implore the blessings of Heaven upon the means used for our safety and defense.[208]

Ron Chernow, in his biography of Washington, summarizes a recollection of Washington's reaction when he heard that General Lee had abandoned his post. Chernow writes:

> "You damned Poltroon," Washington enjoined, "You never tried them!" Always reluctant to resort to profanities, the chaste Washington cursed at Lee, "until the leaves shook on the tree," recalled General Scott. "Charming! Delightful! Never have I enjoyed such swearing before or since." Lafayette said it was the only time he ever heard Washington swear. "I confess, I was disconcerted, astonished, and confounded by the words and the manner in which His Excellency accosted me," Lee recalled.[209]

If Generals Lee and Lafayette are correct about General Washington cursing Charles Lee for abandoning his post at the Battle of Monmouth, then Washington seemed to have envisioned a double standard when it came to profanity and cursing, one standard for his troops, and another standard for his own conduct. In 1900, a new eyewitness account of what Washington may have said to General Lee surfaced in the magazine of the Daughters of the American Revolution. At a dinner party in 1840, Major Jacob Morton, who was then eighty years old, claimed to have been at the scene. He said that Washington "looked like a thunder cloud before the lightning flash." But the major said he was not close enough to the general to hear what he said to General Lee.[210]

The event in question of Washington cursing Major General Charles Lee occurred on the afternoon of June 28, 1778. Washington is said to have "exploded" at his second in command, General Lee, in a moment that became legendary among the officers who were present. Washington had sent Lee with a small force ahead of the main body of the army to harass the British under General Henry Clinton.

> General Lee was ordered to engage the Redcoats until Washington could bring the rest of his men from Valley Forge, where they had spent the previous Winter and Spring. After several hours of fighting, and with the main Army nowhere to be found, General Lee retreated from the Battle field. When Washington finally caught up with General Lee on the road, near the Monmouth Courthouse in New Jersey, he cursed his second in command. General Charles Scott, who was present at the scene, said that Washington was so visibly upset that he reported that the "leaves shook from the trees." General Lafayette later recalled in regards to Washington's service at Monmouth: "I thought then as now I had never beheld so superb a man."[211]

Franklin Ellis, in his *History of Monmouth County*, published in 1885, said this about Washington's response upon Genera Lee leaving the Battle of Monmouth, "If ever anybody did have an excuse for swearing, it was George Washington at the Battle of Monmouth."[212]

Nevertheless, the "light of the Gospels" is a metaphorical passage found at Psalm 119:105, at John 1:5 and 8:12, and Matthew 5:16. The image of being "heirs to eternal glory" is borrowed from Romans 8:17, and it tells us:

> And if children, then heirs; heirs to God, and joint-heirs with Christ; if so be that we suffer with him, that we might also be glorified together.[213]

George Washington appears to have had a prior knowledge of these passages, as well as the connection between them, for he employs the "heir to eternal glory" image on six separate occasions.

In addition to the Bible passages mentioned above, there also were a number of particular versions of the good book that played some roles in the life of President George Washington. The Bible used at his first inaugural address, for example, was borrowed from a local Mason Lodge, Saint John's Lodge No. 1 of the Ancient York Masons, in New York City.[214] Subsequently, this Bible was used in the inaugurations of Presidents Harding, Eisenhower, Carter, and George H. W. Bush. Members of the Saint John Lodge also took part in front of a statue of George Washington on the steps of the Federal Hall to honor the occasion. The Mason Bible since has been known as the "Washington Bible."

Another Masonic Bible was used on the altar when George Washington was initiated into the Masonic Degrees in 1752 and 1753. This Bible is now owned by the Masonic Lodge No. 4 in Fredericksburg, Virginia, not far from St. George's Episcopal Church in that city.

The Library of Congress, in its Archives, houses the Augustine Washington family Bible. This Bible records the birth of George Washington, and was purchased by Augustine Washington. The Library Archives at Mount Vernon owns Martha Washington's family Bible, which contains the genealogy of the Lewis family.[215] George purchased this Bible in New York City on August 18, 1789. This Lewis Family Bible was passed down after the death of Martha Washington until it was finally donated by Esther Maria Lewis to the Mount Vernon Ladies' Association in 1951.[216]

The Lewis Family Bible was printed in 1783. It has a brown leather calf binding, and the pages shine with gold gilt. The Bible has six foldout maps and nearly three hundred copperplate engravings that illustrate the text. Martha Washington clearly cherished this Bible, for she signed it three different times. Her granddaughter, Nelly Custis-Lewis, inherited the Bible.

Another Bible owned by Martha Washington was the family Bible of her first husband's, Daniel Parke-Custis's, family. The Custis Family Bible has a black, leather cover and binding. It was printed in London in 1702. It does not record Martha's marriage to George, but it does have an entry noting her marriage to Mr. Custis. Eventually, the Custis Family Bible became owned by Martha's grandson, George Washington Parke-Custis, called "Washy" by his family. Washy's daughter married none other than Confederate Civil War General Robert E. Lee.[217]

The Lee family cherished the Custis Family Bible. The Bible contains a number of flowers and leaves pressed into the pages. When Union soldiers occupied the Lee family home, Arlington House, which now overlooks Arlington National Cemetery, Mrs. Lee had to leave behind many family treasures, among them that Bible. It then vanished for the next forty-three years, until the year 1904.

In that year, the Custis Family Bible was in the hands of a South Carolina book collector named George W. Kendrick. He claimed to have purchased the Bible decades earlier from a man known only as "Stein." Mr. Kendrick refused to acknowledge the claim to the Custis Family Bible by the Lees. Eventually, however, Kendrick changed his mind, and he returned it to the Lee family.[218]

The Pohick Church was given one of George Washington's original Bibles. In George Washington's will, there is a line that says, "To the Reverend, now Bryan, Lord Fairfax, I give a Bible in three large folio volumes, presented to me by the Right Reverend Thomas Wilson, Bishop of Sodor and Man."[219] To which of the Washington Family Bibles he refers here is not clear, but since it mentions three volumes, it most likely was the Bible purchased by Augustine Washington. What is clear is that at one time or another the Washington Family owned the following Bibles:

1. Augustine Washington's family Bible.

2. Martha Washington's Lewis Family Bible.

3. The Custis Family Bible.

4. The Washington Mason Bible was borrowed for the first oath and inaugural address.

5. The Fredericksburg Masonic Lodge No. 4 Bible.

The Augustine Washington Family Bible mentioned above contains a sheet of paper that is carefully inscribed with the marriage date of Augustine

Washington and his second wife, Mary Ball, as well as the birth dates of their six children. It tells us that George Washington was born "about ten in the morning" on February 11, 1731/32." This is according to the Julian calendar that was then in use. When England adopted the Gregorian calendar in 1752, which we still employ today, this date changed to February 22, 1732—the day Washington considered to be his birthday. The Washington Family Bible is owned by the Masonic National Memorial in Alexandria, Virginia. It can be found on the fourth floor of the museum.

The Bible that was on the altar when George Washington was inducted into the Masonic Degrees in 1752 and 1753 is owned by the Fredericksburg, Virginia, Masonic Lodge No. 4. It can be found in the library there.

A grandson remembers Mary Washington reading to him on Sunday evenings when he was a child. As Kevin J. Hayes, in his *George Washington: A Life in Books*, puts the matter:

> The boy would follow along as his grandmother read aloud from the family Bible. Listening to her, he gazed with childish wonder and admiration at the crude representations of saints and angels, and the joys of the redeemed, and shuddered at the sight of the skeleton death and devils with horns and hoofs, holding in their claws pitchforks of fire.[220]

This grandson's experience sheds some light on his uncle George's relationship to the Bible. It is quite lucky Mary Washington employed the same method to teach her grandchildren about religion and the Bible as she did when instructing her own children, using the Lewis Family Bible or the Custis Family Bible. It could also have been the Augustine Washington's Family Bible. It is not clear which of these was employed by the original First Lady with her children and grandchildren.

In addition to the family Bibles mentioned above, three other items are significant. First, in the Library Archives at Mount Vernon can be found a *Concordance of the Holy Scripture*, dated from 1760. Secondly, in the same location, there is a *Book of Common Prayer* that bears the signature of Martha Washington. Finally, housed in the Rare Book Collection of the Library of Congress is the original "1732 to 1785" *Vestry Book of the Pohick Episcopal Church*. This book contains the continuous record of the activities of every vestry, from its founding in 1732 until January 23, 1785.

Of course, in each of the Episcopal churches that the Washingtons regularly attended, there also were specific copies of the Bible in those churches. When in Williamsburg, George and Martha attended Bruton Parish Episcopal Church. When in Alexandria, they worshiped at Christ Episcopal Church. When in Philadelphia, the Washingtons attended the Christ

Episcopal Church. They worshiped at Saint Paul's on Wall Street when in New York City, where they have preserved Washington's inaugural pew; and when the first president and his wife were attending services in Charleston, South Carolina, it was at pew number forty-three of Saint Michael's Episcopal Church. In nearly all of Washington's churches, his pews are designated by historical markers.

One final aspect of George Washington's views on the Bible concerns a quotation in which he is reported to have said, "It is impossible to rightly govern the world without God and the Bible."[221] Although this quotation has been widely attributed to President Washington, there is absolutely no evidence that he ever actually said it. In checking sources from the University of Virginia, the Library of Congress, and the Mount Vernon Archives itself, it is not clear that Washington ever uttered these words.

Some have attributed this quotation to Washington's "Farewell Address" of 1796. The origin of this misquote, however, is most likely a product of the imagination of Pastor Mason Weems, who will be discussed more thoroughly later in this study. It is enough to point out now that he was the origin of "Pa, I cannot tell a lie" from the story of George chopping down his father's favorite cherry tree, the throwing of a silver dollar across the Potomac River, the view that the general prayed on his knees at Valley Forge, and many other spurious facts about the life of George Washington.[222]

Some writers also have said that, on his death bed, President Washington said to the physician present, "Doctor, I die hard, but I am not afraid to go. Bring me the Book."[223] Presumably, the "Book" is a reference to the Holy Bible, but there is very little evidence that the first president said this on his death bed, as well. The physician in question was Scottish-born James Craik (1727–1814) who was the physician-general of the Continental Army and Washington's personal doctor for forty years. Dr. Craik fought valiantly in a number of battles of the French and Indian War. He also treated General Braddock's fatal wounds in 1755.

Finally, it is important to understand that George Washington was not alone in his judgment of the importance of the Bible for the new American society. In his recent book, *Reading the Bible With the Founding Fathers*, Daniel Dreisbach of American University observes:

> The Bible was the most accessible, authoritative, and venerated text in early Colonial society. Not only was the Bible an essential text for faith and worship, but also it was a primary textbook for education, letters, law, and civil government.[224]

Indeed, John Dickinson (1732–1818), Pennsylvania solicitor and politician, wrote that "The Bible is the most Republican book that ever was written."[225] John Adams, the second president of the United States, observed, "The Bible contains . . . the most perfect morality."[226] When the young John Adams read the Ten Commandments at Exodus 20:3–17 and Deuteronomy 5:7–21, he wrote in his *Diary*:

> A Society that adopted the Bible as its only Law Book and lived according to its precepts would be a Utopia.[227]

Noah Webster echoed the sentiments of the other Founding Fathers when he wrote:

> The moral principles and precepts contained in the Scriptures ought to form the basis of all civil constitutions and laws.[228]

To sum up this third section of this essay on George Washington's religion, we may make the following conclusions. First, the president appears to have had a deep knowledge of the Scriptures, even from early in his life. Secondly, he favored descriptions of the God in the Old Testament to that of the New Testament. Thirdly, Washington rarely mentioned the name of Jesus in his public discourse. Fourthly, the first president had a number of favorite Old and New Testament passages, and chief among these was the image in chapter 4 of Micah about the "vine and the fig tree," Washington's favorite Old Testament phrase, and the narrative of the widow's mite, his favorite New Testament narrative, found in both the Gospels of Mark and Luke.

We also have shown in this section that Washington was not alone in his judgment about the value of the Holy Bible in American life. Many others of the Founding Fathers explicitly stated the worth of Holy Writ to the new nation, and a number of specific Bibles played key roles in Washington's religious life, including the New York Mason Bible he borrowed for his first oath of office; the three-volume family Bible purchased by Augustine Washington in 1819; the Custis Family Bible brought by Martha Washington into the marriage; the Lewis Family Bible George bought for Martha in 1789; and the Mason Bible of Lodge No. 4 in Fredericksburg, Virginia, on which he was inaugurated into the various Orders of the Masons.

One final point about President George Washington and his relationship with the Bible is the fact that his first inauguration address actually was a second draft. A collection of notes owned by Mount Vernon show that the first draft contained at least five other references to the Biblical text. In the first of these, Washington employed Saint Paul's image in Romans 8:27 of the "searcher of hearts."[229]

In another portion of these notes, Washington mentions the garden of Eden in the opening of the book of Genesis and the "Praises of the Most

High," to be found in Psalms 7:17.[230] A third reference in these notes alludes to the thirtieth chapter of the book of Deuteronomy, and its "Blessings of Heaven showered thick around us that should be spilled on the ground."[231]

Washington used images from both Isaiah 40:4 and Luke 3:5, and the "eternal line that separates right from wrong."[232] Finally, in Washington's notes, he appears to mimic Luke 23:46, when Jesus says, "Into Thy hands I commend my Spirit." But Washington substitutes "My dearest Country" for "My Spirit," so that he said in these notes:

> I most earnestly supplicate that Almighty God, to whose holy keeping I commend My dearest Country, will never offer so fair an inheritance to become a prey to Avarice.[233]

With this final observation, we now have made the following general conclusions regarding George Washington's views on the Bible. These may be summarized this way:

1. George Washington had a comprehensive knowledge of the Bible from Genesis to Revelation, beginning in his childhood years.

2. His mother regularly read to her children from the Lewis Family Bible, or the Custis Family Bible she brought to her marriage.

3. Washington quoted directly from the Scriptures over three hundred times in his collected works.

4. He employed a number of Biblical idioms and images, as general and as president.

5. Washington's favorite Old Testament phrase was the "vine and the fig tree."

6. His favorite New Testament passage was that of the widow's mite.

7. A number of particular Bibles played key roles in his life: the Mason's Bible, employed for his first oath of office, the Washington Family Bible bought by Augustine Washington, the Custis Family Bible, and the Lewis Family Bible.

8. Washington favored descriptions of the God of the Old Testament over those of the New Testament.

9. He read regularly from the Bible as an adult.

10. And finally, some quotations about the Bible erroneously have been attributed to him.

Now we shall turn to some remarks on the president's views on religious toleration.

IV

Washington on Religious Toleration

> By common consent, Washington is regarded as not merely the Hero of the
> American Revolution, but also the World's Apostle of Liberty.
>
> —THOMAS PAINE

IN THIS FOURTH SECTION of this study on George Washington's religion, our primary focus will be what the first president believed about religious toleration. There are three major places to look for George Washington's views on religious toleration. The first of these are the many public documents where the first president said or wrote something about the idea. A second source is the climate and environment of the day that exerted an influence on Washington's views on the matter, including John Locke's 1689 *Letter on Toleration*, and the uses that Washington's contemporaries made of these sources.

A number of other Enlightenment thinkers, like Voltaire and Spinoza, as well as other Enlightenment philosophers, may also have played roles in Washington's views on religious toleration, or, as we shall see, what Voltaire called "Intoleration."

However, the third source, Washington's letters, reveal the most information by far of what the first president believed about the issue of religious toleration. Often, as we shall see in this section, these were letters written to the leaders of various religious groups in America, like the Baptists, the Quakers, and Jewish congregations, for examples. Ron Chernow, in his study *Washington: A Life*, describes the first president's views on religious toleration this way:

One thing that hasn't aroused dispute is the exemplary nature of
Washington's religious tolerance. He shuddered at the notion of
exploiting religion for partisan purposes or showing favoritism
for certain denominations.[234]

Mr. Chernow goes on to discuss Washington's letters to various religious congregations in early America in regard to the issue of religious
toleration. Chernow writes:

As President, when writing about to Jewish, Baptist, Presbyterian, and other Congregations—he officially saluted twenty-
two major religious groups—he issued eloquent statements on
religious toleration. He was so devoid of spiritual bias that his
tolerance even embraced Atheism.[235]

More will be said about those letters later, but first we will make some
observations about the practice of religion in early America, followed by an
examination of the public record where President Washington said something about religious toleration.

Most American schoolchildren are taught that the Pilgrims came to
America aboard the *Mayflower* in 1620 in search of religious freedom. The
Puritans, as the story goes, soon followed for many of the same reasons.
Since these religious dissidents arrived at their shining "City Upon a Hill,"
as Governor John Winthrop called it, millions of people from around the
world have done the same thing. Many settlers believed they were coming
to a melting pot, in which everyone was free to practice his or her religion
any way they saw fit, or no religion at all.

The problem with this narrative is that it is an American myth. The
real story of religious practices in early America is often awkward, embar-
rassing, and occasionally a very bloody story that most civics books and
high school textbooks either paper over or shunt to the side. From the earliest times in America, religion has been used to discriminate, suppress, and
even kill the other, the foreigner, the heretic, and the unbeliever—including
the "heathen natives" who already were here.

Moreover, while it is true that the vast majority of the earliest American settlers were Christians, the violent battles between various Protestant
denominations and between Protestants and Roman Catholics presented
an unavoidable contradiction to the widely held notion that America was a
Christian nation. That conclusion, as we shall see in a subsequent section of
this work, is incorrect for several reasons.

First, the initial encounter between Europeans in the future United
States came when the French Huguenots established a colony in 1564 at Fort

Caroline, near present-day Jacksonville, Florida. More than half a century before the arrival of the *Mayflower*, French Protestants came to America in search of religious freedom. The government of Spain, however, had different ideas. They established a colony at Saint Augustine, also in Florida, and they attacked the settlement at Fort Caroline.

The Spanish commander, one Pedro Menendez de Aviles (1509–74), wrote to King Philip II to tell him that he had "hanged all those we had found in [Fort Caroline] because . . . they were scattering the odious Lutheran doctrine in these Provinces."[236] When several survivors of a shipwrecked French fleet washed up on the shores of Florida, they were put to the sword, next to a river that the Spanish called Matanzas, or "slaughters."[237]

We might begin by pointing out that George Washington was of the belief that many fights and animosities among Americans were the products of religious disputes, like those in Florida. In a letter to General Lafayette (1757–1834), who was in favor of religious toleration, Washington wrote:

> Of all the animosities which have existed among mankind, those which were caused by sentiments in Religion appear to be the most inveterate and distressing, and ought most to be deprecated. I was in hopes, that the enlightened and liberal policy, which has marked the present age, would at least have reconciled Christians of every denomination, so far that we shall never again see their religious disputes carried to such a pitch as to endanger the peace of Society.[238]

Here Washington expressed his support for the idea of religious toleration, and also laments over the many skirmishes between Christian denominations, someday hoping they might be settled more peacefully.

In another letter written on June 22, 1792, to Sir Edward Newenham (1734–1814), Irish Protestant politician, Washington also speaks of the acrimony of religious disputes. Lord Newenham had written to Washington about how to handle the practice of Protestantism in the largely Catholic Ireland. Washington wrote back to the Irish statesman:

> I regret exceedingly that the disputes between Protestants and Roman Catholics should be carried to such an alarming height mentioned in your letters. Religious controversies are always productive of more acrimony and irreconcilable hatreds than those that spring from any other causes; and I was not without hopes that the enlightened and liberal policy of the present age would have put an effectual stop to contentions of this kind.[239]

Again, Washington expresses his desire to ameliorate the disputes among believers in various Christian denominations, and he hopes that the acrimony between these denominations should soon be lessened in a place like America.

In another letter to his friend and French nobleman General Lafayette, Washington observed, "I am not less ardent in my wish, that you may succeed in your plan of Toleration in Religious matters. Being no bigot myself, I am disposed to indulge the professors of Christianity in the Church with that road to Heaven, which to them shall seem the most direct, plainest, easiest, and least liable to exception."[240]

In 1775, New England troops of Washington were preparing to celebrate "Pope's Day," an American version of Guy Fawkes Day, in which the soldiers would burn the pope in effigy. When Washington heard of these plans, he said, "[I] cannot help expressing [my] surprise that there should be Officers and Soldiers in this army so void of common sense."[241] Guy Fawkes Day had been instituted after the death of Queen Elizabeth I in 1603. English Catholics who had been persecuted under her reign had hoped that her successor, James I, would be more conducive to the religious rights of Catholics. After all, James's mother had been a Catholic.

Unfortunately, King James did not turn out to be more tolerant than Queen Elizabeth had been. Consequently, thirteen young Catholic men decided that violent action should be their response. The small group was under the leadership of Robert Catesby (1573–1605). He made the suggestion that the group should blow up the Houses of Parliament. In doing so, they also hoped to kill the King, and possibly the Prince of Wales.

To carry out their plan, the conspirators secured thirty-six barrels of gunpowder and stored them beneath the House of Lords. A man named Guy Fawkes (1570–1606) was in the basement with the gunpowder when authorities stormed in, in the early morning of November 5, 1605. Fawkes was captured, tortured, and then executed. On the very night that the conspiracy was foiled, bonfires were set alight to celebrate the safety of the King and the members of Parliament. Since 1605, Guy Fawkes Day is commemorated every year with fireworks and burning an effigy of Mr. Fawkes, for no other reason than that Washington simply saw it as intolerant.[242]

George Washington's men renamed the celebration to call it "Pope's Day." The general, however, found the practice to be repugnant and took measures to keep it from being celebrated under his watch.

While trying to secure some workers for his Mount Vernon Farm, Washington said the following:

If they are good workmen, they may be from Asia, Africa, or Europe; they may be Mahometans, Jews, or Christians, or any Sect, or they may be Atheists.[243]

This passage clearly shows Washington's commitment to religious toleration in suggesting that he would accept workers of any religious persuasion on his property. His only criterion is that they be good workmen from any tradition or none at all.

In fact, there is some evidence that George Washington had a number of slaves at his Mount Vernon estate who may have been Muslims. A tithe table of Washington's from the year 1774 shows slaves named "Fatimer and Little Fatimer," perhaps a mother and daughter pair, who had the same name as the Prophet Muhammad's favorite daughter, Fatima. Another of Washington's slaves, a woman named Letty, had a daughter she named "Nila." Mary V. Thompson suggests this is an adaptation of the female Muslim name "Naailah," which means "someone who acquires something" in the Arabic tongue.[244]

A fourth slave of Washington's, a man named Sambo Anderson, was apparently a descendent of the Hausa Tribe of Northwest Africa. Thompson speaks of Anderson having tribal scars on his face and gold rings in his ears, two characteristics of Hausa warriors from Mali in the eighteenth century.[245] An article published in the *Alexandrian Gazette* on January 18, 1876, called "Mount Vernon Reminiscence," suggests that Sambo "was a great favorite of the master [Washington], by whom he was given a piece of land on which to build a house."[246]

The "Old Citizen of Fairfax" also revealed that Washington allowed Sambo to keep a small boat or skiff to "cross over the Creek in, and for other purposes," a rare privilege for a slave in Colonial America. The account also says that Washington would sometimes use Anderson's boat, "but he would never use it without Sambo's permission."[247] Washington showed unusual treatment toward Sambo Anderson.

Washington biographer Peter Henriques suggests that Sambo Anderson was also an excellent hunter, and he was given permission by Washington to own a rifle, something very unusual for an ex-slave. Although it was likely that Anderson was a Muslim, Washington seemed disinterested in Sambo's religious preference, and more concerned about his trustworthiness and his upright moral behavior.[248]

At any rate, further evidence establishing Washington's views on religious freedom can be seen when a bill was proposed that taxed the residents of the commonwealth to support the Episcopal Church, the denomination he attended; Washington threw his weight against the idea. As the first president wrote at the time:

> Although no man's sentiments are more opposed to any kind of restraint upon Religious principles than mine are, yet, I must confess that I am not among the number of those, who are so much alarmed at the thought of making people pay towards the support of that which they profess, if of the denominations of Christians, or to declare themselves Jews, Mohametans, or otherwise, and thereby obtain proper relief. As the matter now stands, I wish an assessment had never been agitated, and as it has gone so far, that the bill could die an easy death; because I think it will be productive of more quiet to the State, than by enacting it into Law, which, in my opinion, would be impolitic; admitting that there is a decided majority for it, to the disquiet of a respectable minority. In the former case, the matter will soon subside; in the later, it will rankle and perhaps convulse the State.[249]

Washington here expresses his opinion against the idea of a state religion. He hopes that the idea will "die an easy death," and he worries about believers among minority faiths, including Jews and members of the Muslim faith. President George Washington was staunchly against the idea of an established church in America. Clearly he also was in favor of the idea of the proponents of multiple religions in America expressing their rights to worship the divine in any way they saw fit.

From these public statements of Washington, two things should be clear. First, he was in favor of the practice of religious toleration; and secondly, he was against the idea of the state or national government to support one religious group over those of others. These conclusions are in concert with Washington's views of the establishment clause of the First Amendment of the U.S. Constitution, which says:

> Congress shall make no law respecting an establishment of Religion, or prohibiting the free exercise thereof; or abridging the freedom of speech, or of the press, or the right of the people to peaceably assemble, and to petition the Government for a redress of grievances.

It is now generally agreed that one of the major sources of the views of Washington, Jefferson, and others on religious toleration was the 1689 essay by John Locke called *A Letter Concerning Toleration*. The *Letter* was originally published in Latin, but it was soon translated into various European languages, including English. It appeared amidst a fear that Roman

Catholicism may be taking control of Britain, and later responded to the rift by arguing for religious toleration.[250]

Among the main points in Locke's *Letter* are the following: toleration should be the chief attribute of the true church; the gospel of Jesus Christ advocates toleration; the natural rights of human beings should guarantee the ability to worship when and where an individual wishes; and faith and inward sincerity should be the marks of inward commitment to God.[251]

The public statements that George Washington made about religious toleration listed in the above analysis are all consistent with the main proclamation of John Locke's *Letter on Toleration*. Both Thomas Jefferson and George Washington owned a copy of Locke's *Letter*. The English philosopher became the father of modern views on toleration in Britain, America, and France.

Other Enlightenment thinkers, such as Voltaire (1694–1778) in France, and Baruch Spinoza (1632–77) in the Netherlands, also wrote extensively on religious toleration. The latter was a victim of intolerance because he was a Jew in Holland, and he became a vocal advocate of a new idea of religious tolerance that shaped much of modern society. Spinoza defined a new relationship between church and state in his *Theological-Political Treatise* of 1670. The book included a lengthy section on Spinoza's views on religious toleration.[252]

Spinoza's views, however, were significantly different from those of John Locke for at least two fundamental reasons. First, Spinoza's defense of religious liberties is not a defense of a freedom of worship, but rather a defense of the "freedom to philosophize." Freedom of worship is secondary to freedom to philosophize. Secondly, unlike Locke, Spinoza makes a sharp distinction between outward expression of faith and one's internal worship of God. Baruch Spinoza thought that the latter expression of one's faith is vastly more important than one's outward, or the public expression of one's religion.[253]

French philosopher and writer, Francois Marie-Arouet, also known as Voltaire, took the courageous stand of defending a Protestant French family against religious intolerance as well as legal persecution. In his *Treatise on Toleration*, Voltaire argued that religious intolerance was against the laws of nature and was worse than the "right of the tiger."[254]

Voltaire put the matter this way:

> Human law must in every case be based on natural law. All over the Earth, the great principle of both is: Do not unto others what you would that they do not unto you. Now in virtue of this principle, one man cannot say to another, "Believe what I

believe, or thou shalt perish." Thus, do men speak in Portugal, Spain, and Goa. In some other countries they are now content to say, "Believe me or I detest thee. Believe me or I will do all the harm I can to you. Monster, you do not share my Religion, and therefore, you have no Religion. You shall be a thing of horror to thy neighbors, thy city, and thy province." . . . The supposed right of intolerance is absurd and barbaric. It is the right of the tiger; nay, it is far worse, for tigers do not tear to have food, while we rend each other for paragraphs.[255]

Voltaire began a campaign to rectify what had occurred to the Calas family. He brought the case to the attention of the public and petitioned that compensation be paid to the distraught family. He was successful in doing both.[256] It is not clear whether George Washington was familiar with these ideas of Spinoza and Voltaire's, but both thinkers contributed to the Enlightenment ideas of freedom and liberty in that age.

In addition to these public statements on religious toleration mentioned above, President Washington also may have been influenced by the Enlightenment thinkers we have discussed, as well as his Founding Father colleagues in assembling his views of this issue. During the debate over the issue of religious freedom in the Commonwealth of Virginia, for example, George Mason proposed the following religious clause:

> All men should enjoy the fullest toleration in the exercise of Religion, according to the dictates of Conscience.[257]

James Madison suggested an alternative formulation:

> That Religion or the duty that we owe our Creator, and the manner of discharging it, being under the direction of reason and conviction only, not of violence and compulsion, all men are equally entitled to the full and free exercise of it according to the dictates of Conscience.[258]

James Madison also commented on the idea of the separation of church and state in an 1823 letter written from his home. Madison observed:

> The settled opinion here is that religion is essentially distinct from Civil Government, and exempt from its cognizance; that a connection between them is surely injurious to both; that there are causes in the human breast, which ensure the perpetuity of Religion without the aid of the Law; the rival Sects, with equal rights, exercise mutual censorship in favor of good morals.[259]

On June 7, 1776, Richard Henry Lee (1736–99) made a motion to Congress that the American colonies declare their independence. "True Freedom," Mr. Lee asserted, "embraces the Mahomitan and the Gentoo [Hindu], as well as the Christian Religion."[260] The writers of the 1780 Massachusetts Constitution also proclaimed, "The most Liberty of Conscience . . . to Deists, Mahometans, Jews, and Christians."[261] This is a point that Chief Justice Theophilus Parsons (1750–1813) resoundingly affirmed in 1810 in *Barnes v. the Inhabitants of First Parish* in Falmouth, Massachusetts, in which Judge Parsons wrote the majority opinion.[262]

In 1779, as Virginia's governor, Thomas Jefferson had drafted a bill that guaranteed legal equality for citizens of all religions—including those of no religion—in the state. It was at this time that Mr. Jefferson famously wrote, "But it does me no injury for my neighbor to say there are twenty gods or no God. It neither picks my pocket, nor breaks my leg."[263] This plan of Jefferson's, however, did not succeed until after Patrick Henry (1736–99) introduced a bill in 1784 calling for state support of "teachers of the Christian Religion."[264] By this, Henry meant teachers of his Anglican-Episcopal faith. This was a bill to which both Washington and Jefferson were opposed.

In 1786, after Patrick Henry's bill had been defeated, the Virginia Act for Establishing Religious Freedom was passed. The act was one of only three accomplishments that Jefferson wished to include on his tombstone, along with the writing of the Declaration of Independence and establishing the University of Virginia. After the 1786 bill was passed, Jefferson wrote that the law:

> meant to comprehend, within the mantle of its protection, the Jew, the Gentile, the Christian and the Mahometan, the Hindoo, and the Infidel of every denomination.[265]

Jefferson observed that the 1786 bill was designed to respect the religious rights of Christians, as well as those of Jews, Muslims, members of the Hindu faith, and infidels, the term in Jefferson and Washington's day for nonbelievers. Indeed, many in Jefferson's time believed he was one of their number.

Benjamin Franklin, commenting on religion in the Pennsylvania colony, wrote, "Both houses and ground were vested in trustees, expressing for the use of any preacher of any religious persuasion who might desire to say something to the people of Philadelphia; the design in general, so that even if the Mufti of Constantinople were to send a missionary to preach Mohammedanism to us, he would find a pulpit at his service."[266]

Finally, George Mason, the Virginia legislator responsible for the passing of the June 1776 "Virginia Declaration of Rights," declared that:

Religion, or the duty to which we owe our Creator and the manner of discharging it can be directed by reason and conviction, not by force or violence; and therefore, all men are equally entitled to the free exercise of religion, according to the dictates of Conscience; and that it is the mutual duty of all to practice Christian forbearance, love and charity towards each other.[267]

From these remarks, it should be clear that Washington's fellow Founding Fathers also were dedicated to the idea of religious toleration in America. The places where the first president's opinions on religious toleration can most easily be seen is in his letters to various religious groups on the issue. It is to these letters that we now turn. In an August 1789 letter to leaders of the Protestant Episcopal Church, Washington wished to celebrate the religious pluralism of the new nation. Washington wrote:

It affords edifying prospects indeed to see Christians of different denominations dwell together in more Charity, and conduct themselves in respect to each other with a more Christian-like Spirit than ever they have done in any former age, or in any other Nation.[268]

A few months later, Washington assured the Methodist Bishops that "It shall be my endeavor . . . to contribute whatever may be in my power towards the preservation of the Civil and Religious Liberties of the American people."[269] In writing to the Presbyterians, Washington chose the occasion to speak of the duties of all pious citizens. The first president remarked:

While all men within our territories are protected in worshipping the Deity, according to the dictates of their consciences; it is rationally to be expected from them in return, that they will be emulous of evincing the sincerity of their profession by the innocence of their lives, and the beneficence of their actions. For no man, who is profligate in his morals, or a bad member of the Civil Community, can possibly be a true Christian, or a credit to his own Religious Society.[270]

Washington reaffirms his commitment to religious toleration. Then he raises a question about whether people of bad moral character could actually call themselves the real meaning of the word "Christian." He also refers to attending a Dutch Reform Church in New York City. He observed about the sermon, "Being in a language not a word of which I understood, I was in no danger of becoming a proselyte to its Religion by the eloquence of their Preacher."[271]

After being elected president, George Washington also sought to reassure the plights of religious minorities, as well, including Baptists, Quakers, Catholics, and Jews. Writing to the Virginia Baptists, for example, the first president observed:

> Every man, conducting himself a good citizen, and being accountable to God alone for his religious opinions, ought to be protected in worshipping the Deity, according to the dictates of his own Conscience.[272]

Washington favored the Quakers when he said of them, "There is no Denomination among us who are more exemplary and useful Citizens."[273] He did, however, take exception to Quaker Pacifism that sometimes frustrated him in the late war against Great Britain. Washington observed:

> The Liberty enjoyed by the People of these States, of worshipping Almighty God agreeable to their Consciences, is not only among the choicest of their Blessings, but also of their Rights.[274]

The first president makes an intimate connection between the right to worship any way a person wishes and the dictates of that person's conscience. We will say more about this connection in the section of this essay on ethics and virtue, section V of this study on Washington's religion.

In a letter to the Virginia Baptists, who had written to Washington to complain about certain provisions of the Virginia Declaration of Rights, the first president sought to reassure the Baptists by speaking of the "horrors of what he called "Spiritual Tyranny," and that he was willing to do more in the future to protect "everyone's Freedom of Conscience in matters of Religion."[275]

George Washington's administration's response to the Bey and Subjects of Tripoli, concerning religious practices in America, gives further evidence of Washington's views on religious toleration. In Article 11 of the Treaty of Peace and Friendship, signed in November of 1796 by America and January of 1797 by Tripoli, the American government wrote:

> As the government of the United States of America is not in any sense founded on the Christian Religion—as it has in itself no character of enmity against the laws, religion, or tranquility of Musselman—and as the said States never have entered any War or act of hostility against any Mehomitan nation, it is declared by the parties that no pretext arising from religious opinions shall ever produce an interruption of the harmony existing between the two countries.[276]

This treaty implies three major points. First, the United States is not a Christian religion. Second, there is no hostility between America and Muslims. And finally, a harmony existed between Tripoli and the United States, as exemplified in this agreement. The treaty between the United States and Tripoli in 1796 was, in fact, the first agreement between America and another nation.

It is unlikely that these are the actual words of George Washington. Mary V. Thompson has made a persuasive argument in her book, *In the Hands of a Good Providence*, that the words of Article 11 of this treaty were composed by Joel Barlow, poet, former Continental Army chaplain, and diplomat. Mr. Barlow (1754–1812) was a Connecticut-born Yale graduate. He was a chaplain in a Massachusetts brigade during the Revolutionary War. After moving to Hartford, Connecticut in July of 1784, he established a weekly newspaper called the *American Mercury*.[277] Later, during the Washington administration, Barlow became a diplomat. Thus, Thompson believes that Article 11 came from the pen and mind of Ambassador Joel Barlow, who served in North Africa at the end of the eighteenth century. Most likely, then, Barlow was the author of the words of Article 11 of the 1796 treaty with Tripoli.

Mary V. Thompson also comments on Washington's understanding of Joel Barlow as a diplomat. She observes:

> Writing several years later of Barlow's negotiations with the Barbary States, Washington offered his belief that the diplomat had discharged the functions "at that time with ability and propriety."[278]

Another way to see President Washington's attitudes toward religious liberty and toleration are the many treaties that Washington made with various Native American peoples. In many of these agreements, Washington specifically mentioned that his troops should not interfere with the religious practices of the native people. Under his administration, the Indian policy was never very consistent. Washington's secretary of war, Henry Knox (1750–1806), was the first to suggest that any Indian nation, and the treaty with that nation, should be no different than a treaty with any other foreign nation.

By September of 1789, however, America had signed treaties with six separate Indian nations in the Western Territories. Washington, in an attempt to get Congress to ratify these treaties, received a letter from Congress telling him that he should "execute" those treaties, without telling the first president what they meant by "execute." Nevertheless, whenever Washington issued instructions to his military about how to handle Indian tribes, he made it clear, on several occasions, that the sacred religious sites of those Indian nations were not to be disturbed.[279]

Another avenue for showing George Washington's concern about religious toleration is his attempts to soothe the concerns of American Catholics. In a letter to the "Roman Catholics in the United States of America," the first president responded to correspondences from Catholics about anti-Catholicism throughout America, and that they were not being allowed to exercise their First-Amendment religious rights.

The Catholics were entirely justified. The constitution enacted in the state of New Jersey in 1776 forbade Catholics from serving in state offices. Similar laws were passed in Connecticut. Vermont required that all voters be professed Protestants. New Hampshire instituted a series of state constitutions, each containing more anti-Catholic sentiments than the previous law.[280]

The New York State Constitution of 1777 had a proviso barring citizens who refused an allegiance test in spiritual matters to any foreign prince or potentate, obviously with the pope in mind. The proviso in question was inserted under pressure from John Jay, prominent Founding Father. This proviso of the New York Constitution lasted until 1790, when the federal government took over the job of the process of naturalization.[281]

Even the state of Virginia, between May 22, 1754 and July 17, 1755, was conducting an anti-Catholic "test oath" of their own. The document in question included the words "There is no Transubstantiation in the Sacrament of the Lord's Supper, or in the elements of Bread and Wine." The test oath contained a list of subscribers to the declaration denying these Catholic doctrines. And on the list is the signature of one Colonel George Washington.[282]

Washington, then, was fully aware of the many anti-Catholic sentiments in many of the thirteen colonies in the late eighteenth century. Thus, in his response to the Catholics, Washington wrote:

> And may the members of your Society in America, animated alone by the pure spirit of Christianity, and still conducting themselves as the faithful subjects of our free Government, enjoy every temporal and spiritual felicity.[283]

Perhaps the best way to see President Washington's views on religious toleration is to look at his exchange of letters with the Hebrew community of Newport, Rhode Island, in August of 1790. At that time, President Washington paid a goodwill visit to Rhode Island. Joining him were Secretary of State Thomas Jefferson, New York Governor George Clinton (1739–1812), and other government leaders.[284]

On the morning of August 18, officials of Newport and representatives from various religious groups presented messages of welcome to the president. Among them was the leader of the town's Jewish community, Rabbi Moses Seixas (1744–1809). The Rabbi had been born in Portugal and came to America via Barbados. He arrived in New York in 1730, and after establishing a business there, settled in Newport, Rhode Island.[285]

The Rabbi's letter to the president expressed concern that the Jews of Rhode Island, and elsewhere in America, would not be allowed to exercise their religious freedom. Rabbi Seixas wrote:

> Deprived as we heretofore have been of the invaluable rights of free Citizens, we now (with a deep sense of gratitude to the Almighty disposer of all events) behold a Government, erected by the Majesty of the People—a government, which to bigotry gives no sanction, to persecution no assistance—but generously to all Liberty of Conscience, and immunities of Citizenship: deeming every one, of whatever Nation, tongue, or language, equal parts of the great Government Machine.[286]

The Rabbi clearly was concerned about whether the Jews would be able to exercise their religious freedoms, and he seems to favor the rights of those of other religious persuasions in America. A few days after leaving Newport, the president wrote to the citizen groups who had addressed him at the Rhode Island city. He thanked them for their hospitality and graciousness. First among them was a letter back to Rabbi Seixas, as a representative of the Jews. More than simply a courtesy, the letter reflected a policy of the new American Government to those religious beliefs that were perceived at the time as being different.[287]

In Washington's letter, he echoed the Rabbi's phrase "which to bigotry gives no sanction, and to persecution no assistance." The first president began his letter to the "Hebrew Congregation of Newport" this way:

> While I receive with much satisfaction your Address replete with expressions of affection and esteem, I rejoice in the opportunity of assuring you, that I shall always retain a grateful remembrance of the cordial welcome I experienced in my visit to Newport from all classes of Citizens.[288]

At the close of his missive to the Hebrew congregation of Newport, the first president remarked:

> May the children of the stock of Abraham who dwell in this land continue to merit and enjoy the good will of the other inhabitants—while every one shall sit in safety under his own vine and

fig tree, and there shall be none to make him afraid. May the
Father of all mercies scatter light, and not darkness, upon our
paths, and make us all in our several vocations useful here, and
in His own due time and way everlastingly happy.[289]

In this passage, the first president refers to the Prophet Micah's expression concerning the "vine and fig tree," as well as 1 John 1:5 and 2 Corinthians 4:6's references to light and darkness. Washington closed his missive to
the Jews of Newport, Rhode Island with this benediction:

May the Father of all Mercies scatter light and not darkness in
our paths, and make us all in our several vocations useful here,
and in his own due time and way ever-lastingly happy.[290]

In this correspondence to the Newport Jews, Washington again employs deistic language when referring to God as "Father of All Mercies." This
image of the "Light of Truth" was a favorite of President Washington. In a letter to a Swedenborgian Church in Baltimore, for example, he suggested that
"The Light of Truth and Reason had triumphed over the power of bigotry
and superstition."[291] In the same missive, the first president noted, "Every
person here may worship God according to the dictates of his own heart."[292]
As Mary V. Thompson says about this letter to the Baltimore Church:

Washington boasted that the United States was a place where 'a
man's religious tenets will not forfeit the protection of the laws,
nor deprive him of the right of attaining and holding the highest
offices that are known.[293]

In a letter to Benedict Arnold, from September 14, 1775, Washington
cautions Arnold not to interfere with the "free exercise of religion of the
country, and the undisturbed enjoyment of the rights of Conscience in religious matters, with your utmost influence and authority."[294] Washington
appeared in this letter to be mindful of the First-Amendment rights of all
citizens, of every religion—another sign of the first president's view on religious toleration—both during and after the Revolutionary War.

George Washington also wrote a June 14, 1790 letter to the Hebrew
congregation of Savannah, Georgia in which the first president's understanding of Providence is quite clear. Washington wrote:

May the same Wonder-working Deity, who long since delivered
the Hebrews from the Egyptian oppressors, and planted them
in the Promised Land; whose Providential agency has lately
been conspicuous, in establishing these United States as an independent Nation, still continue to water them with the dews of

Heaven, and to make the inhabitants, of every denomination, participate in the temporal and spiritual blessings of that people whose God is Jehovah.[295]

Washington, again, appears to consent to the idea that America is a "new Jerusalem," or "new Promised Land," and he plays the role, by extension, of a "new Moses." Indeed, many slaves after Washington's time called him just that.

The word *Jehovah*, in the above quotation, is a curious term, for it does not appear in the Hebrew Bible. In the ancient world, Jews did not pronounce the name *Yahweh*, so in its stead they said the word *Adonai*, or "Lord." Later Christian scholars did not know what to make of this practice, so they decided to pronounce the consonants of Yahweh, YHWH, and the vowels of Adonai, or A-O-AI. Thus, we get "YAhovah," or "Jehovah."

In an article on "Jehovah" for the *Jewish Encyclopedia*, Emil G. Hirsch suggests the name was derived by:

pronouncing the vowels of the Kere (marginal reading) of the Masoretic Text, along with the Ketib reading of the word "Adonai."[296]

Most modern scholars agree with Professor Hirsch when he observes:

Jehovah is generally held to have been the invention of Pope Leo X, Confessor Peter Galatin, who followed this hybrid use of the term . . . Drusius [1550–1616] was the first to ascribe to Peter Galatin the use of Jehovah, and this view has been taken since his day.[297]

Pope Leo X (1475–1521), who was pontiff from 1513 until 1521, was the second son of Lorenzo the Magnificent, the ruler of the Florentine Republic. His confessor was a cleric called Peter Galatin (1460–1540), who invented the term "Jehovah," or so says Jan Drusius (1550–1616), a Flemish, Protestant divine and Orientalist.

Although a number of contemporary religious groups, like the Jehovah's Witnesses, for example, employ the name "Jehovah" for God, and from the Reformation Era until the time of Washington, this practice apparently also was followed, Jehovah is a made-up name, a product of sixteenth-century Christianity.

On January 27, 1793, George Washington wrote a letter to the New Jerusalem Church in Baltimore, followers of Emmanuel Swedenborg (1688–1772), Swedish philosopher and theologian. In the middle paragraph of that correspondence, the first president again turned to the questions that concern religious liberty and expression. Washington told the members of the New Jerusalem Congregation:

> We have abundant reason to rejoice, that in this land, the light of truth and reason have triumphed over the power of bigotry and superstition, and that every person here may worship God according to the dictates of his own heart. In this enlightened age and in this land of equal liberty, it is our boast, that a man's religious tenets will not forfeit the protection of the laws, nor deprive him of the right of attaining and holding the highest offices that are known in the United States.[298]

In this letter of Washington's—as his secretary, Tobias Lear (1762–1816), tells us—it was written in response to a letter from a Mr. James Wilmer, a member of the New Jerusalem Church. Wilmer's letter had been written on the 22nd of January. Along with the correspondence and a return address, Mr. Wilmer noted that he provided the latter "if necessary."[299]

The New Jerusalem Church had been built in Baltimore to teach the beliefs of the followers of Emmanuel Swedenborg. The first minister of the church was the Rev. John Hargrove. President Thomas Jefferson invited the Rev. Hargrove to preach in the Capitol rotunda before Congress. The invitation came from Jefferson in a letter on March 11, 1801. That sermon was delivered by the Rev. Hargrove (1750–1839) on December 26, 1802, to the president and members of Congress.[300]

Another sign of President George Washington's commitment to religious toleration is the fact that he attended the services of multiple Christian denominations during his mature life. He once publicly supported, for example, an army chaplain who was a Universalist, a view that held that Jesus Christ died for the sins of all people, not just for the elect, in Calvinistic terms.

Besides his attendance at Anglican and Episcopal services, there is also sufficient evidence that the first president attended the religious services of Quakers, the United Baptists, the Presbyterians, the Dutch Reform Church, and Roman Catholics. Michael and Jana Novak speak of the many trips around the country Washington made during his presidency. They comment that he was more easily accepted in the North, where his campaign to liberate Boston had garnered him immense respect. The Novaks say:

> The South, though, was another matter. There he found a less populated landscape, less than adequate roads, and large tracts where he could move about in virtual anonymity.[301]

The Novak pair adds:

At each city, he would attend religious services, sometimes as many as three in one day.[302]

Ron Chernow, in his book *Washington: A Life*, speaks of the first president attending various religious services during the Continental Convention. Mr. Chernow writes:

> While the Convention dragged on, Washington drank enormous quantities of tea at the City Tavern and the Indian Queen, two haunts frequented by delegates. In his social life, he exhibited expert political instincts and embraced a wide spectrum of citizens, as if he already saw the presidency looming dimly on the horizon. On one of his first Sundays, he attended a Roman Catholic Mass and also dined with Mark Prager Sr., a Jewish merchant. On several occasions, he joined fraternal dinners hosted by the Irish-American sons of Saint Patrick.[303]

Thus, even as early as the Continental Convention, George Washington was prescient enough to recognize the validity of religious services outside his own Anglican-Episcopal church. This is a final fact that establishes the first president's dedication to the idea of religious tolerance in early America. Michael and Jana Novak sum up Washington's attitudes toward all the distinctive flavors of religion in his time, when they write:

> As President, he made a point of responding to all the distinct religious groups that wrote to him, and also to some major Masonic Lodges. He wanted all to feel part of the Republic, and to know that they had him a tribune.[304]

Similarly, John Avlon, in his book, *Washington's Farewell*, sums up Washington's views on pluralism and religious toleration when he says:

> Washington believed in the native powers of pluralism and assimilation. He'd learned this lesson early in life. As a young man, working as a Surveyor, he'd seen resistance of German immigrants to move to Virginia unless they were exempted from a uniform tax that went directly into the Church of England's coffers.[305]

Mr. Avlon goes on to point out:

> His beloved older brother Lawrence lobbied the legislature to amend the Law, arguing against 'restraints on Conscience' on the grounds that they were not 'cruel,' but that they put Virginia at a competitive disadvantage against other states as immigrants of different faiths, fled there and grew the local population while

Virginia only 'increased by slow degrees, except for Negroes and Convicts."[306]

Mr. Avlon adds, "This practical as well as moral imperative left its mark on Washington's Mind."[307] Nevertheless, George Washington's preaching on religious tolerance was one of the first president's most prescient and far-sighted ideas about faith—"Being no Bigot myself, I am disposed to indulge the professors of Christianity in the Church with that road to Heaven, which to them shall seem the most direct, plainest, and easiest, and least liable to exceptions."[308]

One final issue in regard to George Washington's beliefs about religious toleration is that the first president made a clear distinction between religious toleration and religious liberty. The latter idea, Washington believed, is a natural, inalienable right possessed equally by all people. It is beyond the reach of civil magistrates because this right was instituted by God.

Religious toleration, on the other hand, assumes an ecclesiastical and/or political origin that extends or withdraws permission to practice one's religion. Religious liberty is irrevocable by the state. Religious toleration, on the other hand, is extended and guaranteed by the state, according to the U.S. Constitution and other documents. Daniel Dreisbach points out that George Washington clearly understood this distinction.[309]

In summing up this section IV of this study on George Washington's religion, we may make the following conclusions: first, George Washington expressed his belief in religious toleration in a variety of his public and private acts. Second, we have shown that many of Washington's contemporaries held similar views to those of the first president on religious liberty and religious expression. Third, one of the principal sources for the American Enlightenment's views on religious toleration was English philosopher John Locke's *Letter on Toleration*, published in Latin in 1689. It is also possible, as we have seen, that Baruch Spinoza and French philosopher Voltaire may have been sources in formulating George Washington's views on religious toleration.[310]

Fourth, another way of ascertaining George Washington's understanding of religious toleration is to examine what his fellow Founding Fathers said about the issue. Among these men, as we have shown, were John Adams, Thomas Jefferson, George Mason, James Madison, and Benjamin Franklin. Each of these Founding Fathers, as well, wrote and spoke publicly about the rights associated with religious liberty and religious toleration.

Fifth, the best way to see George Washington's dedication to the idea of religious toleration in America is to examine the first president's many letters to religious congregations in that period. Sixth, prominent among these letters are those to the Jewish congregation in Newport, Rhode Island, and the Swedenborgian New Jerusalem Church in Baltimore, among many others.[311]

Sixth, George Washington clearly understood the difference between religious liberty and religious tolerance, that the former is a natural right, while the latter is not. And finally, Washington also showed his commitment to religious toleration by attending the services of various religious denominations, including Quakers, Methodists, Presbyterians, Baptists, Anglicans, Swedenborgians, Roman Catholics, and Jews.[312]

Now we shall turn to a fifth section, "Washington on Ethics and Virtue."

V

Washington on Ethics and Virtue

Washington was without an equal and unquestionably he was the greatest
man the world has produced in the last one thousand years.

—WILLIAM WILBUR

IN THIS FIFTH SECTION of this study on George Washington's religion, we will discuss what the first president wrote and thought about
ethics and moral virtue. Among the sources for interpreting Washington's
ethics are the following: what is known as divine command theory; possible early sources for Washington's views of morality, like his copy of the
Rules of Civility, and other family books collected by his mother, Mary Ball
Washington; his written and spoken words; what he had to say on the idea
of conscience; what his contemporaries also had to say about conscience;
what the life of Washington tells us about moral leadership qualities; and
finally, what Washington had to say about the relationship between ethics
and religion. We will begin with this latter question.

In his farewell address, delivered on September 19, 1796, George
Washington spoke of how he understood the relation of ethics to religion.
The first president observed:

> Of all the dispositions and habits which lead to political pros-
> perity, religion and morality are indispensable supports . . . And
> let us with caution indulge the supposition that morality can be
> maintained without Religion. Whatever may be conceded to the
> influence of refined education on minds of peculiar structure,

reason and experience both forbid us to expect that national
morality can prevail in exclusion of Religious Principles.[313]

From this comment in his farewell address, it is clear that George
Washington believed that morality and religion were intimately connected,
and that morality stems from religion. On other occasions, he suggested
that we cannot have one without the other. This comment was, most likely,
engendered by several Enlightenment thinkers who believed that God and
morality were distinct from each other.

In the seventeenth and eighteenth centuries, there were four distinct
philosophical positions on the relationship of ethics to religion. The first
says that religion is more fundamental than morality—that God instituted
ethical principles by issuing divine commands. René Descartes (1596–
1650), John Locke (1632–1704), and English philosopher William Paley
(1743–1805) held this view.[314] These philosophers all believed that ethics
arise from the tenets of religion. This also appears to have been George
Washington's point of view.

The second view on the relationship of religion and ethics is the one
taken by German philosopher Immanuel Kant (1724–1804). According to
Kant, religion is based on ethical principles, and the existence of God is
known only because of the existence of those ethical principles. Kant points
out that human happiness invariably is accompanied by virtue in the achiev-
ing of the highest good. But Kant also realized that happiness is not always
accompanied by virtue. He admits that good people sometimes suffer in a
number of ways when morally bad people enjoy themselves. If the ethical
order is clear and true, however, that should not be the case.[315]

Immanuel Kant's ethics is based on two central ideas: the categorical
imperative and what he refers to as the "Holy Will." From the first of these,
the German philosopher garnered a set of universal moral duties, including
truth-telling, protection of the innocent, and the keeping of one's promises,
as well as many other moral duties. In regard to the latter principle, Kant
suggested that one's moral intentions must be as pure as following the universal moral duties. Kant believed, however, that the categorical imperative
is prior to belief in God. Thus, he was an example of our second theory.[316]

The third Enlightenment view of the relationship of ethics to religion
suggests that the bases of ethics and of religion are different from one another; and this position may or may not be tied to a fourth position that religion
and morality are completely independent of each other. In the eighteenth
century, both Jean-Jacques Rousseau (1712–80) and Voltaire (1694–1778)
held this fourth point of view.[317]

Both Rousseau and Voltaire pointed out that some morally upstanding people do not believe in God. Thus, their views of the good cannot possibly be related to their atheism, and they are against the idea of divine command theory.

In his farewell address, President George Washington obviously favored the first view we have outlined above—that God's laws are the ethical criteria for the moral good, and that the moral good is a reflection of the goodness of God; but this is not the only position that outlines the relationship of ethics to religion, as we have shown in the above analysis. Voltaire, for example, who was a deist, pointed out that sometimes good men are good despite the fact that they may be infidels.

The ancient philosopher Plato was the first to criticize divine command theory. He was starkly against the idea that moral principles are only known by understanding divine commands. In fact, Plato, in his dialogue known as the "Euthyphro," suggested that the propositions that "God is all-Good," and that "Goodness is Good simply because God commands it" are incompatible with each other.[318]

We have argued earlier in this essay, in section III, that the first president's theory of the moral good—in which morality depends upon religion—is divine command theory. Also known as "Theological Voluntarism," it is a meta-ethical theory that proposes that an action's moral status is equivalent to whether or not it is commanded by God. The proponents of this theory assert that what is moral is entirely determined by what God commands. In this view, for a person to be moral, he must follow God's commands and wishes, and nothing else.

Russian novelist and philosopher Fyodor Dostoyevski (1821–81) seemed to have assented to the divine command theory when he had one of his characters in his novel *The Brothers Karamazov*, Dmitri, say, "If God does not exist, then all is permitted."[319] Clearly, the Russian held that morality was little more than the moral provisions outlined by God. Thus, he was a believer in divine command theory. If there is no God, then there is no basis for morality.

Recently, however, David E. Cortesi, in an essay entitled "Dostoevsky Didn't Say It," argues that the phrase in question does not appear in the novel. Cortesi concludes in his 2000 article:

> I say this with confidence because I have searched the online text of the Constance Garnett translation of *The Brothers Karamazov*, examining every use of "God" and "exist" and "lawful." ["Lawful" is how Garnett translates the word that others translate as "permitted."][320]

Even more recently, however, Andrei I. Volkov, in an essay called "Dostoevsky Did Say It" (published in 2011), Volkov, who is a native Russian speaker, argues that Dmitri Karamazov did, in fact, utter the sentence in question in Part IV, book 11, chapter 4 of the *Brothers Karamazov*.[321] Volkov also presents a number of contemporary Russian scholars to support his position, such as Victor Terras, John Bayley, and William Lane Craig.[322]

Historically, numerous versions of divine command theory have been presented by Western philosophers, including Saint Augustine of Hippo (354–430), Duns Scotus (1266–1308), and Thomas Aquinas (1225–74), for example, all of whom have presented various versions of divine command theory. In more contemporary Anglo-American philosophy, Robert Merrihew Adams has proposed what he calls a "modified Divine Command Theory." His theory is based on the concept of the omni-benevolence of God, in which morality is linked to human conceptions of right and wrong.[323]

Robert Adams's version of divine command theory suggests that the following two propositions are equivalent:

1. It is wrong to do X.

2. It is contrary to God's commands to do X.[324]

Like most believers in divine command theory, Professor Adams believes that divine commands precede moral truths, and must be explained in terms of those Commands, and not the other way around. Adams says his theory is an attempt to define what it means to be "morally wrong," and he accepts the view that moral wrong only makes sense in the context of the Judeo-Christian tradition.[325]

At any rate, Washington's 1796 farewell address, quoted above, suggests that the first president was a believer in divine command theory, which is the most important source for Washington's understanding of the moral good. Washington was not alone, however, among the Founding Fathers in his belief in divine command theory. George Mason, for example, seems to have assented to that view as well when he observed the following:

> The Laws of Nature are the Laws of God. Whose authority can be superseded by no power on Earth. A legislature must not obstruct our obedience to Him from Whose punishment they cannot protect us. All human Constitutions which contradict His Laws, we are in Conscience bound to disobey.[326]

In regard to the other sources of the first president's views on ethics and the moral good, we may point to several. One of these is that of the British lawyer and judge Sir Matthew Hale (1609–76.) Washington's mother Mary owned a copy of Hale's *Contemplations, Moral, and Divine.*[327] Her copy is signed in the inside flap, and the book was later to be part of Washington's personal library at Mount Vernon.

The Hale book is full of matters of advice for young men, including this passage about ethics:

> As touching my Conscience, and the light Thou has given me in it, I have been very jealous of wounding or grieving, or discouraging it or deadening it. I have therefore chosen rather to foster that which seemed but indifferent, lest there should be that somewhat in it that it might be useful; and would rather gratify my Conscience with being too scrupulous than to displease or to disquiet it by being too venturous.[328]

Judge Hale continues:

> I have still chosen, therefore, what might be probably lawful, than to do what might possibly be unlawful; because, though I could not err in the former, I might in the latter. If things were disputable, whether they might be done, I rather choose to forbear, because the lawfulness of my forbearance was unquestionable.[329]

Judge Hale makes a number of remarks in his *Contemplations*, many of them about conscience, self-interest, utilitarianism, and the idea of a reputation, particularly in relationship to conscience. In fact, Matthew Hale's works appear to have been one of the sources of the nineteenth-century philosophical movement known as "utilitarianism," which posits that one ought to produce the best consequences for the most number of people.

Another of the sources of moral goodness for Judge Hale was to consult what he called "the Counsel of Mordecai to Esther," by which he means the Holy Scriptures. He refers to them as his "encouragement," and goes on to say:

> Who knoweth whether God hath not given thee this reputation and esteem for such a time as this?"[330]

From this passage, it is clear that Hale's view of ethics was based on divine command theory, as well, in that his view of the moral good seems based on the moral provisions of the Bible, such as the Ten Commandments and the Golden Rule, for examples. It may well be that Mary Ball Washington taught those provisions to her son with the Hale volume.

Sir Matthew Hale also included lessons on humility and modesty. Michael and Jana Novak observed about the English Jurist's book:

Sir Matthew Hale's lessons on humility and modesty uncannily foreshadowed how Washington would later conduct himself, as when he warned the Congress of the many gaps in his knowledge of military matters and his lack of sufficient skills to lead the Army, while pledging to do his best; and how at each stage of his later life he would express publicly an awareness of his limitations. If these are, in fact, lessons that Washington learned at his mother's knee, or from later reading during his school days, his conduct as an adult becomes easier to understand.[331]

We may conclude, then that George Washington could have garnered his emphases on divine command theory and the pragmatism of utilitarianism from Justice Matthew Hale.

Another volume from George Washington's childhood, Thomas Comber's *Commentary of the Book of Common Prayer*, was another source of George Washington's early ethical views. Indeed, Mary Ball Washington, the mother of George, also owned a copy of Comber's book, as well.

Thomas Comber (1645–99) was an English churchman and dean of Durham from 1689 until his death in 1699. Comber's *Commentary* was intended to be a daily prayer book, a large portion of which is taken from the Psalms of the Old Testament. In his introduction to the volume, Comber remarks that "Even the poorest Christians can say them by heart."[332]

Michael and Jana Novak point out that "The backbone of the Book of Common Prayer is Psalm 95, which, as it were, outlines the whole nature and purpose of daily prayer."[333] Comber suggests that Psalm 95 displays what he believed were the four stages of prayer. Comber calls these:

1.   Realizing one is in the presence of God.

2.   Contemplate the sovereignty of God.

3.   We remind ourselves of the compassion of God.

4.   We recognize the integrity of prayer in reforming our lives.[334]

Thomas Comber also outlines a four-part moral decision-making process that suggests one should:

1.   Establish the facts of a given moral situation.

2.   Establish the moral principles at work.

3.   Identify the alternative consequences in the situation.

4.   Make the decision.[335]

This moral decision-making model, of course, is little more than the ethical model outlined by Aristotle in Book III of his *Nicomachean Ethics*, where he suggests that one is fully morally responsible if he or she has

1. moral intentions;

2. knowledge of right and wrong;

3. knowledge of the circumstances;

4. has the ability to do otherwise.[336]

Thomas Comber, in this and in other works, also shows that he is a firm advocate of the moral theory we have called divine command theory, as evidenced by the many Biblical passages with which his works are peppered. Comber also was very familiar with the ethics of Aristotle, as well as the Stoic philosophers, and the Englishman wrote extensively on what could only be called the "Ethics of Dueling," one of the later sources of Washington's views on just war theory.

Again, these remarks and lessons from Bishop Thomas Comber are reflected in the later life of George Washington, particularly when it came to the suffering caused by the war. From his contemplations of Bishop Comber, Washington frequently made remarks like "I flatter myself that a Superintending Providence is ordering everything for the best, and that in due time, all will end well."[337] This remark was made early in Washington's military career; but a year or two later, Washington remarks, under similar circumstances:

> But alas, we are not to expect that the path is to be strewn with flowers ... That Great and Good Being who rules the Universe has disposed matters otherwise and for wise purposes I am persuaded.[338]

Thomas Comber, then, may well be another source of utilitarianism that Washington received at his mother's knee. Michael and Jana Novak, commenting in this regard, speak of the first president's overall theory of theodicy and the problem of evil. They observe:

> Yet in times of suffering and despair, Washington counseled himself that we ought to trust Providence in its unfathomable wisdom, even when its workings remain beyond our comprehension.[339]

The Novaks make three points here. First, in situations involving suffering and despair, we, second, must trust in the wisdom of Providence because, third, the working of the divine are beyond human comprehension. It should be clear that the language concerning "unfathomable wisdom," and "beyond-human comprehension" is directly indicative of the divine plan theory with respect to the problem of evil. Much more will be said of George Washington's appropriation of this theory in section VIII of this work.

The Novaks suggest that George Washington was a believer, then, in a theory sometimes called the "divine plan," with respect to the issues of the problem of evil and theodicy. Much more will be said about the first president's views regarding this question in a subsequent section of this work, section VIII. It is enough now, however, to say that the Novaks are entirely correct about Washington's overall view on the issue.

The Novaks go on to point out that Washington is not referring to "the Deist god . . . but the God Jehovah whose ways are not our ways, and whose wisdom operates on a far higher and deeper wave lengths than we are given access to."[340] Earlier in this essay, however, we argued that the word "Jehovah" is not a Biblical term, but rather a made-up Hebrew name by sixteenth-century Christian thinkers, so it is not entirely clear why Michael Novak employed that name for God.

In addition to Sir Matthew Hale and Bishop Thomas Comber, another source for understanding Washington's views of conscience, ethics, and virtue, were his many contemporaries who shared many of the views on these issues. Justice John Jay (1745–1829) was the first chief justice of the U.S. Supreme Court. He served from 1789 until 1795, signed the Treaty of Paris for the United States, and was the second governor of the state of New York, as well. He was one of the most respected of America's Founding Fathers. He had this to say about conscience:

> Security under our Constitution is given to the rights of Conscience and private judgment. They are, by nature, subject to no control but that of Deity [the Lord] and in that free situation they are now left.[341]

Elsewhere, in his famous "Essay on Property," James Madison observed, "The Religion of every man must be left to the conviction and Conscience of every man; and it is the right of every man to exercise it as they may dictate."[342] Madison also proclaimed, "The Civil Rights of none shall be abridged on account of Religious belief or worship.[343] Madison even argued against the establishment of a state religion when he wrote:

> Nor shall any national Religion be established, nor shall the full and equal rights of Conscience be in any manner, or in any pretext, infringed.[344]

Madison further observes that "Conscience is the most Sacred of all property."

In 1782, Thomas Jefferson referred to what he calls the "Rights of Conscience," when he observed, "But our rulers can have such authority over such natural rights only as we have submitted to them. The Rights of Conscience we never submitted. We are answerable for them to God."[345] In 1809, the third president returned to the same topic when he said:

> No provision in our Constitution ought to be dearer to man than that which protects the Rights of Conscience against the enterprises of the Civil Authority.[346]

John Adams, at the Continental Convention, said the following: "this said Constitution shall never be construed to authorize Congress to infringe the just liberty of the press, or the Rights of Conscience."[347] In commenting about the nature and extent of a militia, Adams again makes mention of conscience when he said:

> A Militia Law, requiring all men, or with very few exceptions besides cases of Conscience to be provided with arms and ammunition . . . is always a wise institution and, in the present circumstances of our Country, indispensable.[348]

On another occasion, the second president observed about religion and conscience:

> And no subject shall be hurt, molested or restrained, in his person, liberty or estate, for worshipping God in the manner most agreeable to the dictates of his own Conscience, or for his religious profession or sentiments; provided he doth not disturb the public peace, or obstruct others in their religious worship.[349]

Here Adams points out one of the limitations of religious freedom. They should only be extended, he argued, against the promotion of the public good, or what he referred to as the "Public Peace." Adams hints at an important moral distinction that is sometimes referred to as the difference between "freedoms from" and "freedoms to," also called negative and positive freedoms. "Freedoms to" are guaranteed by the Constitution, things like freedoms to speak, assemble, etc. "Freedoms from," on the other hand, are those things that citizens desire to be free from, such as crime, poverty, and disease.

Many of America's Founding Fathers, like Adams, Jefferson, and Washington, realized that if a society is to function in a good manner, it must do so in a balance between these "freedoms to" and "freedoms from."

This is not only true of the United States, but it is also true, they believed, of any society.

James Monroe, as well, speaks of the liberty of conscience in a legal context, when he said, "Of the Liberty of Conscience in matters of Religious Faith, of Speech and of the Press; of the Trial by Jury . . . of the benefit of the Writ of Habeas corpus; of the right to keep and to bear arms. If these rights are secured against encroachments, it is impossible that Government should ever denigrate into Tyranny."[350]

Virginia Founding Father, George Mason, also held a similar view to the rights of conscience. He observed:

> All men have an equal, natural, and inalienable right to the free exercise of Religion, according to the dictates of their Conscience; and that no particular Sect of Society of Christians ought to be favored or established by Law in preference to others.[351]

It is important to point out that when the Founding Fathers employed the expression "the Liberty of Conscience," they meant three separate aspects of the idea. First, there is the freedom of belief, by which all individuals are at liberty to choose the religious creed they wish to embrace, or, as Jefferson said, to embrace no creed at all. Second, they are free to attend services or to observe the practice of their religion, any way they see fit, in a lawful manner.

In regard to the third element that makes up the idea of "Liberty of Conscience," every individual has an equal status to worship, consistent with the worship of everyone else. All religions and their believers deserve equal treatment under the law. These elements of the liberty of conscience apply to individuals, as well as to organized churches, synagogues, mosques, temples, and other houses of worship.

Thomas Jefferson and Benjamin Rush (1746–1813; Presbyterian physician, writer, educator, and humanitarian) exchanged a series of letters in April and May of 1803 on the idea of conscience and its relationship to religion. Thus, Rush is another Founding Father who wrote about those issues in early America.[352]

These observations by the other Founding Fathers were similar to George Washington's letter to the General Committee of the United Baptists Churches of Virginia, when the first president wrote, "I have often expressed my sentiments, that every man conducting himself as a good citizen, and being accountable to God alone for his religious opinions, ought to be protected in worshipping the Deity, according to the dictates of his

Conscience."[353] George Washington returns to the idea of conscience and morality in a variety of other places, as well, as we shall see next.

George Washington returns to these three elements of the liberty of conscience in a variety of his writings and speeches. In one speech, the president remarked, "While we are within our territories and protected in worshipping the Deity according to the dictates of their Consciences, it is rational to expect from them in return, that they will demonstrate the innocence of their lives and the beneficence of their actions."[354] Washington speaks here of the protection of the right to follow one's conscience, and that in return the state may wish that the exercising of that right will contribute to the common good.

On another occasion, President Washington remarked:

> While we are contending for our own Liberty, we should be very cautious not to violate the Conscience of others, ever considering that God alone is the Judge of the hearts of men; and to him only in this case are they answerable.[355]

Washington speaks here of something akin to John Stuart Mill's "Principle of Harm," in which he says that a man's freedom only extends as far as the nose of the next man. Mill (1806–73) developed his "Principle of Harm" and articulated it in his work, *On Liberty*, where he argued that "The only purpose for which power may be rightfully exercised over any member of a civilized community, against his will, is to prevent harm to others."[356] A similar idea can be found in France's *Declaration of the Rights of Man and of the Citizen*, of 1789. The French document put the matter this way:

> Liberty consists in the Freedom to do everything which injures no one else; hence, the exercise of the natural rights of each man has no limits except those which assure to the other members of the society the enjoyment of the same rights. These limits can only be determined by Law.[357]

It also should be clear from this discussion that George Washington, as well as many of his fellow Founding Fathers, were dedicated to the three elements of the "Liberty of Conscience" outlined in the above discussion. Another aspect of President Washington's views on ethics and morality are the many times he spoke of "virtue" in his adult life. In his 1796 farewell address, for example, Washington said this about virtue:

> It is substantially true that virtue or morality, is a necessary spring of popular Government. The rule indeed extends with more or less force to every species of Free Government. Who

that is a sincere friend to it, can look with indifference upon attempts to shake the foundations of the Fabric.[358]

For the first president, the foundations of the moral fabric of America was the idea of virtue, particularly the Stoic version of virtue. In his first inaugural address, Washington spoke of the link between virtue and human happiness. He observed:

> There is no truth more thoroughly established than that there exists in the economy and the course of nature an indissoluble union between virtue and happiness; between duty and advantage; between the genuine maxims of an honest magnanimous policy and the solid rewards of public prosperity and felicity; since we ought to be no less persuaded that the propitious smiles of Heaven can never be expected of a nation that disregards the eternal rules of order and right which Heaven itself has ordained.[359]

Washington clearly saw there was a union of virtue and human happiness. He discussed that connection again when he informs us, "The aggregate happiness of the society, which is best promoted by the practice of a virtuous policy, is, or ought to be, the end of all government."[360] This connection between virtue and happiness is also made in many of Washington's contemporaries. Thomas Jefferson wrote, "Without virtue, happiness cannot be."[361] The third president also observed:

> The order of nature is that individual Happiness shall be inseparable from the practice of Virtue.[362]

James Madison also made this same connection. He relates, "To suppose that any form of government will secure Liberty or Happiness without any virtue in the people, is a chimerical idea."[363] John Adams, our second president, remarks that, "Liberty can no more exist without virtue and independence, than the body can live and move without a soul."[364] Few of us can imitate the virtue and self-discipline of George Washington; but some American readers of history know that the virtues about which the Founding Fathers speak are Greco-Roman forms of virtue theory, specifically Aristotle and the Stoic philosophers and poets.

Aristotle's theory of ethics is based on the idea that all moral virtues are a mean between two extremes. One extreme is an excess, and the other a deficiency. Thus, courage is a mean between rashness and cowardice; temperance is the mean between self-indulgence and insensibility; modesty, for Aristotle, stands between shyness and shamelessness; and truthfulness is a mean between falsehood and being overly truthful.[365] For Aristotle, the sum total of the moral virtues is human happiness, exemplified by a man of virtue.

The Stoics, on the other hand, called human happiness "flourishing." For them, there were four principal cardinal virtues that must be cultivated in order to become a morally good person. The four cardinal virtues recognized by the Stoics were: wisdom, courage, justice, and temperance.[366]

The Stoics also made a distinction between events and one's reactions to events. The Stoics believed human beings had no say in events, for they believed in a form of fate, or *Moirai,* but they did believe that human beings can choose about how they react or respond to events.

The ideals of principled leadership were brought into view in the eighteenth century with the 1776 publication of Edward Gibbon's *The Rise and Fall of the Roman Empire.*[367] Gibbon (1737–94), was an English historian, writer, and member of Parliament. He published his masterpiece in six volumes between 1776 and 1788. Upon the book's publication, copies were immediately shipped to America, and its lessons were quickly absorbed by Jefferson, Madison, and Washington, and other Founding Fathers. Gibbon pointed to the many virtues espoused by Roman Emperor Marcus Aurelius in his *Meditations.*[368] After the death of the emperor, Rome began to spiral into an ever-accelerating decay. Civic virtue was replaced by greed, self-interest, and corruption.

George Washington admired Aurelius's Stoic quest for wisdom, virtue, self-restraint, tolerance, and the dignity of men. Some reports say he controlled his fiery temper by practicing Stoic virtues as a religion. Aurelius's central dictum was this: "what matters most is a man's behavior, not his ideas." Serenity, calmness, and an ardent refusal to display the emotions of hate and rage were essential to the survival of morality and good judgment, according to the Stoics.[369]

When George Washington took control of the Continental Army, his response appears to be that of a Stoic. He said, "I hope I shall possess firmness and virtue enough to maintain what I consider the most enviable of all titles—the character of an Honest Man."[370] Washington wrote at the time:

> But lest some unlucky event should happen unfavorable to my reputation, I beg it may be remembered by every Gentlemen in the room, that in this day declare with the utmost sincerity, I do not think myself equal to the Command that I am honored with.[371]

When taking on the job of commander-in-chief of the Continental Army, Washington observed in a letter to Colonel Barakiel Bassett on June 19, 1775:

I can only answer but for three things: a firm belief in Justice of
our cause, close attention in the prosecution of it, and the strict-
est Integrity. If these cannot supply the ability & Experience, the
cause will suffer & more than probable my character along with
it, as reputation derives its principle support from success.[372]

The Stoics had an elaborate taxonomy of virtue. Their principal virtues
were wisdom, justice, courage, and moderation. In his youth, Washington
valued highly the *Rules of Civility*, mentioned earlier in section I, as well as a
compilation of essays known as Seneca's *Morals*. In fact, the *Rules of Civility*
seem often to emphasize the Stoic virtues, and he may well have learned
of those virtues from Matthew Hale and Thomas Comber, as previously
discussed.[373] In his youth, Washington saw himself as the embodiments of
these two works, and he continued to be those embodiments for the remainder of his life.

George Washington owned a copy of Stoic Cicero's complete works "in
a neat edition." Among the things he learned from Cicero was his view of
the soul, that the Stoics divided into two elements—reflection and choice.
The former involves the ability to contemplate, or "reflect," on past and
possible future courses of events. The latter idea entails the ability to make
choices about the proposed possibilities. This distinction between reflection and choice is outlined in the very first of the Federalist Papers.[374] This
distinction, at least for the Stoics, is a corollary to the distinction between
events and reactions to events.

One final point about Washington's respect for Roman Republicanism
and its central virtues is that the first president was enamored with Joseph
Addison's 1713 tragic drama, *Cato*.[375] Addison's play was a dramatization of
the final days of Roman Senator Marcus Cato (95–46 BCE) whom, at least
for Addison, served as an exemplary figure of Roman virtue and opposition
to tyranny.

Addison (1672–1719) was an English essayist, poet, dramatist, and
politician. He also was the guiding spirit behind the *Tatler*, as well as the
Spectator, two biting seventeenth-century English periodicals, popular in
England in the seventeenth and eighteenth-century.

In the Roman Civil War that followed Caesar's crossing of the Rubicon
in 49 BCE, the patrician, Cato, joined the opposition to Caesar's tyranny.
After the defeat at Pompey in 48 BCE, Cato continued to hold out by refus-
ing to join Caesar's forces in North Africa, where he found a ready ally in the
Numidian King Juba I, who lived from 85 to 46 BCE, and reigned from 60
to 46 BCE, was the son and successor of King Hiempsal II. The kingdom of
Numidia is present-day Mauritania. After a decisive defeat at Thapsus in 46

BCE, Cato committed suicide, an act that was considered morally justified for a believer in the Stoic philosophy.

Washington greatly admired Addison's drama. In fact, in May of 1778, a performance of *Cato* took place, at the insistence of General Washington, at Valley Forge. Colonel William Bradford Jr. wrote his sister from his tent at Valley Forge. Colonel Braford wrote:

> The Camp could now afford some entertainment; the maneuvering of the Army is in itself a sight that would charm. Besides these—the Theatre is open—Last Monday "Cato" was performed before a numerous & splendid audience.[376]

At the close of a hard winter at Valley Forge, Washington defied a congressional ban on any theatrical productions and entertainment for his men by organizing the production of Joseph Addison's 1713 drama, *Cato*. As Dr. Robert Hardy has observed about the performance of *Cato*: "Scholars have generally seen the performance of *Cato* at Valley Forge as an attempt to inspire the troops with a stirring dramatization of the self-sacrificing defense of Republican principles against Tyranny."[377]

H. C. Montgomery, in his essay "Washington, the Stoic," published in 1936 in the *Classical Journal*, suggests that Washington quoted Addison's *Cato*, calling the figure "Washington's favorite character in history."[378] Montgomery reported Washington as saying:

> Let me advise thee to retreat betimes
> to thy paternal seat, the Sabine field,
> when the great Censor toil'd with his own hands,
> and all our frugal ancestors were blest,
> in humble virtues, and a rural life.
> There lived retired, pray for the peace of Rome;
> Content thyself to be obscurely good.
> When vice prevails, and impious men bear sway,
> The post of honor is a private station.[379]

More recently, however, Mark Evans Bryan has suggested that the dramatic performance of *Cato* at Valley Forge was meant to stir the virtues of the officers, and not of the troops; he also adds, "It was an emblem of gentility and a deeply attractive indulgence for the burgeoning and contested aristocracy of the Continental Army."[380] Nevertheless, it must be pointed out that the historical Cato was no democratic hero. Rather he was a patrician fighting for the freedoms of the Roman population. At any rate, we will turn to one other issue in regards to George Washington's ethics—his leadership qualities.

In addition to the Roman Republican Stoic virtues mentioned above, George Washington became famous for his moral character for ten leadership traits that he exemplified throughout his adult life, both as a general and as a president. We will list them here, and then discuss them one at a time:

1. He kept to his goal.

2. He embodied exemplary character.

3. He placed his welfare behind that of his troops.

4. He treated others with respect.

5. He was personally invested in his cause.

6. He believed in those around him and his troops.

7. He held his subordinates accountable.

8. He was reluctant to join any cause.

9. Where there is no reason to express an opinion—be silent!

10. Don't surround yourself with yes-men.

George Washington did not waver from his guiding principles. He was against the idea of tyranny. He valued his freedom, and he extended it to include others. He believed in the principles expressed in the Declaration of Independence and the Constitution, and he lived as if those principles were more valuable to him than his own life. Secondly, as Ron Chernow expresses it:

> History records few examples of a leader who so earnestly wanted to do the right thing, not just for himself but for his Country. He avoided moral short-cuts, and he consistently upheld high ethical standards that made him look larger than any other figure in a political sense.[381]

Mr. Chernow refers to the exemplary moral character always on display in Washington's life as a general and as a president. The first president consistently displayed those characteristics as a young man, as a surveyor, in battle in the French and Indian and Revolutionary wars, and in his decision-making as the first U.S. president.

Upon first meeting George Washington, Abigail Adams wrote to her husband on July 16, 1775, her first impressions of the general. In the letter, she included these two paragraphs:

I was struck with General Washington. You had prepared me
to entertain a favorable opinion of him, but I thought the one
half was not told me. Dignity, with ease, and complacency, the
Gentleman and Soldier look agreeably blended in him. Modesty
marks every line and feature of his face. Those lines of Dryden
instantly occurred to me:

> Mark his Majestick[*sic*] fabric. He's a Temple.
> Sacred by birth, and built by hands Divine.
> His Souls the Deity that lodges there.
> Nor is the pile unworthy of the God.[382]

The moral character of Washington can best be seen in two separate
situations that distinctly stand out in exhibiting his great virtue. The first
was when Washington refrained from acting when General Howe occupied
Philadelphia; the second is how Washington kept his army together in the
winter of Valley Forge in 1777–78. The former shows that Washington could
put aside his personal honor to do what is best for the survival of his men.
The latter shows that Washington was unwilling to give up the American
cause in the face of overwhelming power and adversity—against the most
powerful kingdom on Earth at the time, the British Empire.

Thirdly, he always placed the welfare of his men above that of his own.
It was not just the fact that Washington was willing to take a bullet—there is
no glory in that for him. What Washington demonstrated was why he was
willing, and it had nothing to do with his own self-interest. He always put
the interests of his soldiers above that of his own.

Fourthly, Washington always treated others with the utmost respect.
There are even reports that he handled the lowliest private with the dignity
and respect he afforded a visiting dignitary from Philadelphia or Europe.
Later, we will see a good example of this phenomenon in Washington's treat-
ment of the only Jewish soldier at Valley Forge, which we shall see in section
VIII.

Fifthly, the first president always was invested in his cause. The great
general often put his own money where his mouth was. Washington invested in the cause, not only his blood, sweat, and tears, but he also frequently
contributed his own money to the American cause. In an address to the
officers of his army on March 15, 1783, Washington spoke of his dedication
to the American cause. He said:

> You will give one more distinguished proof of unexampled Pa-
> triotism and patient Virtue, rising superior to the pressure of
> the most complicated sufferings; And you will be the dignity of
> your conduct, afford occasion of Posterity to say, when speaking

of the glorious example you have exhibited to Mankind, "Had this day been wanting, the World have never seen the last stage of perfection to which human nature is capable of attaining."[383]

It is clear that, in these lines, Washington foresaw that if his army should fail in fulfilling its cause, the cause might be lost forever. What remained the same for the first president was that this cause was the same as his own—to harbor the will of the people, and nothing more. This speech to his officers was significant in understanding the role of the army, as well as his own role, and the national identity they were in the process of making.

In a letter to his friend, Henry Lamers (1761–1836), on December 23, 1777, while at Valley Forge, General Washington expressed the seriousness of the army's needs. In this letter, you get a great deal of confirmation about the general's dedication to his cause:

> I am now convinced beyond a doubt, that unless some great capital change suddenly takes place in that line, this Army must inevitably be reduced to one or the other of three things—Starve, Dissolve, or Disperse.[384]

Washington made similar pleas to Congress throughout that entire winter of 1777-78. This is not the first time that Congress had been the source of the soldiers' frustration. The events of that winter at Valley Forge occasioned a distrust and doubt on the parts of the soldiers and officers. But through it all, Washington's example of fortitude and steadfastness of character, became the glue that held the army, and the American cause, together.

Ron Chernow, in his *Washington: A Life*, quotes one "Frenchman" who was able to capture Washington's persona at Valley Forge and his dedication to the American cause. Chernow records:

> I cannot describe the impression that the first sight of that great man made upon me, and I could not keep my eyes from that imposing countenance: grave, yet not severe; affable without familiarity. Its predominant expression was calm dignity, through which you could trace the strong feelings of the patriot and discern the father as well as the Commander of his soldiers.[385]

Fifth, Washington also believed in those around him: his officers, his troops, and his cabinet members, as well as his family servants. The first president prided himself in understanding the different gifts of his staff—he was able to employ them most effectively in military situations, not to mention as president.

Sixth, Washington regularly displayed ten central, moral leadership qualities that we have discussed at some length, qualities found in both his time as a general, as well as his moral-decision-making when he was president.

In that regard, Washington always held his subordinates accountable. John Adams observed about Washington, in regard to this seventh trait:

> Every man in the Continental Congress is a great man—an Orator, a Critic, a Statesman, and therefore everyman upon every question must show his Oratory, his Criticism, and his Political Abilities.[386]

What the second president said about all members of the Continental Congress, George Washington believed about all his subordinates, in all of his many walks of life. He held those subordinates accountable for the tasks he had designated to them, another significant aspect of a moral leader.

Eighthly, Washington was reluctant to sign on to just any cause presented to him; however, when he did make a commitment to something, that commitment was full and complete.

A ninth characteristic of Washington's leadership is expressed in his own words. He wrote:

> Where there is no occasion to express an opinion, it is best to be silent, for there is nothing more certain than it is at all times more easy to make enemies than to make friends.[387]

In George Washington's view, when there was no good reason for expressing an opinion about a matter, then it is best to keep silent. Finally, George Washington was keenly aware that no leader should ever surround himself simply with yes-men. He knew that this practice was dangerous, for it stifles creativity—something that is important in leading any organization. Without creativity and innovation, Washington understood, institutions may well not survive.

In summary, in this section of this study on George Washington's religion, we have made the following conclusions: first, Washington believed that religion is more fundamental than ethics, in that he advocated the divine command theory, in regards to ethics. Second, among the other sources of the first president's views on ethics were Matthew Hale and Thomas Comber, as well as his fellow Founding Fathers. Third, a number of his colleagues shared his understanding of conscience and its relationship to the moral good. Among those thinkers were John Adams, Thomas Jefferson, George Mason, James Madison, Benjamin Rush, and, as we have seen, many others.

A fourth conclusion we have made in regard to George Washington's understanding of morality is his view concerning the relationship of virtue to human happiness. In his view, taking his cue from Aristotle and the Stoic philosophers and poets, there can be no happiness where there is no virtue. Fifth, Washington was enamored by the Stoics and their views of virtue. Sixth, Washington exemplified the central Stoic virtues of patience, courage, wisdom, and moderation. Seventh, he often displayed ten separate moral, leadership qualities in his tasks as a general and as a president.

And finally, Washington was fond of Joseph Addison's play *Cato*, so much so that he supervised a performance of the drama during the time of his army at Valley Forge. And the general admired the drama for its presentation of a character that exemplified the ancient Stoic virtues of wisdom, courage, moderation, and justice. We shall now turn our attention to the topic of George Washington's understanding and uses of prayer.

VI

Washington on Prayer

George Washington changed the standard for human greatness.

—FATHER FISHER AMES

AS THE HEADING SUGGESTS, our major aim to this sixth section of this study on George Washington's religion is to say something of what the president said, and apparently believed, about the notion of prayer. We will begin by looking at several places where the first president commented on prayer or engaged in prayer, including two proclamations of thanksgiving and prayer Washington mandated as president in 1789 and again in 1795. Secondly, we will examine several first-person accounts of George Washington at prayer.

These will come, as we shall see from family members and several fellow soldiers of George Washington. This will be followed by examining a few misconceptions about George Washington and prayer, and we will end this section by taking a look at a contemporary artistic view on the first president and prayer.

Among the sources for understanding George Washington's relationship to prayer are his many prayer journals discussed in the section on Washington's uses of the Bible, as well as the prayer book shipped by the Robert Cary Company of London "for the use of George Washington, Potomac River, Virginia, Viz. July 18, 1771."[388] This prayer book of Washington's was described as:

> A Prayer Book with new Version of the Psalms and good plain
> type, covered with red Morocco, to be seven inches long, four

inches wide, and as thin as possible for the greater ease of carry-
ing it in the Pocket.[389]

It appears as though George Washington carried this thin version of
the Psalms in his pocket while in battle, often referring directly to it, or
quoting it, when he did. This text is now owned by the Library of Congress.

George Washington's utterances on prayer are, for the most part, of
two types. The first of these are the many places in his general orders where
he proclaimed that his soldiers should pray. In these general orders that are
extant, in at least twelve instances, the general urged his men to pray for the
good of the nation, as well as to attend religious services, to observe days of
thanksgiving, and to spend days in humility and prayer.[390] One prayer order
came to Washington's troops on May 15, 1776, after the Continental Congress had ordered Washington to proclaim the Day of Prayer. Washington
said at the time:

> The Continental Congress has ordered that Friday the 17th . . .
> shall be a Day of Fasting, Humiliation, and Prayer, humbly to
> supplicate the mercy of Almighty God, that it would please
> him to pardon all our manifold sins and transgressions, and to
> prosper the arms of the United Colonies, and finally establish
> the peace and freedom of America upon a solid and lasting
> Foundation.[391]

Many of Washington's orders to pray to his troops mention three elements in the above passage. First, they often ask God for the forgiveness of
their sins. Second, they ask for the supplication of God's mercy. And, finally,
they make their prayers in a state of fasting and humiliation.

Sometimes Washington prayed for the improvement of America's
arms, as when Washington continued this order from the Continental Congress by observing:

> The exercising of their religious duties, they may pray to incline
> the Lord and Giver of Victory to prosper our arms.[392]

Indeed, one day after receiving his commission as head of the Continental Army, General Washington issued an order to his troops that said:

> All officers and soldiers not engaged in actual duty should at-
> tend Divine Services to implore blessings of Heaven upon the
> means used for their safety and for their defense.[393]

Shortly after the signing of the Declaration of Independence, Washington believed that the blessings of heaven and Providence were manifested
during the Battle of Long Island, where Washington's eight thousand troops

were pitted against 32,000 of the British General Howe. Washington was certain that his prayers, and those of his men, were the true causes of the American escape. Throughout the war, Washington frequently attributed his many victories to have come about due to his many prayers for victory, as well as the prayers of his men.

In another of his general orders just a month or so after he had taken command of the Continental Army, he ordered, or, using one of his favorite verbs, he "enjoined" his men to pray and attend services." The general wrote at the time:

> And in like manner, the General requires and expects, of all Officers and Soldiers, not engaged in actual duty, a punctual attendance on Divine Service, to implore the blessings of Heaven upon the means used for our safety and our defense.[394]

In one of the first acts of the Continental Congress in September of 1774, John Jay, Samuel Adams, and others present made references to beginning with a prayer. There was some disagreement over the kind of prayer and who would give it, until the Rev. Doctor Jacob Duché was proposed by Adams to fulfill the task. Adams said the Anglican minister "has a reputation for good judgment."[395]

Searching through the Book of Common Prayer, the minister settled on a reading from Psalm 35, which in the King James Version proclaims:

> Plead my cause, oh Lord, with those who strive with me, fight against those who fight against me. Take hold of buckler and shield, and rise up for my help . . . Say to my soul, "I am your Salvation." Let those be ashamed and dishonored who seek my life; let those be turned back and humiliated who devise Evil against me.[396]

After reading the Psalm from a lectern, the Anglican minister preached about many of the issues of the day. He began this way:

> O Lord our Heavenly Father, High and Mighty, King of Kings, and Lord of Lords, who dost from thy throne behold all the dwellers on earth, and reignest with power supreme and uncontrolled over all kingdoms, empires, and governments, look down with mercy, we beseech Thee, on these our American States, who have fled to Thee, from the rod of the oppressor.[397]

The "rod of the oppressor," of course, is none other than King George and the British government. A little later on in the sermon, the Anglican reverend observed:

In our own land, the most momentous issues hang on the events
of the passing hours. If oppression, corruption and intolerance
could wear a bolder front and seem to be making rapid strides
toward the mastery of the people, there is on the other hand,
among the thoughtful everywhere a keener perception of the
common danger, and a drawing together of the wise and the
good to resist the advances of Evil.[398]

The Rev. Doctor Duché closed his sermon with these words:

We court for ourselves the alliance of true patriots from all par-
ties to aid in the good work. It is not brute force but intelligence
that governs, and to that we appeal in the hope of rolling back
the tide of Evil that seeks to sweep over the land.[399]

George Washington was present for this first prayer of Congress. We
will say more about this incident later in this section of this essay on the
religion of George Washington. It is enough now, however, to point out that
Washington was there in Philadelphia, along with Samuel Adams (1722–
1803), Henry Lee (1732–94), John Jay, and a number of other Founding
Fathers.

On December 18, 1777, while commanding at Valley Forge, Washington again enjoined his men to observe a day of prayer and fasting. That very
day, one of the general's chaplains, a man named Israel Evans, of the New
Hampshire Brigade, gave a sermon on the character of the general appropriate in the context of a day of prayer and fasting.[400] The Rev. Evans spoke
of General Washington as possessing presence, sovereignty, compassion,
and integrity, and he adds these characteristics are also possessed by God
himself.[401]

The Pennsylvania-born Israel Evans (1747–1807) was a 1772 graduate of Princeton. He was ordained in the Presbyterian Church in 1776, and
served as a chaplain in the Continental Army from 1776 until 1783. He
served under Washington at Valley Forge and also at the Battle of Yorktown.
A letter from Washington to the Rev. Evans is extant from March 18, 1778.[402]

Washington's 1777 prayer proclamation begins with these words:

For as much as it is the indispensable duty of all men to adore
the superintending Providence of the Almighty God; to acknowledge with Gratitude their Obligation to Him for benefits
received, and to implore such further Blessings as they stand in
need of; and it having pleased him in His abundant Mercy not
only to continue to us the innumerable Bounties of His common Providence, but to smile upon us in the Prosecution of a
just and necessary War, for the defense and the establishment

of our unalienable Rights and Liberties; particularly in that He has been pleased in so great a Measure to prosper the Means used for the Support of our Troops and to crown our Arms with most signal a success. It is therefore, recommended to the legislative or executive powers of these United States to set apart, Thursday the 18th Day of December, for solemn Thanksgiving and Prayer.[403]

In this passage, Washington used his most common reference to the divine, "Providence." He expresses his gratitude and indicates his obligations to God. Much of the language in this quotation of Washington looks like terms the deists employed for God; and he mentions the idea of a just war, something we shall return to later in this essay.

Although this prayer was attributed to General George Washington, it is highly unlucky that he composed these lines. As we shall show later in this section, there is no evidence that Washington ever prayed at Valley Forge, on his knees in the snow, by his horse, or otherwise.

In both 1789 and 1795, Washington mandated two days of thanksgiving and prayer for the American people. On October 3, 1789, in New York City, Washington proclaimed that "Both Houses of Congress by their joint Committee requested him to recommend to the People of the United States a day of Public Thanksgiving and Prayer."[404] Thus, it was formally declared on November 26, 1789, "to be devoted by the People of these States to the service of that Great and Glorious Being Who is the Beneficent Author of all the good that was, that is, or that will be."[405]

Although the proclamation enjoined prayer, absent from the document was the name of Jesus Christ. The only indirect use of Jesus Christ was the use of "AD," meaning *Anno domini*, or "the year of Our Lord," to indicate the year it was proclaimed.

Washington's 1789 proclamation does employ, however, language about the divine normally associated with deism, calling God a "Great and Glorious Being," as well as the "Beneficent Author of All that is Good," another bit of evidence that Washington believed in divine command theory.[406] The October 3, 1789 proclamation signed by President Washington begins this way:

Whereas it is the duty of all nations to acknowledge the Providence of the Almighty God, to obey His Will, to be grateful for His benefits, and humbly to implore His protection and favor ... Now I do recommend and assign Thursday, the 26th of November next, to be devoted by the people of these states to the service of that Great and Glorious Being who is the Beneficient Author of all that is Good.[407]

Earlier, the Continental Congress had issued similar proclamations in 1776, beginning with John Hancock, and then in 1777, 1778, 1779, 1780, 1781, and 1782. Of these, the most significant was the one passed by Congress on November 1, 1777. This proclamation set aside December 18, 1777 as a "National Thanksgiving Day of Prayer."

Washington's other thanksgiving and prayer proclamation during his time as president came in 1795. In this proclamation, the first president said:

> I, George Washington, President of the United States, do recommend to Religious Societies and Denominations, and to all Persons whomsoever within the United States, to set apart and observe Thursday, the 19th of February next, as a Day of Public Thanksgiving and Prayer; and on that Day to meet together, and to render their sincere and hearty thanks to the Great Ruler of Nations, for the manifold and signal mercies which distinguish our lot as a Nation.[408]

Like the 1789 proclamation, in the 1795 document, the name "Jesus Christ" is absent of the document. The later proclamation, however, also shares the extensive use of deistic language in regard to the divine. We find the names "Great Ruler of Nations" and the "Kind Author of Blessings" when the latter proclamation refers to God.[409]

After both of these proclamations in 1789 and 1795, controversy arose over the absence of Jesus in the proclamations. The proclamations may have found favor among those who believed in the separation of church and state; but there were some who regarded both proclamations to be affronts to Christianity. Chief among these critics was Parson Ebenezer Bradford, minister of the first church in Rowley, Massachusetts.

Preaching on the morning of the second proclamation from 1795, the Rev. Bradford expressed strong displeasure on the absence of the name Jesus Christ in the document. Bradford observed:

> To leave Christ, therefore, out of the account, is so important a matter as a National Thanksgiving, must be an unpardonable neglect; for he is our Creator, Preserver, Benefactor, and Redeemer, and therefore we are bound to do all this in his name.[410]

The Rev. Bradford (1746–1801) was a graduate of Princeton University. He became a Presbyterian pastor in a church in Danbury, Connecticut for five years. He subsequently became a pastor at the Presbyterian church in Rowley, Massachusetts, where he wrote the letter quoted in the above analysis. Bradford calls the lack of the name "Jesus" in the 1795 thanksgiving proclamation an "unpardonable neglect."

The other way that Washington's views on prayer may be seen are his many prayer journals, letters, and speeches, where prayer was the center of the communication. In his prayer journal from October 3, 1789, for example, while giving a speech in New York City, the first president prayed:

> And also that we may then unite in our most humbling offering our prayers and supplications to the great Lord and Ruler of Nations, and beseech Him to pardon our national and other transgressions . . . to promote the knowledge and practice of the true Religion and Virtue.[411]

In his "Circular Letter to the Governors" in 1783, Washington prayed that God would "protect them and most graciously be pleased to dispose us all to do justice, to love mercy, and to demean ourselves with that charity, humility, and pacific temper of mind, which are the characteristics of the Divine Author of our blessed Religion, and without a humble imitation of whose example in these things, we can never hope to be a happy Nation."[412]

Once again, in this passage, President Washington employed deistic language by calling the divine the "Divine Author of Our Blessed religion." Washington also outlines here the many human virtues that he believed that one must possess in order to be properly engaged in prayer. Among these virtues are justice, mercy, charity, humility, and a peaceful temper.

These uses of deist language in regard to the divine has led some scholars to number the first president among the roles of the deists. We have conclusively argued earlier, however, that George Washington was not a deist.

In another prayer, the first president speaks to God specifically about blessing the United States. He says:

> Almighty God: we make our earnest prayer that Thou will keep the United States in Thy holy protection; that Thou will incline the hearts of its citizens to cultivate a spirit of subordination and obedience to government; and entertain a brotherly affection and love for one another and for their fellow citizens of the United States of America, at large. And finally, Thou will most graciously be pleased to dispose us all to do justice, to love mercy, and to demean ourselves with the charity, humility and pacific temper of mind which were the characteristics of the Divine Author of our blessed Religion, and without those examples of these things, we can never hope to be a happy nation.

Grant our supplication, we beseech Thee, through Jesus Christ
Our Lord. Amen.[413]

Again, the first president puts the emphasis in his private prayers on
the virtues that humans should display in praying. And if these virtues are
not displayed, then America has no hope to be a happy nation. Washington
does bring the prayer to a close, however, by mentioning the name of Jesus Christ. Much more will be said about Washington's views on Jesus and
Christianity in section VII of this essay, to follow.

In another of his prayer journals, Washington mentioned asking for
protection of Israel, when he began:

> Holy and Eternal Lord Who art the King of Heaven, and the
> Watchman of Israel, that never slumberest nor sleepest, what
> shall we render unto Thee for all Thy benefits; because Thou hast
> inclined thine ears unto me, therefore, will I call on Thee as long
> as I live, from the rising of the sun until the setting of the sun.[414]

In this entry from his prayer journal, George Washington quotes directly from Psalms 113:3. The King James Version of the Hebrew original
tells us, "From the rising of the sun unto the going down of the same, the
Lord's names is to be praised."[415] Washington also hints at the idea that, in
the same way, the ancient Jews were a chosen people protected by their God,
America is also a chosen people, with George Washington as America's Moses, or Joshua.

In many of George Washington's prayer journals, he often mentions
the name Jesus Christ, as the first president's belief that he was the Son of
God. In another prayer of Washington's published by William J. Johnson, in
his *Washington's Prayer Journal*, Johnson quotes the first president as beginning a prayer this way:

> Let me live according to those holy rules which Thou hast this
> day prescribed in Thy holy word; make me know what is ac-
> ceptable in thy sight, and therein to delight, open the eyes of
> my understanding, and help me thoroughly to examine myself
> concerning my knowledge, faith, repentance, increase my faith,
> and direct me to the true object, Jesus Christ, the way the truth,
> and the life.[416]

In another prayer, what Washington called "A Prayer for Guidance,"
the president asks, "Of eternal and everlasting God, I presume to present
myself this morning before Thy divine majesty, beseeching Thee to accept Thy humble servant and hearty thanks, that it has pleased Thy great

goodness . . . in which I beseech Thee to defend me from all perils of body and soul."[417]

In addition to these firsthand comments that George Washington made about prayer, or actually prayed, there are also a number of second-hand accounts of Washington's behavior at prayer. We turn now to a few of these accounts.

Jared Sparks records an account from Washington's nephew, George W. Lewis (1774–1852), about the president and prayer:

> Mr. Lewis says he accidentally witnessed Washington's private devotions in his Library, both morning and evening; that on these occasions he had seen him in a kneeling position with a Bible open before him; and he believed such to have been his daily practice.[418]

Major Lewis's older brother, Captain Robert Lewis (1769–1829), who lived with his uncle in the early months of his presidency, also claims to have inadvertently disturbed Washington's prayers and Bible readings, in both the morning and the evening.[419]

Mr. Sparks (1789–1866), American historian, educator, unitarian, and president of Harvard College from 1849 until 1853, also reports that Washington's adopted daughter, Nelly Custis-Lewis (1779–1852), in response to having been asked about the first president's religion, wrote of Washington:

> He attended the Church at Alexandria when the weather and roads permitted a ride of ten miles (a one-way journey of 2–3 hours by horse or carriage). In New York and Philadelphia, he never omitted attendance at church in the morning, unless detained by imposition.[420]

Presumably, by this she meant illness or accident. Ms. Custis-Lewis continued her analysis:

> No one in the Church attended to the services with more reverential respect. I should have thought it the greatest heresy to doubt his firm belief in Christianity. His life, his writings, prove that he was a Christian. He was not one of those who act or pray, that they may be seen of men.[421]

Mary V. Thompson also mentions an anonymous French correspondent with Washington who observed:

> Every day of the year, he arises at five in the morning. As soon as he is up, he dresses himself, and then prays reverently to God.[422]

Other of George Washington's family members remembered the
president praying on the occasion of the sudden death of his sister-in-law,
Hannah Bushrod (1783–1801), as well as that of Martha's granddaughter,
Nelly. About the latter's death, Washington is said to have prayed "fervently
and affectionately" at the side of the girl's aunt, Martha Parke Custis Stuart.
Mrs. Stuart (1777–1854) described the way Washington "solemnly recited
prayers for the dying, while tears rolled down his cheeks and his voice was
often broken by sobs."[423]

Nelly was Mrs. Washington's youngest granddaughter. She later admit-
ted to a Washington biographer that she had always assumed that at least
some of the time the president spent alone between rising and breakfast was
spent in private reflection and prayer.[424] Similarly, at the close of the day,
Nelly also suggests that Washington "communed with his God in secret."[425]
This conclusion is consistent with the reports mentioned above from George
and Robert Lewis about Washington praying daily before breakfast and just
before retiring for the evening.

Julian Ursyn Niemcewicz (1758–1841) was a Polish poet, playwright,
writer of historical novels, and statesman. He spent considerable time with
Washington in the capital and at Mount Vernon, and wrote an 1803 biography of the president. In the biography, the Pole included Washington's daily
schedule, which also said, "He rises at five, dresses himself, and prays with
great piety."[426]

In answer to an inquiry about whether George Washington was a
Christian, Custis-Lewis responses:

> Is it necessary that anyone should certify, "General Washington
> avowed himself to be a believer in Christianity?" As well, may
> we also question his patriotism, his heroic, disinterested devo-
> tion to his Country. His mottos were, "Deeds, not words," and
> "For God and my Country."[427]

In addition to these testimonies from family members that George
Washington regularly prayed in the morning and then in late evening, just
before retiring, there are also a number of testimonies from Washington's
military colleagues. It is to some of these accounts to which we next turn.

Robert Porterfield (1751–1843), for example, a captain in the Seventh
Virginia Regiment, wrote that he "found Washington on his knees, engage
in his morning devotions."[428] Alexander Hamilton agrees that this was the
president's daily ritual.[429]

General David Cobb, on Washington's presidential mansion staff, said
of the president:

Throughout the War, as it was understood in his military family, he gave a part of every day to private prayer and devotion.[430]

In the summer of 1790, President Washington made an address to another Jewish congregation, in Charleston, South Carolina. He closed the address with the following benediction:

> May the Father of All Mercies scatter light and not darkness in our paths, and make us all in our several vocations useful here, and in his own due time and way everlastingly happy.[431]

Over and against these testimonies of family members and fellow soldiers about Washington praying, Oney Judge Staines (1773–1848), who was a Mulatto slave to Martha Washington in New York and Philadelphia, contradicted the claim that Washington daily bent his knees to pray.[432] After Oney escaped from the presidential mansion in Philadelphia on May 23, 1796, Washington advertised for her return in the *Philadelphia Gazette*.[433] The Rev. Benjamin Chase, in a letter to the *Liberator*, also quotes Staines about the general/president's devotion. Mr. Chase quotes Staines as saying in an interview with him, "I sometimes saw him on his knees, but that ain't what I'd call prayer," and "In Philadelphia, while they were packing up to go to Virginia, I was packing up to leave."[434] And that is exactly what she did.

The Maine-born Rev. Benjamin Chase (1715–1807) was a 1737 graduate of Yale College, as well as a 1740 alumnus of Yale Divinity School. Afterwards, he was a member of the Limerick Free Baptist Church of Brunswick, Maine, as was Oney Judge Staines.

These comments by Staines reflect an important change in the religiosity of Americans in what was known as the Second Great Awakening, a religious movement in which religious experience and conversion were at the center of sects like the Baptists and Methodists of the day. As Michael and Jana Novak point out:

> After the Second Great Awakening, the predominant form of American Religion was no longer Anglican or Puritan, but Baptist and Methodist—intimate, expressive experiential, gregarious, friendly, extending a hand, and yet maintaining the discipline of small, morally watchful congregations. To be a Christian came to mean to feel much—and not to be inhibited in saying so.[435]

The Novaks would explain Staines's comment about Washington praying as the difference between a church and a sect in Washington's time. Most likely, Staines understood religion in terms of the intimate, expressive, experiential religion of the new Free Southern Baptists, while she saw Mr.

Washington as taking part in a ritual more to be found in the traditionally staid Anglican Church. She heard the Rev. Elias Smith preach, and she had a religious experience in which she converted to christianity.

Elias Smith (1769–1846) was an Evangelical preacher, journalist, and physician. Smith, along with Pastor Abner Jones, founded a group of churches in New England that came to be known as the "Christian Connexion." Smith also started a Christian newspaper called *The Herald of Gospel Liberty* in 1808. The *Herald* proclaimed that it had two purposes. First, to report news of religious revivals. Second, to promote religious liberty.[436]

These new extroverted religions put to the test the first president's long-time taciturnity. In fact, he seems at times to have been resentful that any man would wish him to profess his faith in a public fashion. In small groups, the Novaks point out, "being asked to declare his feelings, even in relatively small groups, he would politely change the subject."[437] Nevertheless, in the words of the Novaks, Washington was engaged in a religion, while Staines took part in a sect.

Finally, one of the first public images of George Washington at prayer can be seen when the First Continental Congress met at Carpenters Hall in Philadelphia in September of 1774, which was discussed earlier in this section of this study. There Washington knelt alongside Peyton Randolph (1721–75), Henry Lee, John Rutledge (1739–1800), John Jay, and others, as the Rev. Doctor Jacob Duché (1737–98) prayed fervently in a sermon given on the occasion. Duché, the rector of Christ Church in Philadelphia, was also educated at the University of Pennsylvania and Cambridge University, in England, where he received his Doctor of Divinity degree. When the delegates met in Philadelphia, Samuel Adams proposed that they should begin the proceedings with a prayer. The participants then argued about what kind of prayer it should be. It was also Sam Adams who proposed that Duché deliver the prayer.

So, the first meeting of America's government began with a prayer. In addition to the men mentioned above, other Founding Fathers were present, such as John Adams and John Morton (1725–77). Morton was a farmer, surveyor, and jurist from Pennsylvania. He also was a delegate to the First Continental Congress and a signer of the Declaration of Independence.

The Rev. Duché began his prayer with the quoting of Psalm 35:1. "Plead my cause, Oh Lord, with them that strive with me; fight against those who fight against me," a veiled reference to the British crown.[438]

The scene at Carpenters Hall was later immortalized in a painting by T. H. Matteson. The painting was entitled "The First Prayer in Congress." In the center-right of the image, Jacob Duché stands at the lectern; all around him, congressmen are on their knees praying.[439] There is also a memorial plaque dedicated to the centennial of the United States' independence. The plaque has a topping of an arc with a bald eagle.

This brings us to some observations about doubts that have arisen in regard to some of these accounts of Mr. Washington at prayer. First of all, there is absolutely no evidence that George Washington was ever seen praying while at Valley Forge. Most contemporary historians attributed belief in this tale to Pastor Mason Locke Weems, and it is his account in his biography of the first president that acts as the foundation of paintings that depict, and personal accounts that suggest, the scene ever occurred in reality.

The Maryland-born Pastor Mason Weems (1759–1825) was the first biographer of George Washington (the resulting biography was published in 1800), and the owner of a small book shop in Dumfries, Virginia, not far from the Pohick Church. Weems studied theology in London and then was ordained in the Anglican Church. In 1911, Lawrence C. Wroth published a biography of Pastor Weems entitled *Pastor Weems: A Biographical and Critical Study*. For a time, Weems was also the rector of the Pohick Episcopal church on Pohick Creek at the end of the eighteenth century.

Most contemporary scholars on George Washington agree with the conclusion about this issue of Washington praying in the snow at Valley Forge made by John Rhodehamel in his book *George Washington: The Wonder of His Age*, where he observes, "And for what it is worth, there is no reason to believe that George Washington ever prayed on his knees in the snow at Valley Forge, despite the many cornball depictions—ranging from prints and paintings to statues and stain-glass windows—of his doing so."[440]

Mr. Rhodehamel goes on in his book to make another point about Washington and Prayer. He observes:

> He never prayed on his knees, even in church—he always stood during prayers. Besides, it would have spoiled his uniform, a result he would have abhorred. The story is another fabrication of Parson "Cherry-Tree" Weems, appearing for the first time in the seventeenth edition of his enormously popular life of Washington.[441]

Secondly, there is a contemporary claim that George Washington added to the U.S. Presidential Oath of Office the words, "So help me God," as a prayer confirming his religious commitment to the divine. In point of fact, it was President Chester A. Arthur who, in 1881, was the first president to add the phrase to the oath, not George Washington.[442]

It also was not George Washington who instituted the practice of Thanksgiving in America. In fact, thirteen years before Washington's first Thanksgiving and prayer proclamation in 1789, John Hancock (1737–93) did the same on March 16, 1776. Hancock was then the president of the Second Constitutional Congress.

Finally, the "Prayer for the United States," mentioned above—often attributed to George Washington—conclusively was not written by him. This prayer is frequently employed and quoted by American politicians, including contemporary representative Michelle Lojan Grisham, a Democrat from the First Congressional District of New Mexico. It also has been used at a national prayer breakfast. Again, in point of fact, this prayer has been shown to be a hoax by writer Franklin Steiner in his 1936 book, *The Religious Beliefs of Our Presidents.*[443]

Mr. Steiner began his research into the "Prayer for the United States" when, in 1925, he visited Saint Paul's Chapel in New York City, in which it is said that George Washington sat when he worshiped in that city. Steiner relates that, "On a bronze tablet attached to the wall, as well as on a card in the pew where he sat, I saw the following inscription, 'George Washington's Prayer for the United States.'"[444]

After writing to officials at the church in Manhattan, who, after several rounds of being put off by several clergymen and scholars, Mr. Steiner finally concluded that the prayer was a hoax, designed "to make George Washington more religious than he actually was."[445] In sum, then, there is absolutely no evidence that Washington prayed in the snow at Valley Forge, that he uttered "So help me God" at the end of his presidential oath, that he instituted the first Thanksgiving, or that he was the author of the popular "Prayer for the United States."[446]

There is contradictory extant evidence on whether George Washington said grace before meals at Mount Vernon. One guest, Amariah Frost, said that no prayers were said on the particular day he ate dinner at the Virginia Estate.[447] Mr. Frost, who was a 1770 graduate of Harvard College, was from Milford, Massachusetts. He visited Mount Vernon in June of 1797.

Another guest, the Rev. James Latta (1732–1801), an Irish-born Presbyterian chaplain from Pennsylvania, wrote that the president asked him to "officiate in his clerical character," both before and after the meal he ate at Mount Vernon.[448] Still another member of the clergy, mentioned by Mary V. Thompson in her book *In the Hands of a Good Providence*, suggested that George Washington himself stood and said grace before congressional dinners.[449]

In a French journal kept by Claude Blanchard, who served in the Revolution on the American side, the French soldier noted that, during dinner at Washington's military head- quarters in the summer of 1781, a clergyman said grace at the close of the meal, "after they were done with eating and had brought out the wine."[450] Blanchard tells us that he was informed that it was

General Washington's practice to offer a prayer for the meal "if no Clergy was available."[451] Mr. Blanchard was a commissary of the French Auxiliary Army under General Rochembeau. The Paris-born Blanchard (1742–1803) wrote a substantial journal while in America. Thomas Balch translated the journal into English in 1876 in Albany, New York. In 1969, the *New York Times* also published an English version of Blanchard's journal.

New Hampshire Senator Paine Wingate, in his "Diary," left a description of the first official dinner that the first president hosted at the executive mansion in New York City. Wingate tells us, "As there was no Clergyman present, Washington himself said grace on the taking of his seat."[452] Senator Wingate (1739–1838) was a member of the Federalist Party, as well as being an early American preacher, farmer, and statesman, from Strathan, New Hampshire.

There has been a debate over the years about whether George Washington prayed on his knees when he worshiped in his Anglican churches. Bishop White, whose church Washington attended in Philadelphia for many years, reports that "I never saw him on his knees in Church."[453] David Holmes, in a recent book, offered this opinion about the matter:

> Many who have left descriptions of Washington at worship specifically note that he insisted on standing in his pew for prayers, instead of (as was usual for Anglicans) kneeling. Washington's choice of posture represents a puzzling idiosyncrasy, unless it stemmed from childhood upbringing, from a knowledge that Christians (like Jews) originally stood for prayer, or from his field experience on Sundays in the English Army.[454]

What to make of Mr. Holmes's suggestions as to why Washington stood when praying in church is not clear. A number of eyewitness reports, however, including that of Bishop White, claimed that Washington always prayed while standing erect in his pew. Another plausible explanation for why that was true is that General Washington did not want to get the knees of his uniform soiled or creased in any way—something about which he would have been very perturbed, so he stood erect in church during services.

In the final portion of this section on Washington and prayer, we shall look at another, this time contemporary, painting of George Washington in regard to the general/president praying. Despite the invalidity of the four examples above, a much more interesting depiction of President George Washington praying comes from contemporary American painter Mark Keathley. Mr. Keathley calls his painting, which was completed in 2011, "Praying for America."[455]

In the image, General Washington stands, along with his grey horse, before Saint Paul's Chapel in lower Manhattan. He holds the reins in his left hand and he gazes off in the direction of what today would be Ground Zero. Mr. Keathley gives this description of the painting:

> In my newest painting, "Praying for America," I have chosen to portray President Washington taking a moment to pray for his new nation. I imagine him praying the aforementioned purpose and destiny of this new republic would survive against the evil forces of the world. He stands in front of the Church he attended when the nation's capital was in New York, at Saint Paul's Chapel, which remains to this day and rests in the shadows of Lower Manhattan. If one could follow his gaze today, the President would be looking directly at the empty space of the World Trade Center that one day would fall in an evil plot to usurp America's Liberty . . . Saint Paul's Chapel served as a resting place for first responders during the 9-11 Crisis, and symbolizes the best that is only possible when people are free from Tyranny.[456]

There are two other apocryphal stories related to Washington and prayer, both found in Parson Weem's text. In the first, a young Quaker man named Isaac Potts happened upon the general while praying aloud and alone in the woods. The young man was so moved by the general's sincerity that he renounced his Quaker Pacifism and became a supporter of the war.[457] Isaac Potts (1750–1803) is also the name of the man who, along with his wife, Martha Bolton, rented the A-frame stone house that Washington used as his headquarters at Valley Forge.

Presbyterian Minister Rev. Nathaniel Randolph Snowden (1778–1850) left an account of the Isaac Potts narrative. He claims that Potts told him the story directly. He observed, "I knew personally the celebrated Quaker Potts who saw General Washington alone in the woods at Prayer. I got it from himself, myself."[458] The Rev. Snowden then repeats the narrative of Washington praying in the snow at Valley Forge, "with his sword in one hand and his hat cocked in the other." Like Mr. Potts, Snowden closes the narrative by saying, "Such a prayer I never heard from the lips of man. I left him alone praying."[459] The Reverend Snowden attended Dickinson College and then received his Divinity degree from Princeton Seminary. Afterwards, he worked as a Presbyterian Minister in several American churches. He was also the author of the book *George Washington, Son of the Republic*.[460]

The second tale was reported by a French soldier who tells the story of the French General Lafayette and an American general coming upon General Washington knelt in deep, silent prayer inside a horse barn. The two generals reportedly observed the scene, closed the barn door, and then silently walked away so as not to disturb Washington. At this point, it is said that they conducted a serious conversation about how much they admired General Washington for seeking divine guidance and support in the conducting of the war.[461]

An old file of the *Aldine Press*, a periodical published in New York in the 1870s, contains a version of the two generals who come upon Washington at prayer in a barn. The account is credited to "An Ex-Pension Agent." This agent identified the other general as Peter Muhlenberg (1746–1807.) Muhlenberg fought in a number of battles in the Revolutionary War, including the Battle of Charleston in 1776 and the Battle of Yorktown in 1781. The remainder of the facts are precisely the same as those outlined in the above analysis. The fact that Peter Muhlenberg was also a preacher and studied in Germany, and was familiar with German and French, lends more credence to this idea.

Mary V. Thompson points out that among the books of the Mount Vernon Collection are two Anglican prayer books that may help us in describing the environment of American Anglicanism of Washington's day. The first is called *A Prayer for a Sick Person, When There Appears No Hope of Recovery*.[462] The prayer makes a plea to "fly to Thee for succor in behalf of this Thy Servant."[463]

The second volume of interest is *A Commendatory Prayer for a Sick Person at the Point of Departure*. The person making the prayer again asks for succor for one on his deathbed, "in the name of the blood of that Immaculate Lamb, that was slain to take away the sins of the World," an obvious reference to the Atonement of Jesus Christ.[464] It is not clear, however, if Washington ever employed either of these volumes for devotional purposes, but at least Mary V. Thompson raises the possibility that the first president did find some religious use for them.[465]

One final issue on George Washington's views on prayer. Alexander Hamilton, who died several years after Washington in a duel, requested the presence of an Anglican bishop from whom he wanted the Eucharist while professing his faith in Christ. George Washington's Secretary Tobias Lear points out that no clergy was present at the first president's deathbed, nor were there made any prayers at the scene.[466] This, of course, raises questions about Washington's commitment to the Christian faith at the end of his life. We will say more about this issue in the next section of this work on whether Washington should be considered as a Christian.

In summary, in this sixth section on Washington and prayer, we have made the following conclusions. First, we have shown that George Washington was a firm believer in the efficacy of prayer. Secondly, Washington mandated two separate days of Thanksgiving and prayer in 1789 and 1795. Thirdly, Washington was of the belief that prayer had an effect in producing the victors in military skirmishes. Fourthly, Washington, while a general, regularly gave orders that his soldiers and officers should pray. Fifthly, there are a number of apocryphal stories about finding Washington at prayer, at Valley Forge, for example. And finally, a number of his family members and other people close to him suggested that Washington prayed daily, both in the morning and at night, while his former slave, Oney Judge Staines, claimed that George Washington was not a daily prayer—at least not what she would call "praying."

In section VII, there will be an analysis of the questions "Was George Washington a Christian?" and "Was America founded as a Christian nation?" This will be followed by section VIII, on Washington's views on the problem of evil, followed by section IX on some conclusions we have made in this essay.

VII

Was George Washington a Christian, and Was America Founded as a Christian Nation?

The world furnishes no other example to stand with that of Washington's.

—THOMAS JEFFERSON

IN THIS SEVENTH SECTION of this study on George Washington's religion, we wish to answer the two questions at the title of this section. In short, as we shall see, our answers to these queries are "yes" to the former, and a resounding "no" to the latter. We will begin this section by making some remarks about whether George Washington was a Christian. Following that, we shall turn our attention in the second half of this section to the latter question, "Was America founded as a Christian nation?" This will be followed by a summary of the major conclusions we will make.

One of the major foci of what are called the "culture wars" in contemporary America is whether George Washington, as well as many other of the Founding Fathers of America, was/were Christians. A concomitant inquiry to this question is "Was America founded as a Christian nation?" In regard to the first question, many of Washington's contemporaries also wondered about whether Washington was or was not, a Christian.

The Rev. Timothy Dwight (1752–1817), for example, the president of Yale University, and one of the leaders of the Evangelical revival known as the Second Great Awakening, felt confidently that Washington was a Christian, but then the Rev. Dwight adds, "But I am also aware that doubts may and will exist about the substance of his faith."[467]

The Rev. Doctor Wilson of Albany, New York, in a sermon on October 27, 1831, said, "Washington was a man of valor and wisdom. He was esteemed by the whole World as a great and good man, but he was not a professing Christian, at least not until after he became President."[468] Dr. Wilson goes on to quote the Rector James Abercrombie, who we have introduced earlier in this work, to the effect that Washington left Abercrombie's Philadelphia Anglican Christ Church prior to the communion service. For Dr. Wilson, this is further evidence that George Washington was not a practicing, Orthodox Christian. As indicated earlier in this essay, this was evidence enough for the Rev. James Abercrombie, as well.

As we have seen earlier in this work, Thomas Jefferson also had some doubts about the orthodoxy of George Washington's faith; but Jefferson calls the first president "too sly a fox publicly to reveal too much of himself." In contemporary America, Evangelical minister Tim LaHaye, coauthor of the *Left Behind* series of books, has called Washington "A devout believer in Jesus Christ" who, in good Evangelical fashion, "had accepted Him as His Lord and Savior."[469]

After researching the life of George Washington, Dr. LaHaye wrote, "Our First President was a godly man of humble character and sterling commitment to God." LaHaye goes on to quote Robert Lewis, one of Washington's nephews, who accidentally witnessed his uncle's private devotions in his library before breakfast.[470] We discussed Captain Robert Lewis back in section VI of this study on Washington's religion.

Professor Peter Lillback, the president of Westminster Theological Seminary in Philadelphia, has recently completed his *George Washington's Sacred Fire*. In a February 22, 2017 interview with Mark Martin, Dr. Lillback observed:

> If you go through his 30-plus volumes of writings, which I have done, both pain-stakingly by computer and by reading, I've discovered that he claims to be a Christian on many occasions.[471]

Professor Lillback adds:

> He speaks of Jesus as "the Divine Author of our Blessed Religion. He gives the phrase divinity to Him, and then finally, he calls the Bible, the "Word of God."[472]

There is a great deal at stake when discussing and deciding both of the questions that began this section. If George Washington was a Christian, many argue, then America must have been seen as a Christian nation. If Washington was not a Christian, some contemporary secularists argue, then America was a secular nation, as well, at its founding. As indicated earlier, more will be said about this issue in the second half of this seventh section of this study on Washington's religion.

In the first half of this seventh section of this work on Washington's religion, we will explore and discuss an answer to the question at the heading of this seventh section: was George Washington a Christian? In order to answer that question, we must first raise the question of what counts as a Christian; and we must point out that the answer has changed a great deal since the time of George Washington.

Several months ago, while in a conversation with a young man, he asked me, "Are you a Christian?" Having been a Roman Catholic for close to seven decades, I hesitated in answering. Then he asked, "What I mean by that is, 'Is Jesus Christ your personal Lord and Savior? Are you born-again?'"

What it means to be a "Christian" for many Americans living in the early twenty-first century is to assent to a collection of several propositions, including

1. belief in the literal meaning of the Biblical text;

2. belief that Jesus Christ is one's personal Lord and Savior;

3. belief in Biblical inerrancy;

4. belief that one is born-again; and

5. belief that the end times will involve an age of tribulation, and the end of the world as we know it.[473]

In the late eighteenth century, after the First Great Awakening, some Protestant denominations, like the Primitive and Separate Baptists of the American Midwest, for example, to which Abraham Lincoln and his family belonged, held to all five of these propositions, with their emphasis on conversion and ecstatic religious experience. It was the case, however, that what counted as a "Christian" in Washington's time, at least for Virginia Anglicans, had little to do with these five beliefs. Some critics point out that contemporary Evangelical Christians commit the informal fallacy of Presentism. That is, what counts as the truth today has always been what counted as the truth, in any age.

What it meant to be a Christian in the Anglican circles in which Washington lived and worked was to believe in the following propositions: First, that Jesus Christ is God. Second, that Jesus is the Second Person of the Christian Trinity. Third, that Jesus was crucified, was buried, and then resurrected, so that he may have atoned for the sins of humanity. And, finally, contemporary Anglicans of Washington's time were firm believers in resurrection and survival after death. If these were the Anglican standards of the day, then these are the context in which we may answer our first question.[474]

We also may add that, in Washington's day, a Christian was one who took part in the Sacraments. In the late eighteenth century, the Anglican Church of Washington's day professed belief in five Sacraments: baptism, the Eucharist, confirmation, matrimony, and the anointing of the sick. Given the debate over whether Washington regularly received communion, and the fact that there was no clergy present on Washington's death bed, and if we add to these the facts that George Washington was not confirmed in the Anglican Church, the conclusion can only be that the first president took part in two of the Anglican Sacraments in late eighteenth-century Virginia: baptism and matrimony.

Nevertheless, there was very little discussion in Anglican circles of the late eighteenth century about whether the Bible is without errors, or of whether one could find among Washington's contemporaries any language about Jesus being one's "Lord and personal Savior," nor about being "born-again." One reason for this is that, after the Second Great Awakening, Protestant Denominations often made a distinction between what were called the "New Lights" and the "Old Lights." The New Lights were the staid and traditional Anglicans, Unitarians, and Congregationalists. The New Lights were those Protestants who placed central emphases on conversion and religious experiences, much like late-twentieth- and early-twenty-first-century born-again Christians. Many of the New Lights in the eighteenth century were Methodists and Southern Baptists.

The Old Lights, also called the "Old Sides," downplayed emotion and placed more emphasis on rationality in religion. The New Lights placed a primary emphasis on emotion in religion. The most important New Light preachers in the mid-eighteenth century were George Whitefield, James Davenport, and Gilbert Tennent. Davenport added loud music, the burning of idols, and extemporaneous sermons in his New Light services.

Thousands of New Lights traveled to see the Rev. Whitefield from all over the colonies, and Gilbert Tennent placed primary emphasis on the personal religious conversion experience. In 1743, Gilbert Tennent was expelled from the Presbyterian Synod of Philadelphia by Old Light ministers, primarily because of New Light leanings.[475]

By 1745, Gilbert Tennent formed a New Light synod in New York to carry on their work. By 1758, the Philadelphia and the New York synods had reconciled, and the Rev. Tennent was elected as their first moderator. Gilbert Tennent died in 1762 in Philadelphia. If we ask whether George Washington was a Christian by the standards of the New Lights, our answer would probably be no. If the standard was that of the Old Lights, it most likely would be yes.

If we ask if George Washington was a Christian using the standards of contemporary Evangelical Christians in America, the answer to our question would be a resounding "no," as well. But in terms of the theological principles of his own time mentioned in the analysis above, there is sufficient evidence that George Washington believed in those four propositions that Jesus is God, that he is part of the Trinity, that he died for our sins, and was resurrected from the dead. We now will examine these four propositions to see what George Washington had to say about these matters.

It is generally believed among contemporary Washington scholars that the first president rarely spoke of Jesus in his private and public papers. This is certainly true, with some very specific exceptions, particularly in regard to his private papers. William J. Johnson, in his 1919 *George Washington: The Christian*, reproduced a portion of Washington's prayer journal, from May 14–16, 1787, which we have discussed in section 6.[476] In that journal, we find some comments on all four of the theological propositions in the above analysis. More will be said about this journal next.

In Washington's first general order to his troops after taking over as head of the Continental Army, the general called upon "Every officer and soldier . . . to live and act, as becomes a Christian Soldier, defending the dearest rights and liberties of his Country," implying that both he and his men were Christians.[477]

In an entry from May 14, 1787 in the prayer journal, Washington, speaking to the delegates of the Constitutional Convention, observed: "If to please the people, we offer what we ourselves disapprove, how can we afterward defend our work. Let us raise the standard to which the Wise and the honest can repair, the event in the Hand of God, and His Son," an obvious reference to Jesus Christ.[478]

In a separate prayer journal from October of 1789, Washington, after addressing God in prayer, mentioned "Thy Son, Jesus Christ."[479] A few paragraphs later, in the same prayer journal he again speaks of "Jesus Christ, our Lord," and in the next two paragraphs he speaks of Jesus another three times.[480] In the same prayer journal from the following Monday evening, Washington again speaks of "Thy Son, Jesus Christ" and being defended from all evil for "Jesus Christ's sake."[481]

Later, the first president asserts his belief in the Gospels, in the view that Jesus is God, and belief in survival after death. Washington indicated:

> Increase my faith in the sweet promises of the Gospel . . . daily
> frame me more into the likeness of Thy Son, Jesus Christ, that

living in Thy fear, and dying in Thy favor I may in Thy appointed
time attain the Resurrection of the Just unto Eternal Life, bless
my family, friends, and kindred.[482]

The expression "The resurrection of the just" is taken from Luke 14:14.
The expression also appears in several places in Acts. The King James Version's translation of Luke 14:13–14, on which Washington relied, tells us
this:

But when thou makest a feast, call the poor, the maimed, the
lame, the blind. And Thou shall be blessed; for they cannot rec-
ompense thee, for thou shall be recompensed at the Resurrection of the Just.[483]

Thus, Washington was a firm believer in our fourth proposition, that
Jesus resurrected from the dead. In the prayer journal reproduced by William Johnson, Washington mentioned that he wished God to:

I beseech Thee to remove my sins from Thy presence, as far as
the East is from the West, and accept me for the merits of Thy
Son, Jesus Christ.[484]

As we have shown in the section of this work entitled, "Washington's
Uses of the Bible," the first president here is quoting directly from the book
of Psalms 103:12, which begins, "As far as the East is from the West."[485] As
we have shown, this is one of George Washington's favorite Old Testament
passages.

A few lines later, in the same prayer journal, Washington spoke of asking God to "Give me Grace to hear Thee calling to me in Thy word, that it
may be wisdom, righteousness, reconciliation, and peace, to the saving of
the Soul in the day of the Lord, Jesus Christ."[486] And a few lines after this,
Washington asked the Divine "to be his God and Guide on this day and
forever, for His sake who lay down in the grave and rose again for us, Jesus
Christ, Our Lord, Amen.[487] These are obvious references to Jesus Christ, the
Trinity, his death, and the resurrection of the dead.

Later on, in a passage from the following evening, the first president
spoke to God about:

Thy dear Son, that those sacrifices which I have offered may be
accepted by Thee, in and for the sacrifice of Jesus Christ offered
upon the Cross for me.[488]

Again, the first president speaks here of Jesus as the son of God, his
Crucifixion and death, as well as the Atonement for human sins, on the
Cross. Washington ends this prayer by commenting, "These weak petitions

I humbly implore Thee to hear and to accept and to answer for the sake of Thy dear Son, Jesus Christ, Our Lord, Amen.[489] The following day, again in the same prayer journal, Washington again speaks of the atonement, as well as survival after death, when he wrote:

> But daily frame me more into the likeness of Thy Son, Jesus Christ, that, living in Thy fear, and dying in Thy favor, I may, in Thy appointment time attain the Resurrection of the Just unto Eternal Life.[490]

This, of course, is another reference to Saint Luke's idea of the Resurrection of the Just, at the end of time. From the next day, in the same "Prayer Journal," on a Monday evening, Washington again spoke of "pardoning me for Jesus Christ's sake," and he asks to be filled with "the knowledge of Thee and of Thy Son, Jesus Christ."[491] In the same book, *George Washington: The Christian*, William Johnson speaks of a "Book of prayers by Washington in his own hand, that was sold at auction in 1891. Johnson adds:

> It is not known whether Washington composed the prayers himself, or simply copied them.[492]

As we have seen earlier in this study, in section I, many of the poems of George Washington's childhood were not original creations by the young Washington, but rather were often copied from British poets; and Mr. Johnson appears to be referring to that fact here.

In one of the prayers in question, however, Washington again asks God to pardon his sins, and to "remove them from Thy presence . . . and accept me for the merits of Thy Son, Jesus Christ." Washington adds, "that when I come into Thy temple and compass Thine altar, may prayers come before Thee as incense."[493] By "temple" here Washington was referring to the heavenly residence of God.

This also appears to be a reference to an ancient Hebraic idea that the smoke from the incense rises from the earthly temple to God himself. Thus, Washington appears to be comparing believers in his day to Old Testament Jews who thought they were the closest to God because the incense travels to be closest to him—from one temple to another.

In a letter from February 1, 1800, a few weeks after George Washington's death, in an entry in his journal, Thomas Jefferson speaks of Washington's religious beliefs. The third president speaks of the first president that he did not "declare at length publicly whether he was a Christian, or not."[494] Jefferson seems to assent to the idea that Washington may have been an infidel, but then Mr. Jefferson added the following:

The old fox was too cunning for them. He answered every article
of their address particularly except that which he passed over
without notice.[495]

Mr. Jefferson implied that George Washington kept his religious cards
tightly to his vest. He also does not appear to speculate about just what those
religious views of the first president were.

In a letter written at the end of his life, George Washington speaks
of religious rights at the Constitutional Convention. He wrote, "If I could
have entertained the slightest apprehension that the Constitution framed in
the Convention, where I had the honor to preside, might possibly endanger
the Religious Christian rights of any ecclesiastical Society, certainly, I never
should have placed my signature to it."[496] This seems to imply that Washington thought that he, as well as his companions, were Christians.

In a letter from October 19, 1777 to Major-General Israel Putnam,
upon the death of his wife, Washington wrote, in part, "I hope you will
bear the misfortune with the fortitude and complacency of mind that becomes a man and a Christian," two principle Christian and Stoic virtues.[497]
Israel Putnam (1718–90) was a Massachusetts-born American general in
the Revolution. He also fought courageously in the French and Indian War.
Washington had high hopes for Putnam after his near-legendary feats as an
Indian fighter. But General Putnam proved to be a taciturn leader, and failed
to plan and coordinate operations. Consequently, after 1777, Washington
was forced to withhold crucial commands from him.[498]

In a letter from the General Assembly of the Presbyterian Churches,
written on May 26, 1789, Washington is called an "avowed friend of the
Christian Religion . . . who adorns the doctrines of the Gospel of Jesus
Christ."[499] And in a footnote in Paul F. Boller's *George Washington and Religion*, George Washington is quoted as saying, "I believe in God, the Father
Almighty, Maker of Heaven and Earth, and in Jesus Christ, His only Son,
Our Lord."[500] In all of these, George Washington clearly was a Christian, by
the standards of what were called the Old Lights at the end of the eighteenth
century.

In countless other of his letters and his public words, it is clear that
George Washington appears regularly to have assented to the four central
Christian beliefs mentioned in the above analysis. That is:

1.   The divinity of Jesus.

2.   Jesus as a member of the Trinity.

3.   The atonement.

4.   Survival after death.

A number of other people close to George Washington verified the conclusions we have made here. John Marshall of the Supreme Court said about Washington, "Without making ostentatious professions of religion, he was a sincere believer in the Christian faith, and a truly devout man."[501] Historian and president of Harvard College Jared Sparks said, "Washington was a Christian in Faith and in Practice."[502]

One of the principal reasons that Jared Sparks is important for our purposes is that he was the first organizer of the collected works of George Washington, as well as literature related to other aspects of early America. In January of 1827, Bushrod Washington, Washington's nephew, gave Jared Sparks permission to publish some of Washington's papers. During his work on the project, Sparks moved many of the Washington papers to Cambridge, near Boston, as he visited many Washington locations in America and Europe to search for letters and other papers associated with the first president.

Between 1833 and 1837, Sparks published the Washington papers in eleven volumes, under the title, *The Writings of George Washington*.[503] Sparks was heavy-handed in editing Washington's words. He changed spelling, grammar, phrasing, and at times, even entire sentences. One thing was clear, however: Jared Sparks thought that George Washington was a committed Christian.

The fourth president of the United States, James Madison, agreed. He observed:

> Washington was constant in the observance of Worship, according to the received forms of the Episcopal Church.[504]

Even a description at Washington's home, Mount Vernon, describes the first president as "A Hero, a Patriot, and a Christian. In 1745, when George Washington was thirteen years old, he copied some verses of the "Christmas Day" poem mentioned earlier in section 1. The young Washington copied:

> Assist me, Muse Divine, to sing the Morn, On which the Saviour of Mankind was born.[505]

Washington was thirteen when he copied those words. Even the adult Washington clearly would say, "Amen to That!"

To sum up this section so far on the relation of George Washington to the Christian faith, we will turn to John Avlon's book, called *Washington's Farewell*. Mr. Avlon observes:

> Washington's real vision of faith, virtue, and morality is far more interesting. There is no doubt that he was a Christian, raised in the Anglican Church, and served for a time as a member of

his local Vestry. But as President, Washington declined to take Communion, despite the protests of prominent ministers, and he avoided specific mention of Jesus Christ in public and private letters. Nevertheless, he regularly praised the good fortune that "Providence" provides in a spirit of gratitude, freely acknowledging the larger forces outside our control.[506]

Mr. Avlon was convinced that George Washington was a Christian, and he fully believed in the four propositions mentioned earlier in regard to the Anglican-Episcopal Church. Avlon also reiterates the point that Washington's preferred term in referring to the divine was Providence.

Three final arguments that can be given to support the view that George Washington was a dedicated Christian are, first, advice that General Washington gave in a speech to the Delaware nation during the Revolutionary War, in which he wished to give the Native-Americans some advice. Washington told them:

> You do well to wish to learn our arts and ways of life, and, above all, the Religion of Jesus Christ. These will make you a greater and a happier people than you now are.[507]

General Washington believed the greatest gift he could give to the Delaware nation was the religion of Jesus Christ, so he must himself have been a Christian. The second argument for believing in George Washington's commitment to the Christian faith are his many financial records which, over the years show the many Christian groups to whom he gave funds over the years. In March of 1790, for example, he gave five dollars to help in the building of a church in Albany.[508] A year later, he contributed ten dollars toward the purchase of an organ in Old Christ Church, in Philadelphia.[509] In March of 1792, he gave four dollars for the building program at a Roman Catholic Church in Baltimore.[510]

The church in question was the Baltimore Basilica. Washington included his donation in a letter to Archbishop John Carroll on March 15, 1790. The church was completed between 1806 and 1821, and was the first see in the colonies of the American Catholic Church. If George Washington was not a dedicated Christian, then what other reason can we come up with to explain these contributions?

John Carroll (1735–1815) was the first Catholic bishop and archbishop in the United States. He also was the founder of Georgetown University, the oldest Catholic University in America. Archbishop Carroll was educated at Saint Omar's in French Flanders, on the southern edge, near Belgium. Carroll was also the only Catholic signer of the Declaration of Independence.

Finally, George Washington agreed to be a godfather on at least eight different occasions. During the ceremonies of each, he was required to guide the child in the doctrines of the Anglican Church of the day. Mary V. Thompson writes about what was required of Anglican godparents at the end of the eighteenth century. She observes, "The ritual associated with Christenings spelled out the very duties expected of Anglican, and later Episcopal, Churches. The minister would approach the child's sponsors (the godparents) in these words:

> Dearly beloved, you have brought this child here to be baptized; you have prayed that Our Lord Jesus Christ would vouchsafe to receive him, to release him from sin, to sanctify him with the Holy Ghost, to give him the Kingdom of Heaven and Everlasting life . . . This infant must also promise by you that are his Sureties (until he comes of age to take it upon himself), that he will renounce the Devil and all his works, and constantly believe God's holy Word, and obediently keep his commandments.[511]

The godparents were then asked a series of theological questions related to central Anglican doctrine. On at least nine different occasions, Washington answered in the positive to these religious queries. Thomas Jefferson, on the other hand, refused to consent to being a godfather, precisely because of these theological requirements. The theological questions were related to the four propositions outlined earlier. Thus, in short, the answer to our first question at the heading of this section is a resounding "yes!"—at least by the standards of Old Light Episcopals.

Our second question at the head of this section is one of much controversy today on the American political scene. On the one side of the debate about whether the United States was founded as a Christian Nation, many Conservatives like Attorney General Jeff Sessions, for example, insist that America was founded as a Christian nation. Sessions, in arguing against the nomination of Sonia Sotomayor to the Supreme Court, wrote that "those with 'a secular mindset' . . . do not understand 'who we are' and advance a worldview 'directly contrary to the founding of our republic.'"[512]

Those who argue on the Sessions side of the debate, like conservative Christian Evangelist Tim LaHaye, suggest that the Founding Fathers, by and large, were practicing Christians. LaHaye says about John Adams, for example, "He was deeply committed to Jesus Christ and the use of Biblical principles in governing the nation."[513] About George Washington, LaHaye writes:

If he were alive today, he would freely associate with the Bible-believing branch of Evangelical Christianity that is having such a positive influence upon our nation.[514]

On the other side of this contemporary debate—the side that argues against America being founded as a Christian nation—are thinkers like historian Frank Lambert and University of Chicago law professor, Goeffrey Stone. The former writes, "The significance of the Enlightenment and Deism for the birth of the American Republic, and especially the relationship of Church and State within it, can hardly be overstated."[515]

In a similar vein, Dr. Stone avers that "Deistic beliefs played a central role in the framing of the American Republic" and that "The Founding generation viewed religion, and particularly religion's relation to government, through the Enlightenment lens that was deeply skeptical of organized religion."[516] Both Lambert and Stone suggest that the first generation Founding Fathers, for the most part, assented to a secular form of deism, and thus America was not founded as a Christian nation. The historical record of this issue, however, is much more complicated than either of these contemporary views.

In regard to this other question raised at the beginning of this section about whether America was founded as a Christian nation, the record appears to be mixed. On the one side is the First Amendment of the U.S. Constitution, as well as the 1797 Treaty with Tripoli that said, "The Government of the United States is not, in any sense, founded on the Christian Religion." On the other hand, there have been many attempts in the history of America to declare that the United States is a "Christian nation." One example is the 1892 Supreme Court decision, written by Justice David Brewer, that argued that America is a Christian nation.

This decision is known as the *Church of the Holy Trinity v. the United States* case. In the unanimous decision, Justice Brewer concluded:

> There is no dissonance in these declarations. There is a universal language pervading them all, having one meaning; they affirm and reaffirm that this is a religious nation. These are not individual sayings, declarations of private persons: they are organic utterances; they speak the voice of the entire people . . . These, and many other matters which might be noticed, add a volume of unofficial declarations to the mass of organic utterances that this is a Christian Nation.[517]

Eight years later, after many had criticized Brewer's decision, in a 1905 book entitled *The United States: A Christian Nation*, Justice Brewer sought to clarify his 1897 decision. In the book, Judge Brewer said:

But in what sense can it be called a Christian nation? Not in the sense that Christianity is the established religion or that people in any matter are compelled to support it. On the contrary, the Constitution specifically provides that "Congress" shall make no laws respecting an established religion, or the prohibiting of the free exercise thereof." . . . Nevertheless, we constantly speak of this republic as a Christian nation. This popular use of the term certainly has significance. It is not a mere creation of the imagination. It is not a term of derision, but has substantial basis—one which justifies its use.[518]

Justice Brewer's argument seems to have been that America was founded as a Christian nation because most people of that age were Christians, and believed that it was a Christian nation. In point of fact, at the time of the founding of the United States, 98 percent of Americans were Protestant Christians; 1.4 percent were Roman Catholics; and the remaining 0.6 percent were Jews and members of the Muslim faith.[519]

In other periods of American history, there have been other attempts to verify that the United States is a Christian nation. In the mid-nineteenth century, for example, a group called the National Reform Association attempted to push a "Christian Amendment" in Congress in 1864. The members of the NRA believed that the sufferings of the Civil War were best explained as divine retribution for failing to mention God in the Constitution, and they saw their proposed amendment as a way to atone for that omission.[520]

The Amendment in question called for Congress to "humbly acknowledg[e] Almighty God as the source of all authority and power in civil government, the Lord Jesus Christ as the Ruler among nations, [and] His revealed will as the supreme law of the land, in order to constitute a Christian government."[521]

Ten years later, the House Judiciary Committee voted against the adoption of the NRA's amendment. At the time, the Committee noted "The many dangers which the union between church and state had imposed upon so many nations in the Old World." And in light of this fact, the Committee believed that "It is inexpedient to put anything in the Constitution which may be construed as a reference to any religious creed or doctrine."[522] The Committee here, of course, refers to the many religious wars in Europe in the seventeenth and early eighteenth centuries.

A number of similar proposals in Congress over the years also have attempted to place language about God in the Constitution. The most recent of these came in 1950. At that time, there was a proposal in the Senate that might have added the following words to the Constitution:

> Devoutly recogniz[ing] the authority and law of Jesus Christ,
> Savior and Ruler of nations, through Whom are disposed the
> blessings of liberty.[523]

The proposed amendment never made it to a vote outside the committee that proposed it. Efforts to revive the amendment in the 1960s were not successful. Even today, some efforts are made to established the United States as a Christian nation. Governor Kirk Fordice of Mississippi, for example, in a recent speech, said, "The early days of this Union . . . were totally based not only on religion, but on one particular religion—the Christian Religion."[524] Televangelist D. James Kennedy, to cite another example, quoted a small American Jewish community of 1776 as proof that the United States was intended to be a "Christian Nation."[525]

Ralph Reed, the director of the Christian Coalition, the most vocal group of religious activists on the contemporary American scene, often has observed that America was founded as a Christian nation. At one point, Mr. Reed wrote, "What Christians have to do is to take back this country," and to "Again make it a country governed by Christians."[526] Pat Robertson, another prominent spokesman for the religious right, also has insisted that America was founded as a Christian nation. But he believes this view was replaced by an "un-American secular state, 20th-century liberals and free thinkers."[527] Like Ralph Reed, Robertson also uses the language of "return." In that regard, Robertson once remarked:

> If all Christians worked together they can succeed during this
> decade in winning back control of the institutions that have
> been taken from us over the past seventy years.[528]

In another speech in 1993, Pat Robertson remarked that "The wall of separation is a lie of the American Left," and "There is no such thing in the Constitution."[529] In point of fact, he is correct about the Constitution. The phrase first was introduced by Thomas Jefferson, as we shall see below.

At the 1984 Republican National Convention, a Dallas Baptist preacher delivered the benediction. During his comments, he observed:

> There is no such thing as a separation of Church and State. It is
> merely the figment of the imagination of Infidels.[530]

Presumably the Reverend James Robison meant that the class of infidels in early America included Roger Williams, Thomas Jefferson, James Madison, William Penn, and George Washington, as well as many other early American patriots.

One of the Christian Right's most visible spokesman, the evangelist/psychologist James Dobson, who distributes Christian literature through his group Focus on the Family, includes a history lesson that proclaims that "The concept of a Secular State was virtually non-existent in 1776, as well as 1787, when the Constitution was written, and no less so when the Bill of Rights was adopted."[531]

In point of fact, the expression "the separation of church and state" does not appear in the U.S. Constitution. There are some colonial precedents, however, to the idea among some early American statesmen. When Roger Williams, for example, was banned from the Massachusetts Bay Colony for his religious beliefs in 1636, he went on to found the colony of Rhode Island on the premise that people of all religious persuasions would be welcomed.[532]

In the Maryland Colony in 1649, Lord Baltimore drafted the "Maryland Toleration Act." This act was designed to "protect the citizens' rights to worship as they pleased."[533] William Penn's Pennsylvania Colony, which was founded in 1681, also welcomed persons of diverse religious beliefs. But only Anglicans and Quakers could hold political offices at the time.[534]

As indicated above, it was Thomas Jefferson who coined the expression "the separation of church and state" in an 1802 letter to the Danbury Baptist Association of Connecticut. In this correspondence, Jefferson observed that religion "is a matter which lies solely between Man & his God," and that government should not have any influence over opinions. Therefore, Jefferson concluded:

> I contemplate with sovereign reverence that act of the whole American People which declared that their legislature should make no law respecting an establishment of Religion, or prohibiting the free exercise thereof, thus building of separation between Church & State.[535]

Mr. Madison, of course, is referring here to the many religious wars in Europe in the seventeenth and eighteenth centuries that were often bloody and violent, both during the Reformation and the Counter-Reformation in that period.

Besides Jefferson and Washington, other Founding Fathers spoke of the separation of church and state. James Madison, for example, in a letter that objected to the use of government land for churches, commented, "The purpose of the separation of Church and State is to keep forever from these shores the ceaseless strife that has soaked the soil of Europe in blood for centuries."[536]

In a letter to Edward Livingston, on July 10, 1822, Madison again turns to the phenomenon of church and State. He wrote:

> Every new and successful example therefore of a perfect sepa-
> ration of ecclesiastical and civil matters is of importance. And
> I have no doubt that every new example, will succeed, as ev-
> ery past one has done, in shewing that Religion and Govern-
> ment will both exist in greater purity, the less they are mixed
> together.[537]

All of these passages go quite nicely with Washington's observation in the Treaty with Tripoli that "The Government of the United States is not, in any sense, founded on the Christian Religion."[538] Nevertheless, as indicated earlier, there are some contemporary Evangelical theologians who do not believe in the separation of church and state because it is not in the Constitution. One other prime example of this view is Dr. Mark Noll and his book *The Scandal of the Evangelical Mind*.[539] In that work, Noll argues vociferously against the idea of separation. And he is not alone.

Chief Justice William Rehnquist, on June 4, 1985, in a dissenting opinion in *Wallace v. Jaffree*, wrote, "The wall of separation between church and state is a metaphor based on bad history, a metaphor which has proved useless as a guide in judging. It should be frankly and explicitly abandoned."[540] Justice Antonin Scalia, in his June 27, 2005 dissenting opinion in *Kentucky v. American Civil Liberties Union*, also wrote extensively against the idea of separation of church and state.[541]

Still, in the 1947 decision *Everson v. Board of Education*, the Supreme Court unanimously affirmed the separation of church and state, and it employed the wording of Jefferson's letter to the Baptists in the writing of their opinion. The opinion came from the pen of Justice Hugo L. Black, who said, "The wall must be kept high and impregnable."[542] Justice Black also wrote:

> Neither a State nor the Federal Government can, either secretly
> or openly, participate in the affairs of any religious organization
> or group and vice versa. In the words of Thomas Jefferson, the
> clause against the Establishment of religion By law was intended
> to erect a "wall of Separation between Church and State."[543]

In more modern American times, several U.S. presidents were also of the belief that the United States was founded as a Christian nation. Theodore Roosevelt, for example, remarked:

> The teachings of the Bible are so interwoven and entwined
> with our whole civil and social life that it would be literally . . .

impossible for us to figure ourselves what that life would be if these teachings were removed.[544]

By these "teachings," President Roosevelt meant the Judeo-Christian tradition and the major theological principles of the Old and the New Testaments. President Woodrow Wilson was even more explicit about the question when he said clearly, "America was born a Christian Nation. America was born to exemplify that devotion to the elements of righteousness which are derived from the revelations of the Holy Scriptures."[545]

While president, Herbert Hoover proclaimed, "American life has been built, and can only survive upon . . . the fundamental philosophy announced by the Savior nineteen hundred years ago."[546] He meant, of course, Jesus Christ.

President Harry S. Truman, in an exchange of messages with the pope, wrote, "This is a Christian Nation."[547] Richard M. Nixon, in some "Remarks at a Prayer Breakfast" on August 28, 1947, remarked, "Let us remember that as a Christian nation . . . we have a charge and a destiny."[548] Even our second president, John Adams, made the remark:

> The general principles on which the fathers achieved independence were . . . the general principles of Christianity.[549]

Despite these remarks from American presidents and various representatives of the contemporary American Christian Right, who believe(d) that America was founded as a Christian nation, Justice John Paul Stevens surely was correct when he wrote:

> When the underlying principle has been examined in the crucible of litigation the Court has unambiguously concluded that the individual freedom of Conscience protected by the First Amendment embraces the right to select any religious faith, or none at all.[550]

Like Justice Stevens, we believe that only a separation of church and state can protect America's degree of religious freedom. The individual rights and diversity we enjoy could not be maintained in this country if the government of the United States promoted Christianity, or if the government takes on the trappings of a theocratic state.

In conclusion, then, we believe that the United States was not founded as a Christian nation, nor was it designed to espouse any official religion. Instead, the powers that be, in the late eighteenth century, left religious decisions to be made by individual citizens. We will answer our question concerning whether America was founded as a Christian nation, then, with a resounding "no."

In summary of this second question, then, we only can conclude that although some American presidents and contemporary leaders of the Religious Right in America believe(d) that America was first founded as a Christian nation, these thinkers are/were just plain wrong about that issue.

From our analysis in the seventh section of this study on George Washington's religion, we have made five major conclusions. First, George Washington was a devout member of the Anglican and Episcopal churches his entire life. Second, Washington assented to four core religious beliefs of those churches: Jesus was God; he was a member of the Christian Trinity; he was crucified, died, and was buried; and he resurrected from the dead to atone for the sins of human believers in him.

A third conclusion we have made in section VII of this essay is that the first president of the United States was against the idea of America having a state religion. Concomitant to this third conclusion is Washington's expressed belief that America was not founded as a Christian nation. And fifth, Washington clearly would have been in favor of Thomas Jefferson's idea, and that of the U.S. Supreme Court, that there ought to be a wall of separation between church and state.

This now brings us to section VIII, "Washington on the Problem of Evil."

VIII

Washington on the Problem of Evil

Washington appears to have believed that while God/Providence directed
the course of events on Earth, human beings could not always understand
why certain things occurred.

—MARY V. THOMPSON, *IN THE HANDS OF A GOOD PROVIDENCE*

ONE OF THE MANY apocryphal stories about the childhood of George
Washington provided by the Pastor Mason Weems is the tale that Augustine
Washington taught his son a theological lesson by planting cabbage seeds
in a plot, so that when the plants grew out, the plot would spell our G-E-O-
R-G-E. Augustine had his son water the plot, not knowing anything of the
father's plan.

Not surprisingly, when the pattern finally appeared, the Pastor Weems
tells us, the boy wondered how the pattern got that way. "Do you believe it
happened by chance?" the father asked, leaving the boy in a state of wonder-
ment. "This is a great thing," the father concluded, "which I wanted you to
understand. I want, my son, to introduce you to your real, true father."[551]

In Pastor Weems's telling of the tale, it is the Father who is at the center
of the story, "instructing his son's head and his heart, at the same time."[552]
Another way to interpret the tale, however, is to say that Augustine Washington was teaching his son the workings of divine Providence, and that
God has a divine plan for which everything works out for the good, in the
same way that the father had a plan for the cabbages.

As we shall see, this is the major response in this section of this essay, that George Washington made to the problem of evil, in both his private and public papers—the divine plan point of view.

This alternative way of understanding the cabbage seeds is also consistent with the eighteenth-century theory known as the teleological argument for God's existence. This argument, championed by British philosopher William Paley (1743–1805) in his 1802 work *Natural Theology*, and by others, say that since the constituent parts of the universe appear to be in order, then they must be "designed." If designed, there must be a designer. In Paley's view, and others who held this theory, that designer is God. Paley used Newton's watch analogy, as well as the human eye, to argue for God's existence based on design.

In Augustine Washington's mind, God is the Gardener of the seeds, and the pattern of the cabbages that eventually appears is a sign of the Gardener's design. For Washington's father, the cabbages are also a "sign" of George's "true Father." George Washington's father Augustine may well have been aware of Paley's theory, and he demonstrated it for his son George with the cabbage seeds.

The main goal of this eighth section of this study on George Washington's religion is to explore and discuss what our first president had to say about the philosophical issue known as the problem of evil, or "theodicy," a word we will discuss later in this section. The problem of evil is usually understood by the consenting of four propositions. If God is 1) all-good, 2) all-knowing, and 3) all-powerful, then 4) why is there so much evil and suffering in the world?[553]

Most of the world's religious traditions attempt to respond to evil and suffering by answering three fundamental questions:

1. What is it, or how is it defined?

2. Where does it come from, or what are its origins?

3. How should we respond to, or find meaning, in evil and suffering?

Nearly all of the religions of the world attempt to answer, or respond to, the issues of evil and suffering. Some, like Vedantic Hinduism and Hinayana Buddhism, posit that evil is an illusion, or what those traditions call *Maya*. If it is an illusion, then there is no evil. If there is no evil, then there is no problem of evil. Thus, the problem of evil is dissolved in these religious traditions.

A second kind of religious response to evil and suffering is dualism. This theory suggests that reality is divided according to the control of two Gods, two forces, or a combination of a God and a Force. Prime examples of this view are the ancient Persian religion, Zoroastrianism; the Roman religions, Mithraism and Manicheanism; as well as the metaphysics of Plato, who combined a god (the demiurge), and a force ("chaos") with respect to the problem of evil.[554] Plato discusses his doctrine of creation in several works, including sections 30a to 48 of the *Timaeus*, Book 10 of the *Laws*, and Book 2 of the *Republic*.

We will call this second position "religions of solution," for in this view, proponents suggest there are two gods, usually a good god and a bad god. In Zoroastrianism, these are called Ahura Mazda, the good god, and Angra Mainya, the evil god. Evil, in this second view, originates in the bad god. The best way to respond to evil in this view is to turn to the good god.[555]

The third view of the world's religious traditions on evil and suffering, we shall call the "religions of paradox." The chief traditions committed to this third position are Judaism, Christianity, and Islam. In each of these three traditions, proponents are committed to four propositions mentioned above: the three about God and the one about the world. The three about God are that he is said to be all-good, all-knowing, and all-powerful. The proposition about the world is that evil exists, in moral, natural, and psychological forms.[556]

Moral evils are those examples of evil and suffering caused by human agents—things like murder, rape, and stealing, for example. Natural evils are those caused by nature, like cancer, floods, heart disease, and earthquakes, for example. Psychological evils are those caused by mental events. Examples of psychological evil are anguish, worry, and despair.

The religions of paradox have that name because assenting to the four propositions mentioned above appears to be a paradox—that is, all four cannot be true at the same time. If any of these four propositions are not true, then it would be easy to say that God did not know about it (and thus is not omniscient), could do nothing about it (and is not omnipotent), is not really so good (not omni-benevolent), or, like the religions of dissolution, there really is no evil.

In Judaism, Christianity, and Islam, there have been a number of traditional responses to the problem of evil for the religions of paradox. Some of those responses looked back to the past, and some look forward to the future, to understand the causes or meaning of suffering and evil.[557]

Among the backward-looking responses to the problem of evil for the religions of paradox are the following: retributive justice, the influence of demonic forces, the free-will defense, and original sin theory. The first of these argues that God brings evil and suffering to those who have sinned, as a kind of retribution, or retaliation. Sometimes this theory is applied to individuals, and at other times to groups, such as a family, a clan, or even a nation.

In contemporary life, those who say "What goes around, comes around" or "Karma's a bitch" are assenting to this view. Retributive justice is the oldest view in the Old Testament for explaining evil and suffering, as indicated earlier, and it may involve individual or collective evil and suffering. It is also the theory that lies beneath the question "What have I done to deserve this?"—for this question assumes that someone's sin is the cause of the evil or the suffering of an individual.

The influence of demonic forces theory suggests that Satan, or his minions, tempts and influence human beings to sin. Those who say "The devil made me do it" are proponents of the influence of demonic forces view. This explanation for evil and suffering plays a much more central role in Islam than in Judaism or Christianity. The Qur'anic names for the demonic are *Iblis* and *Shaytan*. These concepts appear far more often in the holy book of Islam than in the Bible.

Another backward-looking theory—the free-will defense—relates that God gave human beings free will, and they sometimes used it to commit sin. In this view, human moral choices are the cause of much human evil and suffering.

Finally, the original sin theory, which seems to be favored by Saint Paul in his letters, says that all human beings after Adam and Eve inherit the sin of these first human parents.[558] Saint Paul employs this theory in Romans 5 and 1 Corinthians 15. This perspective is also featured in the works of Saint Augustine of Hippo and Thomas Aquinas in the thirteenth century, as well as in Reformation thinkers like Martin Luther and John Calvin.

Among the most frequent forward-looking responses to the problem of evil in the religions of paradox are the following: the contrast perspective, the test view, the moral qualities view, and the divine plan theory. We call these answers forward-looking because they look ahead to see the reason, or purpose, of evil and suffering.

The proponent of the contrast view maintains that we have to have evil to know what the good is. You cannot have one without the other.[559] This response can be seen in the Bible, the Qur'an, and in the Eastern religion, Taoism, where reality is bifurcated between Yin and Yang.

The test view says that God uses evil and suffering to "test" the moral characters of human beings. The book of Job is often seen in light of this theory. In the moral qualities perspective, God employs evil and suffering as a way of developing certain moral qualities like fortitude and patience. The contemporary expression "If it does not kill you, it makes you stronger" is a tip of the hat in the direction of this theory. Thus, in this view, evil and suffering are used by the divine to make people better.

Finally, the advocate of the divine plan perspective says that something may appear to be an example of evil or suffering in the short run, but in the long run, we eventually will see that everything works out for the good.[560] Those in contemporary American religious life who say "God has a reason for everything" or "God has his own purposes" are assenters to this philosophical position.

Among the religions of the world, most of them can be described as being on a continuum that goes from religions of dissolution to religions of solution, with religions of paradox to be found between the two poles. Thus, the continuum looks like this:

Figure 8.1

Religions of Solution	Religions of Paradox	Religions of Dissolution
[_____X_____]		
Zoroastrianism and Manicheanism	Judaism, Christianity, Islam	Vedanta Hinduism and Hinayana Buddhism
Dualistic	Mixed	Monistic.[561]

In Figure 8.1 above, religions of solution are on the left because they are dualistic, with a good god and an evil god. In this view, there is a place to point to the origins of evil because it comes from the evil god (Angra Mainya in Zoroastrianism). In this view, then, the problem is "solved." The religions of dissolution, on the other hand, dissolve the problem of evil because ultimately evil is not real. Thus, the problem is "dissolved."[562]

We have placed the religions of paradox between the two poles because they are a paradoxical mix of monism and dualism. On the one hand, like the religions of dissolution, the religions of paradox say that everything comes from God, and that God is all-good. On the other hand, the religions of paradox believes in the existence of the devil and the demonic, so there is a kind of moral dualism.

We raise this background information here so that we may more easily employ traditional vocabulary in the religions of paradox when discussing the problem of evil in the context of the life of George Washington.[563]

We will attempt to show what George Washington had to say about this philosophical problem of evil in the religions of paradox by looking at the following factors. First, how did evil and suffering occur in Washington's life? Second, how did evil and suffering affect the lives of those around him? And finally, what philosophical and theological responses did the first president employ to answer, or respond to, the classical problem of evil? By this, we mean the philosophical positions we have outlined in the opening of this section.

That George Washington was no stranger to suffering in his life is made clear by the fact that he suffered from diphtheria at age fifteen, "Ague and Fever" at sixteen, malaria at age seventeen, and smallpox when he was eighteen. Indeed, when George accompanied his older brother Lawrence to Barbados in 1751, George contracted smallpox and it laid him out for a full three weeks. While waiting in bed for the progression of the disease, the young Washington watched lizards scuttling across the walls and floor. After three weeks, the first president had survived the attack, unlike many others in colonial times.

Washington's face, however, would be permanently scarred from the disease with the distinctive pock-marks, a common disfigurement in the mid-eighteenth-century New World. Perhaps a greater danger, however, was the effects that smallpox had on Washington's immune system; but at least he now was safe from one of the scourges of the armies of the time.

Washington also suffered from a disease called "Quinsy," what we would call tonsillitis; "carbuncle," another name for skin cancer, for much of his later life; and epiglottitis, a virulent influenza that ultimately killed him.[564] James Flexner suggests that "carbuncle" may in fact have been an outbreak of hide-porter's disease caused by *Bacillus anthracis* spores, or anthrax. A lesion appeared on Washington's thigh in the spring of 1789. A few weeks later, it was lanced by a father and son team of physicians whose names are unknown.[565]

Flexner tells us that the younger of the pair performed the surgery, the father instructing him to "cut deeper" throughout. All the while, of course, the first president took the surgery—and its accompanying pain—as a Stoic. Eventually, Washington recovered from the lesion and went on to live another decade.[566]

Even at General Braddock's Defeat in 1755, at the age of twenty-one, after suffering from the flu and dysentery for two weeks in his tent, Washington rallied to go on to accompany Braddock's troops. However, Washington found his hemorrhoids so painful that he had to attach pillows to his saddle before mounting his horse for the first time in a month. By the end of Braddock's defeat, fifteen of Braddock's eighteen officers were dead, as well as Braddock himself. Washington received nary a scratch.

Two weeks after burying the body of General Braddock in a secret grave, Washington struggled back to Mount Vernon, collapsing again into his sickbed. A few weeks later, Washington got the word that a commission in Williamsburg had decided that he should lead the entire Virginia Colony Regiment. At first, Washington demurred, saying, "I am unequal to the task." But a short time later, the newly appointed General Washington defended the Virginia Frontier in the autumn of 1755, just a few scant months after General Braddock's fiasco on the Mobogahela River.

While on the frontier at the end of 1757, Washington was seized by a another violent attack of dysentery, which occasioned him to leave the army.[567] In 1761, he was attacked by a disease known as "River Fever," and later referred to as "Break-bone Fever." Hoping to cure the fever, which we now know as malaria, Washington traveled over the mountains to the Warm Springs, "being much overcome with the fatigue of the ride together."[568]

In 1787, a new foe appeared in the form of "rheumatism," to the point where "I could not raise my hand, nor turn in bed."[569] While president, Washington came down with the flu during the Battle of Boston, and he had a bad cold in the time of the Battle of Trenton.[570] For much of his adult life, both before and after the war, he suffered from lung problems, as did many of his relatives on his father's side before him. In fact, Lawrence died of a lung ailment, most likely tuberculosis.

At the end of his life, George Washington was extremely hard of hearing and his eyesight was failing. Not only was Washington knowledgeable about the suffering of his own, but he was also around for the suffering and deaths of many of his own family members, including his sister Jane when he was a toddler, his father's death when he was eleven years old, and his brother Lawrence's death, mentioned in the previous paragraph, when George was twenty years old.

Additionally, Martha Parke Custis, or "Patsy," as she was known, the only surviving daughter of Martha Washington and her first husband, began showing symptoms of epilepsy when she was twelve years old. She experienced frequent seizures, sometimes as many as twice a day. George and Martha consulted with a group of at least six physicians and specialists, and tried a variety of unsuccessful treatments. These medical procedures included treatment with heavy metals, purging pills, special diets, and trips to bathe in mineral springs, but Patsy suddenly died at the age of seventeen during a seizure in 1773.[571] All of these personal sufferings were nothing compared to that brought to his eyes in the course of battle.

There are a number of extant first-person narratives of the evil and suffering at Valley Forge. We will examine some of these later in this section. The winter of 1777–78 was clearly the low point of the Continental Army. After winning the Battle of Brandywine in September of 1777 and the Battle of Germantown on October 4, 1777, the British went on to occupy the American capital, and then Philadelphia. The Continental Army was in shambles.

On December 19, 1777, George Washington led eleven thousand troops to the winter encampment at Valley Forge in Pennsylvania, outside Philadelphia. The army suffered terrible deprivations in the six-month period in Valley Forge. Shortages of food, clothing, firewood, and a lack of adequate shelter saw the deaths of three thousand men. Prospects for the Americans looked bleak as morale plummeted, with frequent death and a high desertion rate. Nevertheless, the Continental Army did not crumble.

Although there were brutal conditions, General Washington used the six months in Valley Forge to improve his army. Troops drilled and were trained by a Prussian officer, the Baron Von Steuben, who implemented a system of standardized military training into the Continental Army. The level of military discipline vastly improved for the remainder of the war.[572]

Von Steuben (1730–94) taught Washington's troops how to maneuver in the field and the proper use of the bayonet. He was very strict with the Americans and, in the beginning, he had little knowledge of English. Indeed, he is said to have cursed at the Continental soldiers for hours at a time. Nevertheless, the Americans appreciated the Baron's devotion to the American cause, and he instructed the Continental Army with some improvements. To this point, the American troops had been given very little training.[573]

The Marquis de Lafayette, a French nobleman, also volunteered his services to the American cause. In December of 1777, Washington gave the Frenchman the command of a division of troops from Virginia. Because of his initial successes, Lafayette was given even more men. The French Government also sent Louis Lebeque Duportail (1743-1802), an army engineer who designed the Valley Forge encampment. Duportail also was responsible for fortifying Boston Harbor before the Battle of Boston, and he constructed the siege works at the Battle of Yorktown.[574]

By February of 1777, the Americans began building huts at Valley Forge. These huts were to provide shelter for the troops, and in some cases, for the families that came along. By the spring, when the weather turned warmer, Washington made sure that each hut had two windows.

Surgeon's mate Jonathan Todd sent a letter to his father on January 19, 1777, describing the hut in which he lived at Valley Forge. He tells us that it was completed with "one dull axe and when done we know not with what then."[575] About the dimensions of his hut, Todd tells us:

> I will give you a description of our hut which is built nearly after
> the same model of the others. It is 18 feet long & 16 broad, two

rooms and two chimneys at opposite corners of the house. The
floor is made of split logs, as are the partition and the door. The
whole of it was made with one poor axe and not another tool.
We were not more than a fortnight in making it, although never
more than three men worked on it at once. The roof is not the
best in wet weather, oak slabs covered with turf and earth—Our
innards work is not yet completed.[576]

During his time at Valley Forge, General Washington wrote a letter to
Governor George Clinton of New York about the conditions and the verve
of his men there. Washington wrote, "As naked and as starving as they are,
we cannot enough admire the incomparable patience and fidelity of the
soldiers."[577] Patience and courage, of course, were two of the principal Stoic
virtues.

In the same letter, General Washington tells Governor Clinton:

What methods you take to assist us, you will be the best judge;
but if you can devise any means to procure a quantity of cattle,
or other kind of flesh, for the use of this Army, to be at camp in
the course of a month, you will render a most essential service
to the common cause. I have the honor, etc.[578]

A few days after Christmas, during the months at Valley Forge, General Washington wrote to delegates of New Hampshire for aid. At the close
of this letter from December 29, 1777, the general wrote:

No pains, no efforts on the part of the states can be too great for
this purpose. It is not easy to give you a just and accurate idea
of the suffering of the Army at large—of the loss of men on this
account. Were they to be minutely detailed, your feelings would
be deeply wounded, and the relation probably would not be received without a degree of doubt & discredit. We had in Camp
on the 23rd passed, by a Field Return then taken, not less than
2898 men unfit for duty, by reason of there being barefoot and
otherwise naked. Besides this number, sufficiently distressing of
itself, there are many Others detained in Hospitals and crowded
in Farm Houses for the same cause.[579]

Lieutenant William Barton of the Fourth New Jersey Regiment wrote
to his father from Valley Forge, on February 18, 1777. Barton told his father:

I have not received a letter from you since I left home. I would
be very glad if you could favor me with a few lines if convenient
and likewise with a few pounds of sugar and a little chocolate.

There is a scarcity of these articles in this place . . . Camp does
not very much agree with me.[580]

Six days later, Barton's friend at Valley Forge, Lieutenant John Blair,
wrote to Barton's family to tell them that Barton is "unwell these ten days
with no appearance of getting better, and he is very desirous that you would
send a wagon for him, as he is too weak to ride on horseback."[581]

Through all of this, George Washington had firsthand knowledge of
the suffering of his men; and he appears to have dealt with that suffering
with equanimity, patience, and courage. One of the prayers he recited for
his troops has been recorded by his men. General Washington observed:

Tis pride with these old men

To tell what they have seen.

Twill be pride, when we be old

To say that in our youth

We heard the tales they told

And looked on them in their truth.

Valley Forge was yet the darkest hour

Before the dawn, yet

The Continental Army never did give up.[582]

In a letter written at Valley Forge on April 21, 1778, Washington wrote
about the explicit conditions of his men in the encampment. He observed:

To see men without clothes to cover their nakedness, without
blankets to lie upon, without shoes . . . without a house or hut to
cover them until those could be built, and submitting without
a murmur, is a proof of patience and obedience, which, in my
opinion, can scarcely be paralleled.[583]

In his diary kept at Valley Forge, George Washington commented
on the conditions of his men and the progress of the war. In the following description, written in the winter of 1777, he gives the struggles of the
Continental Army a theological context. Washington wrote:

Ours is a kind of struggle designed, I dare say, by Providence
to try the Patience and Fortitude, and Virtue of men. None,
therefore, who is engaged in it, will suffer himself, I trust, tis
sink under difficulties, or to be discouraged by hardships. If he
cannot do as he wishes, he must do what he can.[584]

In this passage, General Washington shows belief in a number of responses to the traditional problem of evil in Judaism, Christianity, and Islam,

as outlined earlier. One of these views, the moral qualities perspective, suggests that his soldiers develop patience and fortitude by God bringing evil and suffering to them. However, the expression "discouraged by hardships" in the above passage is more akin to a view called the test perspective. In this latter view, as we described earlier in this section, God sometimes brings evil and suffering to believers as a way of "testing" their characters.

In this passage, we also see an overall view of George Washington's understanding of evil and suffering in relationship to the war—that is, that Washington was a believer in divine plan theory when it came to the conundrum of the problem of evil. In another letter, Washington told his correspondent that "I will not lament or repine at any act of Providence because I am in a great measure a convert to Mr. Pope's opinion that 'whatever is, is right.'"[585] This comment of Washington's is a reference to Alexander Pope's poem "An Essay on Man," in which the Englishman proclaims:

> All nature is but Art, unknown to Thee.
> All chance, direction, which thou canst not see;
> All discord, harmony not understood;
> All partial Evil, universal Good.
> And spite of pride, in erring reason's spite,
> One Truth is clear, 'Whatever is, is Right.[586]

When it came to the problem of evil, Alexander Pope was a devotee of German philosopher G. W. Leibniz and his idea of divine plan theory. In Washington's overall picture of the problem of evil, the first president was also a believer in this theory. We remember that, according to this point of view, something may appear to be evil and suffering in the short run, but in the long run, God has a divine plan by which all examples of evil will, in the end, work out for the good.

In the course of his adult life, George Washington regularly responded to examples of evil and suffering by pointing out that all is "in the Hands of Providence," another catchphrase in the eighteenth century for the divine plan theory. In terms of the scheme we have introduced in the opening of this section, Alexander Pope and G. W. Leibniz were adherents to the religions of dissolution, in that all evil will work out for the good in the end, for "Whatever is, is Right."

Washington's nephew, William Augustine Washington, wrote his uncle after losing his young son and daughter, that the "Mysteries and decrees of an All-Wise Providence are unsearchable to short-sighted Mortals."[587] Washington wrote back in the same vein, when he wrote, "It is the duty of humankind to be resigned to the Divine Will."[588] In these letters, both

Washington and his nephew are assenting to the divine plan theory. The idea of being resigned to the will of God, of course, is another indication of Washington's commitment to divine plan theory.

In a letter to Martha before the Battle of Boston, Washington again shows his assent to divine plan theory. The first president wrote:

> My Dearest, . . . as it has been a kind of Destiny that has thrown me upon this service. I shall hope that my understanding is de-signed to answer some good purpose . . . I shall rely, therefore, confidently on that Providence, which has heretofore preserved and has been bountiful to me, not doubting but that I shall re-turn safe to you.[589]

Washington may have been referring to the *morei*, or "destiny," of the Stoics, or he may be indicating his assent to divine plan theory with his mention of having a "good purpose." At any rate, after the fall of Charleston to the British in May of 1780, Washington offered up a prayer that again has hints of divine plan theory, with respect to the problem of evil. The first president observed:

> Providence—to Whom we are infinitely more indebted than we are to our wisdom, or to our own exertions—has always dis-played its power and goodness, when clouds and thick darkness seemed ready to overwhelm us. The hour has now come when we stand much in need of another manifestation of its bounty, however little we deserve it.[590]

There is also considerable evidence that Martha Washington's overall view on the issues of theodicy and the problem of evil was also divine plan theory. She expressed similar views on these issues, for examples, when she responded to a widowed niece who now was contemplating remarriage. Martha advised, "I really don't know what to say to you on the subject; you must be governed by your own judgment; and I trust that Providence will direct you for the best."[591]

Martha Washington wrote to her sister-in-law, Hannah Bushrod Washington, the widow of the first president's younger brother, that "In car-ing for the sick and dying members of my family over the years, my grief is in some degree mitigated by reflecting that I have been & still am useful to those I love and perhaps I am answering the purpose for which I was made."[592] There can be little doubt that, like her husband, these purposes Martha had in mind were related to the divine plan of Providence.

Mary V. Thompson sums up this penchant that George Washington had in respect to the first president's understanding of Providence and its relationships to the problem of evil, when she writes:

> Washington appears to have believed that, while God/Providence directed the course of events on earth, human beings could not always understand why certain things occurred and simply had to turn to their reasoning powers and their religious beliefs in order to make sense of it all, and, in the end, come to the acceptance of God's Will.[593]

Again, the acceptance of God's will is little more than assenting to the divine plan point of view with respect to the issues of evil and suffering, for, as Alexander Pope puts the matter, "Whatever is, is Right!"

Although George Washington's overall view of the problem of evil was the divine plan view, he also employed a number of other responses outlined earlier—for example, the moral qualities perspective and the test view. In addition, Washington also employed two other traditional responses in regard to that issue. This first of these can be seen in Washington's response to the injuring, killing, or stealing from prisoners of war. In an order, or charge, to the Northern Expeditionary Force on September 14, 1775, Washington observed:

> Should any American soldier be so base and infamous as to injure any prisoner . . . I do most earnestly enjoin you to bring him to such severe and exemplary punishment as the enormity of the crime may require. Should it extend to death itself, it will not be disproportional to its guilt at such a time and in such a cause . . . for by such conduct they bring shame, disgrace, and ruin to themselves and to their Country.[594]

In this passage, Washington seems to rely on retributive justice. In this theory, the adherent suggests the Biblical dictum of "An eye for an eye, and a tooth for a tooth"; in this case, to the treatment of POWs. In his military career, General Washington frequently resorted to the practice of this theory when he believed that a misfortune, or an example of injustice, had been caused by his men.[595]

John A. Nagy, in his book *George Washington's Secret Spy War*, points to another of Washington's uses of retributive justice theory. Nagy describes the context this way:

> Another serious issue that required Washington's immediate attention was the grave-robbing of American Soldiers to steal

GEORGE WASHINGTON'S RELIGION

salable items. He had to issue a General Order to stop this repulsive practice.[596]

The Washington General Order in question said this:

> Complaint has been made to the general, that the body of a soldier Col[onel] [Benjamin] Woodbridge's [Massachusetts] Regiment, has been taken from his grave by persons unknown; the General and the friends of the deceased are desirous of all the information that can be given, of the perpetrators of this abominable crime, that he, or they, may be made an example, to deter others from committing so wicked and shameful an offense.[597]

Early on in the Revolutionary War, both sides of the skirmish were keen to endear to the sentiments of the local populations, and Washington held his men accountable for behavior on and off the battlefield. Another way to see the first president's employment of retributive justice was when he told his men that stealing from local gardens would be "punished without mercy."[598] For Washington, anyone who causes harm to innocent people in times of war should be severely punished for it, in a kind of tit for tat.

These observations about the treatment of POWs and local populations during times of war point to another moral issue about which the first president had much to say—namely, just-war theory tradition. Washington was fully aware of the long-time classical just-war theory that stemmed from Cicero and Augustine of Hippo. Washington's theory suggested seven criteria for a war to be morally justified. These were the following:

1. Last resort.

2. Legitimate authority.

3. Just cause.

4. Probability of success.

5. Right intentions

6. Proportionality.

7. No noncombatant casualties.[599]

When General Washington took command of the Continental Army, he believed that the goals of the rebellion could only be accomplished by military means. He thought the thirteen colonies and their leaders were legitimate authorities. Moreover, he thought the American cause was a just one, the Continental Army went into the fray with a belief they would win, and the main intention was to reestablish peace in the colonies.

Washington also advised his troops never to use more force than was necessary, and that civilian and noncombatants were to be avoided as military targets. In short, Washington understood the Revolutionary War as a just war, according to the just-war tradition of Augustine, Thomas Aquinas, and others, like Hugo Grotius who Washington admired. In 1757, the British Royal Navy had published their own Articles of War.[600] These Articles originally were established in the 1650s, then amended in 1749, and again in 1757.

Through Congress, the American colonies also established one hundred and one "Articles For the Government of the Armies of the United States." These articles prohibit a soldier from striking a superior officer; outline the treatment of POWS; and enjoin that a soldier ought not to use more aggression than is necessary and must always keep the goal of peace at the forefront, as well as a number of other provisions.

When Washington launched America's first invasion in a foreign land by dispatching troops to Quebec in September of 1775, he sent his men, led by General Benedict Arnold, with "Rules for the Behavior of Officers and Soldiers." The five principal rules for combat in a foreign land were these:

1. Don't assume you are welcomed.

2. Cultivate local support.

3. Respect local religious practices.

4. Don't abuse prisoners

5. Withdraw if your goal is not attainable.[601]

From this analysis, it should be clear that General Washington was again dipping his ladle into the just-war tradition. Number 5 above, for example, is intimately connected to just cause, probability of success, and proper intentions. The "Articles for the Government of the Armies of the United States" explicitly speak of legitimate authority, last resort, and the treatment of noncombatants. Thus, General Washington was deeply entrenched in fulfilling the precepts of the just-war tradition.

Finally, a third and final response that George Washington sometimes employed in regard to the classical problem of evil is a response to evil and suffering that we most often have seen in the beliefs of Jesus in situations that involved evil and suffering, especially in regard to the poor and the disadvantaged in the Gospel narratives, a view we have not yet discussed. This position may be called the practical approach to the problem of evil. This view essentially argues that, like Jesus, we should fight evil and suffering wherever and whenever we can. We call this approach practical because

Jesus seems to always be primarily concerned about ameliorating suffering in those who are downtrodden.

Altogether, there are thirty-one individual healings by Jesus Christ in the New Testament. Out of the 3,779 verses of the New Testament, 727 of them relate specifically to a physical or mental healing by Jesus, or about 20 percent of the total number of verses. Nearly all of these episodes display the same four parts. These may be summarized this way:

1.   Jesus and the person, or persons, to be healed greet each other.

2.   The identity of the mental or physical condition to be healed is identified.

3.   Jesus devises a plan for healing the condition.

4.   Jesus executes the plan.

Three examples of healing that show this above pattern are the dead son of the widow of Nain in Luke 7:11–16; the healing of the two blind men at Capernaum in Matthew 9:27–31; and Peter's mother-in-law being healed of a fever at Capernaum. In the first example, the condition to be healed is death; in the second, it is the blindness of two people; in the third, it is a fever. In each of these three cases, Jesus devises a healing plan, and this is followed by the executions of those plans.

In each of these examples, Jesus seems to fight suffering and evil wherever he finds it; and in each of these cases, he does it in a very practical way. This practical approach to suffering is also one that can be seen in the life of George Washington, as we shall see next in some other narratives involving the first president.

In another letter from Valley Forge, Washington gives us some insight into this practical approach to evil and suffering. The first president observes:

> Let your heart feel for the afflictions and distresses of everyone, and let your hand give in proportion to your purse; remembering always the estimation of the Widow's Mite, but that it is not everyone who asks that deserves Charity.[602]

In this letter, Washington clearly seeks for comfort for the afflicted at Valley Forge. The reference to the widow's mite story, told in Luke 21:1–4 and Mark 12:41–44, calls back to an earlier section of this essay (section III). The important point of this Biblical narrative, for our present purposes, is that Jesus points to the widow's desire to treat the poor in as practical a way as she could, even though she gave all that she had. In the Gospel narrative, Jesus says this is "more" than what the rich man gives.

Another place where the first president exhibits this practical approach to evil and suffering is in the many letters of advice he wrote to young people. On January 15, 1783, for example, Washington wrote his nephew, Bushrod. Among his pieces of advice to the nephew were these words:

> Let your heart feel for the afflictions and distress of everyone, and let your hand give in proportion to your purse, remembering always the estimation of the Widow's Mite, that it is not everyone who asks that deserves charity; all, however, are worthy of inquiry, or the deserving may suffer.[603]

Again, the first president refers here to his favorite New Testament narrative, the widow's mite, but he also conveys to his nephew the importance of taking a practical approach when handling those who are suffering, much like the approach that Jesus often took toward the downtrodden in the Gospel stories, the poor and the disabled. A good example of Jesus' practical approach can be seen in his behavior towards the blind man at Bethsaida in Mark 8:22–25. Jesus first takes the blind man outside the city, so the two may be alone. Next he puts mud on the man's eyes, and when asked if he could see, the man says, "I see what looks like trees walking." Then Jesus again puts mud on the blind man's eyes, and instantly "His sight was restored and he saw everything."[604] Jesus used a trial and error method to restore the man's sight.

Washington also employed the practical approach to suffering in a letter to General William Woodford. In the correspondence, Washington tells his subordinate, "Be strict in your discipline, that is, require nothing unreasonable of your officers and men, but see that whatever is required is punctually done."[605] Brigadier General William Woodford (1734–80), from Caroline County, Virginia, served as an ensign under Washington during the French and Indian War. Two counties in the United States, one in Illinois, and the other in Kentucky, are named after General Woodford.

In these letters, as well as many others like them, General Washington showed his preference for practicality in most aspects of his life, including how to proceed with those in the throes of evil and suffering.

Perhaps the best way to see this practical approach to evil and suffering in the adult life of George Washington comes from an unlikely source—the only, or one of the only, Jews at Valley Forge. This man left a chronicle of his time in the Pennsylvania encampment. He begins one of his entries this way:

> A difficult winter. Terrible cold. We are sitting in Valley Forge and waiting. Why? I don't know. Perhaps for better days than

these. I am the only Jew here. Perhaps there are other Jews among us, but I have not seen any. We hunger for bread. We have no warm clothing or shoes to protect our feet. Most of the soldiers curse George Washington for going to War against Britain.[606]

The Jewish soldier goes on to discuss a Chanukah menorah his father had given him when he left home back in Poland. His father said at the time, "My son, when you light the Chanukah candles, they will illuminate the way for you."[607] The young man waited for all his *Goyim* compatriots, non-Jews, to fall asleep before he lighted the candles. As he was doing so, the soldier revealed:

> Suddenly, I felt a gentle hand touching my head. I lifted my eyes and it was He—He was standing over me and he asked, "Why are you crying soldier? Are you cold?"[608]

The Jewish soldier continued his analysis. He wrote:

> Pain and Compassion were in his voice. I could not bear to see him suffering. I jumped up, forgot that I was a soldier standing before General Washington, and I said what came from my heart, like a son speaking to his father. "General," I said, 'I am crying and praying for your victory. And I know that with the help of G-D we will win. Today they are strong, but tomorrow they will fall because justice is with us. We want to be free in this land. We want to build a home here for all those who flee from the hands of *Poritzim,* for all who suffer across the ocean. The *Poritzim* will not rule over us! They will fall and you will rise. Then General Washington pressed my hand.[609]

The Hebrew term *poritzim* was a word used by Polish Jews to stand for wealthy, anti-Semitic land owners. Thus, the use here is a plea to escape from the clutches of the *Poritzim,* so that they no longer "ruled over" the Jews in Eastern Europe.

To return to the Jewish soldier's tale,

> "Thank you, Soldier," he said to me. Then he sat next to me on the ground, in front of the Menorah. "What is this candlestick?" he asked. I told him I brought it from my father's house.
>
> "The Jews all over the world light candles on this night, on Chanukah, a holiday of a great miracle." The Chanukah candles lit up Washington's eyes, and he asked joyfully, "Are you a Jew from the nation of the Prophets?"[610]

The Jewish soldier was referring to the story of a tyrant king from Damascus ruling over the Jews and forcing them to worship Greek gods. Jewish rebels called Maccabees fought for their freedom for three years, and after becoming victorious, they reclaimed control over the temple in Jerusalem. In order to rededicate the temple, they needed oil to light the menorah, but they could only find enough oil to keep the fire burning for a single night. However, the oil lasted for eight nights. They were then able to make more oil and to keep the eternal flame lit.

The ancients Jews, as well as those Jews ever since the Maccabees, see the lighting of the menorah as one of God's great miracles, brought by the divine for his chosen people. Washington, of course, saw America as a new chosen people, and some saw him as a new Moses.

The Jewish soldier responded:

> "Yes, sir," I answered with conviction. "We will win just like the Maccabees won, for themselves and for all of those who come here after us to build a new land and new lives." The General got up and his face was shining. He shook my hand, and disappeared into the darkness.[611]

The Jewish soldier began a family and a business in New York City after the war on Broome Street. One year, while he was lighting the Chanukah candles for his family's devotion, there was a sharp knocking at the door.

> When I opened the front door, My General, now President Washington, was there, standing at my threshold. In all his Glory, the president said: "Behold the wonderful candle, the candle of hope of the Jewish People."
>
> Then the President put his hand on my shoulder and said, "This candle and your beautiful words ignited a light in my heart that night. Soon you will receive a Medal of Honor from the United States of America, together with all the brave men of Valley Forge. But tonight, please accept this token from me." Then he hung a golden medallion on my chest and shook my hand. Tears filled my eyes and I couldn't speak. The President shook my hand again and departed.
>
> I came to, as if from a wonderful dream, then I looked at the medallion and saw an etching of a beautiful Chanukah Menorah. Under it was written, "A token of gratitude for the light of your candle, George Washington."[612]

In both the scene at Valley Forge and the one in New York City, the president, like Jesus and the widow of the widow's mite tale, dealt with suffering in the most practical way possible. Although the divine plan theory was Washington's overall view on the problem of evil, certainly this practical approach is also a large part of the first president's responses to the issues of theodicy and the problem of evil.

To sum up this eighth section of this study on George Washington's religion, we have made the following conclusions. First, in the opening of this section, we introduced the classical problem of evil and three religious persuasions in regard to that problem—religions of solution, dissolution and paradox. Second, we have introduced and discussed eight major responses to evil and suffering often employed by the religions of paradox—Judaism, Christianity, and Islam.

Third, we have shown that George Washington was quite familiar with occasions of evil and suffering in his own life, as well as those around him.

And finally we have explored the variety of traditional responses to evil and suffering that George Washington seems to have employed in his life and works. Among those theories, we have seen retributive justice, the test view, the moral qualities theory, the practical approach, and the divine plan theory, as used by the first president in his writings, his letters, and even in his military life.

Now we will turn to the major conclusions of this study in section IX.

IX

Major Conclusions of This Essay

Two hundred years after the deaths of the men and women who founded the United States, the question of their Religious Faith still elicits strong opinions.

—MARY V. THOMPSON, *IN THE HANDS OF A GOOD PROVIDENCE*

THE MAJOR AIM OF this study has been to describe and discuss the religious life of the first president of the United States, George Washington. To that end, we began this essay by making a number of observations about Washington's earliest religious life, including his family background, his early education, and his baptism and attendance at church as a child, as well as books owned by his family that contributed to his early religious education. Included among these volumes was his copy of the *Rules of Civility*, made as a boy, and other books owned by Mary Ball Washington, the first president's mother, known for her piety.[613]

We have shown that Washington appears to have used his copy of the *Rules of Civility* as a handwriting exercise around the year 1744, and that the text of the *Rules* used by Washington was an edition edited by Francis Hawkins in London in 1640. The original text of the work, however, was developed by French Jesuits at the very end of the sixteenth century.

We also have indicated in the first section of this work that Washington attended two different Anglican churches as a child: one near Mount Vernon, called the Pohick Church, on the creek by that same name, and the other in Fredericksburg, Virginia, called Saint George's Episcopal Church, located across the Rappahannock River. Early on, there is evidence that Augustine Washington's family attended both of these churches fairly regularly, and George appears to have received communion at both these churches, as well, early in his life.

When he became a surveyor at age sixteen, however, George Washington's church attendance ceased until after his marriage to Martha Washington on January 6, 1759, when the president was twenty-seven years old. After that time, as we have indicated, Washington's attendance at Sunday services was a fairly regular occurrence, although, as we have shown, he no longer attended the communion service, for reasons that are not entirely clear.[614]

There is also evidence that George Washington was read to from the three-volume family Bible that his father purchased, and that his mother, Mary, also employed devotional literature in the early moral education of her children.[615] Among these volumes, as we have indicated, were works by Sir Matthew Hale and Thomas Comber, as well as other popular British writers.

We also have indicated several other aspects of Washington's early life: another book that may have influenced his literary interests was a copy of Aesop's *Fables*; in his early surveying career, his mentor was Englishman George Hume; Washington was embarrassed by the lack of his higher education for the remainder of his life; and he was the executor of the estate of the Rev. Charles Green after the latter's death in 1765. Washington was also the executors of a number of other friends and family members over the years.

The major goal of the second section of this study on George Washington's religion was to explore what the first president had to say about God, or what he usually referred to as "Providence," though he did employ at least one hundred other names when speaking of the divine.[616] Many of these names, as we have shown, had deistic overtones. Indeed, we have pointed out in this study that Michael and Jana Novak have supplied a catalogue of these divine names employed by George Washington in an appendix of their volume on Washington's religion.[617]

In this second section of this work, we have maintained that George Washington was a firm believer in the propositions that God is all-good, all-knowing, all-powerful, the Creator of the universe out of nothing, and that God acts in history by answering prayers, performing miracles, and sometimes choosing sides in battles and wars.[618]

Indeed, we have argued that, because Washington believed that God acts in history, the first president was not a deist. If he were a deist, as we have maintained, then he would have believed that God created the universe, and the rules it runs by, and then withdrew to let it run on its own.[619] Along the way, in the second section of this study on George Washington's religion, we also have maintained that deism, like dualism and atheism, grew out of a metaphor that Sir Isaac Newton introduced at the end of his *Principia Mathematica*—that is, that God is to the universe as a watchmaker is to his watch.[620]

At the close of section II, we have examined the major arguments that some scholars make that Washington was a deist, and we responded to them by clearly and conclusively saying that he was not.[621] In fact, the main reason for our view is that George Washington believed that his God acted in history by performing miracles, answering prayers, and by choosing sides in military skirmishes.

One final aspect of Washington's view of God we have shown in section II is the belief that the first president firmly believed that divine Providence had brought special graces to the American side of the Revolution. Two letters of Mr. Washington's, which we have cited earlier, confirm this point. The first letter was written to Congregationalist minister and president of Harvard College, Samuel Langdon, on September 28, 1789.

Washington wrote:

> The man must be bad indeed who can look upon the events of the American Revolution without feeling the warmest gratitude towards the Great Author of the Universe whose divine impositions were so frequently manifested in our own behalf.[622]

In another correspondence written to the Reverend John Rodgers (1727–1811), Presbyterian pastor to congregations in New England and New York City, on June 11, 1783, the first president again reiterated this point about Providence offering special graces to the American cause when he wrote, "Glorious indeed has been our Contest: glorious if we consider The Prize for which we have contended, and glorious in its Issue; but in the midst of our joys, I hope that we shall not forget that, to Divine Providence is to be ascribed the Glory and the praise.[623]

George Washington's knowledge of, and uses of, the Bible were the subject matter of the third section of this essay. In that section, we have explored the places in his many works where he quotes from both the Old and the New Testaments in the King James Version of the Bible. In fact, Washington quoted regularly from Genesis, Exodus, Numbers, Deuteronomy, 1 and 2 Kings, Samuel, Isaiah, Esther, Joel, Daniel, the Psalms, and Micah, and many other Old Testament books.

In regard to the New Testament, we have shown that George Washington made uses of passages in the four Gospels, as well as Hebrews, Romans, James, Revelation, and a number of other New Testament books, though, like other Enlightenment thinkers (such as Jefferson, for example),

Washington was not nearly as fond of the letters of Paul as he was of the Gospels.[624]

Indeed, we also have explored the many uses of phrases and idioms that Washington employed in both of his public and private lives, including several favorite Biblical passages, as we have shown, including the many references to the "vine and the fig tree" in the book of Micah, as well as the narrative of the widow's mite in chapter 12 of Mark and chapter 21 of Luke.[625] These were Washington's two favorite Biblical narratives, as we have shown.

At the end of the third section of this study on Washington's faith, we have made some comments about a number of copies of the Bible that seemed to have played some roles in the religious education of George Washington. Among those Bibles were one borrowed from the Masons to use in his first oath of office; the family Bible, purchased by his father, Augustine Washington; the Custis Family Bible brought to the Washington marriage by Martha Washington; and the Lewis Family Bible he bought as a gift for Martha.[626]

Religious toleration, and Washington's views on that matter, were the stuff of the fourth section of this work. In that section, we have shown the many places in his public life and in his private papers where the first president refers to the idea of religious toleration in early America. We also have shown in this fourth section that the major source for Washington's thoughts about religious toleration were the many letters that the president wrote to various and sundry religious congregations, including the Baptists, Presbyterians, Congregationalists, Catholics, members of the Dutch Reform Church, the Swedenborgians in Baltimore, and the Jewish congregations of Savannah, Georgia and Newport, Rhode Island, among many others.[627] Indeed, as we have shown, Ron Chernow suggests that Washington wrote letters on toleration of religion to two dozen different congregations or denominations.[628]

We also have indicated that the writings of several other Enlightenment thinkers, like John Locke, Francois-Marie Arouet (better known as Voltaire), and Baruch Spinoza, may also have contributed to the attitudes of George Washington concerning religious toleration.[629]

We have also pointed out in section IV that a number of Washington's fellow Founding Fathers also had much to say about religious toleration, particularly John Adams, Thomas Jefferson, and James Madison; and these Fellow Founding Fathers may have influenced Washington's beliefs about religious toleration, as well as the separation of church and state and other religious issues.

We also have catalogued in section IV the many references to religious tolerations in the founding documents of this country, including the U.S. Constitution and its First Amendment. In addition, we also have provided a number of personal letters written by Washington in which he discusses his beliefs about toleration in religious matters. In that regard, we have mentioned letters to Lafayette, James Madison, and Patrick Henry, among others, in regard to that issue.[630]

In the fifth section of this study on George Washington's religion, we have explored the first president's many observations about ethics and republican virtue. Among the sources we have indicated for Washington's views on these matters were his 1796 farewell address, his circular letter, and the works of Matthew Hale and Thomas Comber. Along the way, in section V, we also have shown Washington's fondness for Stoic philosophy and poetry, as well as Joseph Addison's play *Cato*, which was performed at Valley Forge in May of 1778.[631] In fact, as we have shown, Addison's *Cato* was George Washington's favorite play. We also have indicated that George Washington had a number of works of Stoic philosophy in his personal library at Mount Vernon.[632]

We also have indicated in section V of this work that George Washington employed the theory known as divine command theory, which posits that moral standards are determined by the moral wishes and commands of divine Providence. We further suggested that Washington appears to have been an advocate of utilitarianism when it came to moral theory. Washington saw that both moral principles and moral consequences were important in judging the moral good in a given situation.

At the close of section V, we have explored ten leadership qualities that were embodied in the life of George Washington, both as a general and as a president. As we have shown, these ten qualities contributed in great ways to Washington's success in war time and in peace.[633] Among these leadership qualities embodied by President Washington were that Washington always kept to his goal; that he exhibited exemplary moral character and integrity; that he put the welfare of his men before his own; that he always treated others with respect; that Washington frequently invested his own money to the cause; that Washington believed in those around him; that he held his subordinates accountable; that he was reluctant to join any cause without reason; that if there were no reason to express an opinion, then he thought it best to remain silent; and finally, that Washington realized that there are drawbacks in surrounding oneself with yes-men—particularly that it stifles creativity in an organization.

George Washington's views on prayer were the subject matter of section VI. In this section, we have described both the many places where the first president mentioned prayer, as well as several times when he is said to have prayed. Indeed, we have introduced the first-person narratives of a number of family members and fellow soldier who claim to have seen the first president pray.[634]

We also have shown in our analysis that many of the latter—like praying on his knees at Valley Forge, composing the "Prayer for the United States," and adding "So help me God" to the Presidential oath—all appear to have been apocryphal tales, perhaps made up by Pastor Mason Locke Weems.[635]

In the seventh section of this study, we have raised the question about whether George Washington was a Christian, and whether America was founded as a Christian nation. In regard to the former question, after pointing out that what counts as being a Christian has changed over the years, using the standards of George Washington's day, he was indeed a believer in the Christian faith—at least by the standards of the Old Lights of the Second Great Awakening.[636]

We have arrived at this conclusion mostly by examining the many prayer journals of George Washington from both his youth and his later life. We added the caveat, however, that the notion of contemporary Evangelicals concerning what a Christian is has radically changed from what it meant at the end of eighteenth-century America among members of the Anglican and Episcopal churches.[637]

Indeed, among Anglicans in the late eighteenth century, there were few discussions concerning Biblical inerrancy, the second coming, and whether Jesus was one's Lord and personal Savior. Nor did late-eighteenth-century Anglicans profess to having been "born again," even though the phrase appears in the Gospel of John at the story of Nicodemus in chapter 3.[638] Indeed, in that regard, we have shown that contemporary Evangelical Christians come out of the New Lights tradition of the Second Great Awakening, whereas George Washington was an "Old Light," to use the terms employed by Michael and Jana Novak.[639]

We began our discussion of whether America was founded as a Christian nation by citing Attorney General Jeff Sessions, who argues that it was. We then countered this view by those of historian Frank Lambert and University of Chicago law professor Geoffrey Stone, who both suggest that the United States was founded on Enlightenment and deistic principles. Not only is this question controversial in contemporary America, but it also has been rather complicated in the history of the nation.

In fact, in regard to the latter query about whether America was founded as a Christian nation, we have shown that the evidence to settle this issue is contradictory, both in colonial times and in contemporary America.

Despite the evidence offered by Justice David Joseph Brewer (1837–1910) and several modern American presidents we nevertheless have sided with the Supreme Court for much of the latter twentieth century, and have concluded that our latter query should be answered "no." Certainly the Treaty of Tripoli suggests that that is the proper answer to our second question.[640]

In section VIII, we have analyzed and discussed the views of George Washington on the classic philosophical conundrum in the West known as the problem of evil. Namely, if God is all-good, all-knowing, and all-powerful, then why is there so much evil and suffering in the world? After introducing the distinctions among the religions of solution, dissolution, and paradox, and their metaphysical persuasions of dualism, monism, and mixed metaphysics, we discussed the three traditional kinds of evil—moral, natural, and psychological.

We then sketched out nine traditional responses to the problem of evil to be found in the religions of paradox—that is, Judaism, Christianity, and Islam—and we have shown that Washington employed six of those responses. Four of those responses, as we have shown, are backwards-looking, and four look forward, while the ninth response—the practical approach—is one that Jesus most often seems to employ in the Gospel narratives where he relates to the poor and the disabled.

In the course of this eighth section, we have argued that Washington's overall view of the problem is the divine plan point of view; but we also have maintained that the first president assented to several other responses to the problem of evil. We have called these two views retributive justice and the practical response to evil and suffering. Earlier in this essay, in section II, we maintained that the first president also endorsed a theory we then called the moral qualities view, and another known as the test perspective. These theories, as we have shown, say that God sometimes uses evil and suffering to improve the moral characteristics of his followers, or simply to test them.[641]

As we have shown, Washington thought that patience and fortitude, both stoic virtues, can only be developed by experiencing tragic events. We also have shown that, at times (though very rarely), Washington mentions the actions of demonic forces that may have effects on the lives of men. Although these latter two views were employed by George Washington, they are not nearly as important as retributive justice and divine plan theory when understanding the first president's views on the problem of evil.

In this eighth section, we have also indicated that, with regard to the issue of the problem of evil, George Washington frequently fell back on what we have called the practical approach to evil and suffering, one most often exemplified in the healing powers of Jesus in the four Gospels.[642]

Altogether, then, we have maintained that George Washington endorsed, or assented to, the following explanations and responses in regard to the traditional problem of evil in the Judeo-Christian-Islamic traditions:

1. The retributive justice view.

2. The test perspective.

3. The moral qualities theory.

4. The divine plan perspective.

5. The influences of demonic forces.

6. The practical approach to evil and suffering.[643]

Thus, we have seen that the first president of the United States was baptized and worshipped in two separate Anglican-Episcopal churches as a child. He was a firm believer in monotheism—that is, he believed in a God who is all-good, all-knowing, and all-powerful. We also have shown that George Washington, along with fellow Founding Fathers such as Jefferson and Madison, was deeply devoted to the idea of religious toleration, so much so that he had Muslim slaves on his farms at Mount Vernon.

We also have shown here that Washington embodied a set of Stoic virtues that are unparalleled in American history, and chief among these were courage and honesty. We also have indicated that the first president was a man of prayer, even to the point of his relatives telling us that he set aside time every day before breakfast, and again before retiring to bed, when he prayed.

Additionally, in this essay, we have maintained that George Washington was clearly a Christian, while not believing that the United States was established as a Christian nation. Nevertheless, we have seen that Washington often employed the divine plan response to the problem of evil, and that he was a believer in some form of the afterlife, but the nature of that belief, at least for master of Mount Vernon, is not entirely clear.

Endnotes

Section I

1. Weems and Cunliffe, *Life of Washington*. Weems's text is the original source for the story of the chopping of the cherry tree, the silver dollar thrown by Washington across the Potomac River, and a number of other myths about the early life of George Washington.

2. Slaughter, *History of St. George's Parish*.

3. Hayes, *George Washington: A Life*, 23.

4. Hayes, *George Washington: A Life*, 23.

5. Hayes, *George Washington: A Life*, 23–24.

6. Dickinson, *Fairfax Proprietary*, 1–49.

7. Dickinson, *Fairfax Proprietary*, 1–49.

8. For more on David Piper, see Hayes, *George Washington: A Life*, 17.

9. Hayes, *George Washington: A Life*, 17.

10. Hayes, *George Washington: A Life*, 18.

11. Hayes, *George Washington: A Life*, 18.

12. George Washington, *Rules of Civility*.

13. Nagy, *George Washington's Secret Spy War*, 13.

14. St. George's was an Anglican church from 1741 until 1789, at which time it became an Episcopal church.

15. Toner, *Washington's Rules of Civility*.

16. Toner, *Washington's Rules of Civility*.

17. Toner, *Washington's Rules of Civility*.

18.   Toner, *Washington's Rules of Civility*.

19.   Toner, *Washington's Rules of Civility*.

20.   Toner, *Washington's Rules of Civility*.

21.   Toner, *Washington's Rules of Civility*.

22.   Toner, *Washington's Rules of Civility*.

23.   Toner, *Washington's Rules of Civility*. This Old Testament idea of God writing the conscience on the hearts of all human beings is often tied to another idea called the Theory of the Two *Yetzerim*. This theory says that God placed two "imaginations" or "inclinations" into all human hearts. These are called the *yetzer ha ra*, or "evil imagination," and the *yetzer tov*, or the "good imagination." Two places where this idea is employed in the Old Testament are Genesis 6:5 and Genesis 8:21.

24.   *Pohick Church*.

25.   Scott, *Christian Life*; Hervey, *Meditations and Contemplations*; Boyle, *Occasional Reflections*. Scott (1639–95) was a writer of devotional literature and a defender of Anglican Orthodoxy; Hervey (1714–58) was educated at Lincoln College, Oxford, and also wrote devotional literature.

26.   *Pohick Church*, 19.

27.   Moore, "Introduction to Washington's Copy." A more modern edition has been published by Applewood Books in 1989.

28.   Toner, *Washington's Rules of Civility*.

29.   Toner, *Washington's Rules of Civility*.

30.   Marye, *Minutes of the Vestry Truro Parish*. The vestry book of Pohick Church was originally published by Gateway Press in 1974.

31.   Mount Vernon was named after Admiral Vernon, a Commanding Officer of Lawrence Washington.

32.   Lillback and Newcombe, *George Washington's Sacred Fire*.

33.   Commander Jumonville (1718–54), was a French-Canadian military officer who was defeated by Washington at the Battle of Jumonville Glen. This was one of the sparks for the Seven Years' War.

34.   Packer and Beckwith, *Thirty-Nine Articles*.

35. Coughlin, "Old Pohick Church." See also Coughlin, *Colonial Church-es in the Original Colony*. These remain the best sources on the church at Pohick Creek in Virginia.

36. This scolding of Washington by the Rev. Abercrombie took place on December 28, 1794.

37. "History of Pohick Church."

38. "History of Pohick Church."

39. Coughlin, "Old Pohick Church."

40. French (1812–78) and Wren (1728–1815), designed many public buildings and homes in Colonial Virginia.

41. *Diaries of George Washington*. The diaries were published in 1976 (vol. 1) and 1978 (vol. 2). There is also an abridged version, also by the University of Virginia Press.

42. The Mason Family Bible currently resides at Gunston House. This Bible is the folio edition of Thomas Baskett's Bible, published in London in 1759. The inside flap of this Bible contains the birth and death dates for many Mason family members.

43. Packer and Beckwith, *Thirty-Nine Articles*, 7–9, 10–15.

44. "The Reminiscences of a Former Slave: Sambo Anderson; Part I," *Fredericksburg News*, October 12, 1858.

45. "The Reminiscences of a Former Slave: Sambo Anderson; Part II," *Fredericksburg Weekly Advertiser*, October 12, 1858.

46. Packer and Beckwith, *Thirty-Nine Articles*, 16–25.

47. Packer and Beckwith, *Thirty-Nine Articles*, 26–33.

48. Packer and Beckwith, *Thirty-Nine Articles*, 35–41.

49. Packer and Beckwith, *Thirty-Nine Articles*, 42–46. This miscellaneous category was a kind of catch-all for anything not covered in the other sections.

50. Packer and Beckwith, *Thirty-Nine Articles*, 47–50.

51. Packer and Beckwith, *Thirty-Nine Articles*, 51–56.

Section II

52. Novak and Novak, *Washington's God*, 243–45.

53.   Vicchio, *Jefferson's Religion*, 70.

54.   Vicchio, *Jefferson's Religion*, 70.

55.   Vicchio, *Jefferson's Religion*, 71.

56.   Vicchio, *Jefferson's Religion*, 71.

57.   Benjamin Franklin to Ezra Stiles, March 9, 1790.

58.   Benjamin Franklin, "Speech at the Constitutional Convention," June 28, 1787.

59.   Samuel Adams, "Rights of Colonists," November 20, 1772.

60.   Alexander Hamilton, "Dying Words," July 12, 1804.

61.   Vicchio, *Jefferson's Religion*, 65. Lord Henry St. John Bolingbroke (1678–1851) was an English politician, political philosopher, and government official.

62.   Vicchio, *Jefferson's Religion*, 64.

63.   Vicchio, *Jefferson's Religion*, 65.

64.   Vicchio, *Jefferson's Religion*, 65.

65.   George Washington, "First Inaugural Address," April 30, 1789.

66.   George Washington, "Farewell Address," September 19, 1796.

67.   Burton, *Anatomy of Melancholy*. Burton (1577–1640) was an Oxford Don best known for this volume.

68.   George Washington to Colonel Barakieth Bassett, April 25, 1773.

69.   George Washington to John Augustine Washington, July 18, 1755.

70.   Franklin, *Articles of Belief and Acts of Religion*, 53.

71.   Franklin, *Articles of Belief and Acts of Religion*, 53.

72.   Allen, *Reason*, 53. Allen (1738–89) was a Revolutionary War hero, philosopher, writer, lay theologian, and one of the founders of the state of Vermont.

73.   George Washington to his troops, October 3, 1789.

74.   Herbert, *De Veritate*. Herbert (1583–48) was an English baron and historian, poet, and religious philosopher.

75.   Holmes, *Faiths of the Founding Fathers*, 131.

76.   Johnson, *Dictionary of the English Language*, 71. Also see Brian Swearer's quote in Kilmeade, *George Washington's Secret Six*, 189–90. Johnson (1709–84), was a British editor, poet, and journalist. G. W.

Leibniz (1646–1716) was a German professor of moral philosophy, and, along with Isaac Newton, also discovered integral calculus.

77. Newton, *Principia; Mathematical Principles*, 421–55.

78. Pierre Bayle (1647–1706) was a French Protestant philosopher. He discusses Manicheanism in his *Historical and Critical Dictionary*, where he is quite enamored of the idea, principally because of the answer in regards to the problem of evil. More will be said about that problem in section VIII of this essay. The original Manichean faith was established by a Persian philosopher named Mani in the latter half of the third century. The key to his system was his cosmology, which separates the universe into good and evil that later became personified as gods.

79. The Baron D'Holbach (1723–89) was a French-German author and encyclopedist. Denis Diderot (1713–84) was a French philosopher and coeditor of *Encyclopedie.*

80. Washington was very familiar with Alexander Pope's poem "An Essay on Man," in which he gives a sort of tutorial on the divine plan response to the problem of evil.

81. Bayle, *Historical and Critical Dictionary*, 100. G. W. Leibniz (1646–1716) was a German polymath, rationalist philosopher.

82. Byrne, *Natural Religion and the Nature of Religion*, 3–4.

83. Kirk, *Roots of American Order.* Kirk (1918–94) was a conservative American political theorist.

84. Kirk, *Roots of American Order*, 293.

85. Kirk, *Roots of American Order*, 293.

86. Vicchio, *Jefferson's Religion*, 61. Francois-Marie Arouet, also known as Voltaire (1694–78), was one of the leading figures of the French Revolution. He also wrote plays, novels, and philosophical works.

87. Novak and Novak, *Washington's God*, 119–42.

88. Holmes, *Faiths of the Founding Fathers*, 132.

89. Holmes, *Faiths of the Founding Fathers*, 132.

90. Schwartz and Sharpe, *Practical Wisdom*, 39.

91. Frazer, *Religious Beliefs of America's Founders*, 93.

92. Boller, *George Washington and Religion*, 134. Ashbel Green (1762–1848) was an American Presbyterian minister and academic.

93. The Rev. James Abercrombie (1758–1841) was assistant rector at Christ's Church, Philadelphia, from 1794 until 1831.

94. Thompson, *In the Hands of a Good Providence*, 33–35.

95. George Washington, "Letter to the Hebrew Congregation of Newport," August 21, 1789.

96. Vicchio, *Jefferson's Religion*, 97–117, 121–43.

97. George Washington, "Circular Letter of Farewell to the Army," July 18, 1783.

98. Dwight, *Conquest of Canaan*. Dwight (1752–1817) was a Congregationalist minister, theologian, and writer, and the eighth president of Yale College from 1795 until 1817.

99. Dwight, *Conquest of Canaan*.

100. George Washington to the Hebrew Congregation of Savannah, Georgia, June 14, 1790.

101. George Washington to Samuel Langdon, September 28, 1789.

102. George Washington to Samuel Langdon, September 28, 1789.

103. Chernow, *Washington: A Life*, 206–9.

104. Chernow, *Washington: A Life*, 206–9.

105. Chernow, *Washington: A Life*, 206–9.

106. Chernow, *Washington: A Life*, 206–9. General William Howe (1729–1810) was one of Britain's most notable Generals during the American Revolution.

107. Novak and Novak, *Washington's God*, 71–78.

108. Novak and Novak, *Washington's God*, 71–78. John Witherspoon (1723–94) was a Scottish-American, Presbyterian minister, and signer of the Declaration of Independence.

109. Novak and Novak, *Washington's God*, 71–78.

110. Novak, *On Two Wings*.

111. George Washington to John Augustine Washington, July 18, 1755.

112. George Washington, "First Inaugural Address," April 30, 1789.

113. Smith, *Theory of Moral Sentiments*; Smith, *Wealth of Nations*. For more on Washington and the invisible hand, see Lillback, "Invisible Hand," 20. Adam Smith (1723–98) was a Scottish social philosopher and economist.

114. George Washington, First Inaugural Address, April 30, 1789.

115. George Washington to Thomas Nelson, Jr., August 20, 1778. Nelson (1738–89) was a planter and soldier. He reportedly told General Washington to fire on his own home.

116. George Washington, "Day of Thanksgiving and Prayer," October 3, 1789.

117. George Washington to Thomas Nelson, Jr., August 20, 1778.

118. George Washington, "General Order to Troops," quoted in Novak and Novak, *Washington's God*, 30.

119. Novak and Novak, *Washington's God*, 30.

120. Novak and Novak, *Washington's God*, 65.

121. Novak and Novak, *Washington's God*, 66.

122. George Washington to Martha Washington, June 18, 1775.

123. George Washington to Martha Washington, June 18, 1775.

124. Novak and Novak, *Washington's God*, 110.

125. Novak and Novak, *Washington's God*, 110.

126. Plato, *Euthyphro and Clitophon*. Plato seems to think it is impossible to believe that "Goodness is Good because the gods say so," and "God is All-Good, at the same time."

127. Novak and Novak, *Washington's God*, 103.

128. Novak and Novak, *Washington's God*, 103.

129. Vicchio, *Voice From the Whirlwind*, 129–31.

130. Vicchio, *Voice From the Whirlwind*, 131–37.

131. Although Robert Gingrich uses this quotation as an epigram for chapter 4 of his *Faith and Freedom*, this one appears to be bogus, as well.

132. George Washington to Alexander Spotswood, November 22, 1798. Spotswood (1676–1740) was a lieutenant colonel in the British Army and later lieutenant governor of Virginia.

133. Quoted in "God in the White House."

134. For more on Washington's views on God, see Thompson, *In the Hands of a Good Providence*, 108–23; Novak and Novak, *Washington's God*, 211–28; and Avlon, *Washington's Farewell*, 151–56, 158–76.

Section III

135. George Washington, *Memorandum Books*, esp. folios 1–10. See https://www.loc.gov/item/mgw500001/.

136. Novak and Novak, *Washington's God*, 15.

137. Sanders, *Washington Manuscript of the Psalms*.

138. Sanders, *Washington Manuscript of the Psalms*.

139. Sanders, *Washington Manuscript of the Psalms*, 14 and 160, for examples.

140. Ps 67:1–7 (KJV).

141. George Washington, Letter to Congress, December 20, 1776.

142. 1 Kgs 4:25; 2 Kgs 18:3 (KJV).

143. George Washington to Robert Morris, May 25, 1778.

144. George Washington to Mary Ball Washington, February 15, 1787.

145. George Washington to Martha Washington, June 18, 1775.

146. George Washington to Samuel Purviance, March 10, 1786.

147. George Washington to General Thomas Nelson Jr., February 8, 1778.

148. George Washington to Daniel Bowers, May 28, 1779.

149. George Washington to Richard Sprigg, June 28, 1776.

150. George Washington to Francois Barbe-Marbois, July 9, 1783.

151. Novak and Novak, *Washington's God*, 160.

152. Num 11:12; Isa 49:33.

153. George Washington, *Memorandum Books*, folio 12. See https://www.loc.gov/item/mgw500001/.

154. Washington to Burwell Bassett, quoted in Grizzard, *George Washington*, 24.

155. Grizzard, *George Washington*, 24. Washington is referring to the figure of Haman in the book of Esther, at 3:1–6; 7:6–19; and 9:5–14.

156. Grizzard, *George Washington*, 24.

157. Gen 15:16 (KJV).

158. George Washington, Circular Letter to the Governor of the States, June 8, 1783.

159. Mic 6:8 (KJV).

160. 1 Macc 14:12 (KJV).

161. Avlon, *Washington's Farewell*, 162.

162. Washington to John Augustine Washington, November 19, 1776.

163. Washington to Charles Thomson, January 22, 1784.

164. Washington to Landon Carter, October 17, 1796.

165. Washington to John Q. Adams, June 25, 1797.

166. Washington to Oliver Wolcott, May 15, 1797.

167. Washington to Charles Pinckney, June 24, 1797.

168. Washington to Sarah Cary Fairfax, May 16, 1798.

169. Washington to Hebrew Congregation of Newport, August 21, 1790.

170. Washington to William Vans Murray, December 3, 1797.

171. Washington, Circular Letter to the Northern States, January 31, 1782.

172. Mal 1:11 (KJV).

173. Ps 29:2 (KJV).

174. Washington, Circular Letter to the Northern States, January 31, 1782; Ps 14:34; Mic 6:8 (KJV).

175. 1 Tim 2:2 (KJV).

176. Deut 15:11; 24:14; and Ps 35:10 (KJV).

177. Zech 4:6 (KJV).

178. Prov 16:19 (KJV).

179. George Washington to David Stuart, June 15, 1790.

180. Washington, Circular Letter to the Northern States, January 31, 1782.

181. Heb 4:16 (KJV).

182. Heb 4:16 (KJV).

183. Washington, Circular Letter to the Northern States, January 31, 1782.

184. Matt 22:35–40; Mark 12:28–34.

185. Matt 6:19–20 (KJV).

186. Matt 7:12; Luke 6:21 (KJV).

187. Washington to John Augustine Washington, May 31, 1776.

188. Eccl 3:1–2 (KJV).

189. Mark 12:41–44; Luke 21:1–4 (KJV).

190. Washington to Bushrod Washington, January 15, 1783.

191. Washington to Bushrod Washington, January 15, 1783.

192. Rom 8:28 (KJV).

193. George Washington, Order to His Troops, October 17, 1779.

194. Thompson, *In the Hands of a Good Providence*, 24.

195. Jas 1:2–3 (KJV).

196. Deut 6:16; Matt 4:7 (KJV).

197. Deut 6:16; Matt 4:7 (KJV).

198. Carrier, "Widow's Mite and the Widow's Might," para. 1.

199. Carrier, "Widow's Mite and the Widow's Might," para. 1.

200. Washington to Bushrod Washington, January 15, 1783.

201. Deut 28:1–4 (KJV).

202. Gen 49:13 (KJV).

203. Washington to Hebrew Congregation of Newport, August 21, 1790.

204. John 11:25–26 (KJV).

205. George Washington, General Order to Troops, November 27, 1779.

206. George Washington, General Order to Troops, July 4, 1778.

207. George Washington, General Order to Troops, September 10, 1778.

208. George Washington, General Order to Troops, September 10, 1778.

209. George Washington, General Order to Troops, November 9, 1778.

210. "Did George Washington Swear," para. 2.

211. Quoted in Flexner, *George Washington in the American Revolution*, 305. See also Lengel, *General George Washington*, 300.

212. 2 Chr 18:18; Matt 5:34 (KJV).

213. Rom 8:18 (KJV).

214. "George Washington Inaugural Bible."

215. See "Martha Washington's Bible" at https://www.mountvernon.org/preservation/collections-holdings/browse-the-museum-collections/object/w-1659/.

216. Ibid.

217. George Washington Parke Custis (1781–1857) was the grandson of Martha Washington. His daughter, Mary Anna Randolph Custis, married General Robert E. Lee.

218. For more on these various Bibles of Martha Washington, see Conley, "Faith and Family."

219. George Washington Parke Custis donated a two-volume 1796 edition of the Bible owned by George Washington to the Pohick Church in 1802.

220. This is George Washington Parke Custis's account.

221. This spurious quotation has appeared many times as attributed to George Washington.

222. Weems and Cunliffe, *Washington*, 97.

223. Lear, "Last Illness and Death of George Washington," 163.

224. Dreisbach, *Reading the Bible*.

225. Taylor, "What America's Founders Really Thought," para. 6.

226. Taylor, "What America's Founders Really Thought," para. 21.

227. Taylor, "What America's Founders Really Thought," para. 6.

228. Taylor, "What America's Founders Really Thought," para. 6.

229. Rom 8:27 (KJV).

230. Ps 7:17 (KJV).

231. Deut 30:12; Isa 40:4; Luke 3:5 (KJV).

232. George Washington, *Memorandum Books*, folios 24–26. See https://www.loc.gov/item/mgw500001/.

233. George Washington, *Memorandum Books*, folios 24–26. See https://www.loc.gov/item/mgw500001/.

Section IV

234. Chernow, *Washington: A Life*, 132.

235. Chernow, *Washington: A Life*, 132.

236. Quoted in Davis, "America's True History of Religious Tolerance," para. 7.

237. Quoted in Davis, "America's True History of Religious Tolerance," para. 7.

238. Washington to Lafayette, February 1, 1784.

239. Washington to Sir Edward Newenham, June 22, 1792.

240. Washington to Lafayette, July 25, 1785.

241. Novak and Novak, *Washington's God*, 230.

242. Novak and Novak, *Washington's God*, 230.

243. George Washington to Tench Tilghman, March 24, 1784.

244. Thompson, "Islam at Mount Vernon," para. 9

245. "The Reminiscences of a Former Slave: Sambo Anderson; Part I," *Fredericksburg News*, October 12, 1858.

246. "The Reminiscences of a Former Slave: Sambo Anderson; Part I," *Fredericksburg News*, October 12, 1858.

247. "The Reminiscences of a Former Slave: Sambo Anderson; Part I," *Fredericksburg News*, October 12, 1858.

248. Henriques, "George Washington's Enslaved Workers."

249. George Washington to Jared Sparks, August 19, 1789.

250. Locke, *Letter Concerning Religious Toleration*.

251. Locke, *Letter Concerning Religious Toleration*.

252. Quoted in Rosenthal, "Is Toleration Possible," para. 5.

253. Israel, *Radical Enlightenment*, 265–70.

254. Israel, *Radical Enlightenment*, 265–70.

255. Voltaire, *Treatise on Toleration*.

256. Voltaire, *Treatise on Toleration*.

257. George Mason, "Proposal for Religious Toleration," State of Virginia, June, 1776.

258. James Madison, "Proposal for Religious Toleration," State of Virginia, June, 1776.

259. James Madison to Joseph C. Cabell, September 18, 1828.

260. Richard Henry Lee, "Motion to Congress," June 7, 1776.

261. See the Massachusetts State Constitution of 1780.

262. Theophilus Parsons, "Barnes V. Inhabitants of First Parish in Falmouth, Massachusetts," 1810.

263. Thomas Jefferson, *Virginia Act for Establishing Religious Freedom,* 1786.

264. Patrick Henry, "State Support for Christian Religion," 1784.

265. Vicchio, *Jefferson's Religion,* 45, 65.

266. "Benjamin Franklin on Interfaith Engagement," para. 2.

267. George Mason, "Virginia Declaration of Rights," June, 1776.

268. George Washington to Protestant Episcopal Church, August 19, 1789.

269. George Washington to Methodist Bishops, May 15, 1789.

270. George Washington to Presbyterians, January 1, 1789.

271. George Washington to Dutch Reform Church, November 1, 1789.

272. George Washington to Virginia Baptists, May 8, 1789.

273. George Washington to Quakers, October 13, 1789.

274. George Washington to Quakers, October 13, 1789.

275. George Washington to Virginia Baptists, May 8, 1789.

276. "Treaty of Peace and Friendship Between America and Tripoli," November 1796.

277. Joel Barlow (1754–1812) was an American poet, diplomat, and politician who supported the French and the American Revolutions.

278. Thompson, *In the Hands of a Good Providence,* 166.

279. George Washington to Congress, September 17, 1789.

280. Washington visited Newport, Rhode Island on August 18, 1790.

281. Vicchio and Geiger, "Origins and Development," 89.

282. Vicchio and Geiger, "Origins and Development," 89–90.

283. Virginia Colony Anti-Catholic Test Oath, July 17, 1755.

284. George Washington to the Catholics of the United States of America, March 15, 1790.

285. George Washington, "Letter to the Hebrew Congregation in Newport," August 21, 1789.

286. Rabbi Moses Seixas to George Washington, August 18, 1790.

287. George Washington, "Letter to the Hebrew Congregation of Newport," August 21, 1789.

288. George Washington, "Letter to the Hebrew Congregation of Newport," August 21, 1789.

289. George Washington, "Letter to the Hebrew Congregation of Newport," August 21, 1789.

290. George Washington, "Letter to the Hebrew Congregation of Newport," August 21, 1789.

291. George Washington, "Letter to the Hebrew Congregation of Newport," August 21, 1789.

292. George Washington, "Letter to the Hebrew Congregation of Newport," August 21, 1789.

293. Thompson, *In the Hands of a Good Providence*, 158.

294. George Washington to Benedict Arnold, September 14, 1775.

295. George Washington to Hebrew Congregation of Savannah, June 14, 1790.

296. Hirsch, "Jehovah," 87–88.

297. George Washington to New Jerusalem Congregation in Baltimore, January 27, 1793.

298. George Washington to New Jerusalem Congregation in Baltimore, January 27, 1793.

299. George Washington to New Jerusalem Congregation in Baltimore, January 27, 1793.

300. George Washington to New Jerusalem Congregation in Baltimore, January 27, 1793.

301. Novak and Novak, *Washington's God*, 39.

302. Novak and Novak, *Washington's God*, 39.

303. Chernow, *Washington: A Life*. See also Washington's 1780 "Saint Patrick's Day Proclamation."

304. Novak and Novak, *Washington's God*, 218.

305. Avlon, *Washington's Farewell*, 142.

306. Avlon, *Washington's Farewell*, 142.

307. Avlon, *Washington's Farewell*, 142.

308. Washington to Lafayette, February 1, 1784.

309. Dreisbach, "Three Letters Offering a Window," paras 17–23.

310. Dreisbach, *Reading the Bible*, 222–23.

311. Dreisbach, *Reading the Bible*, 222–23.

312. Dreisbach, *Reading the Bible*, 222–23.

Section V

313. George Washington, "Farewell Address," September 19, 1796.

314. The best place to see Descartes's views on ethics is his book *The Passions of the Soul*; see also Locke, "Essay Concerning Human Understanding," and Paley, *Principles of Morality in Politics and Philosophy*.

315. Kant, *Groundwork For the Metaphysics of Morals*.

316. Kant, *Groundwork For the Metaphysics of Morals*.

317. Rousseau, *Emile*; Voltaire, *Philosophical Dictionary*.

318. Plato, *Euthyphro*.

319. Dostoyevski, *Brothers Karamazov*, 99. He also uses the same phrase in his novel *Crime and Punishment*.

320. Dostoyevski, *Brothers Karamazov*, 99.

321. Volkov, "Dostoevsky Did Say It."

322. Volkov, "Dostoevsky Did Say It."

323. Adams, *Laws of Virtue*.

324. Adams, *Laws of Virtue*.

325. Adams, *Laws of Virtue*.

326. George Mason, "Draft of the Virginia Declaration of Rights," 1777.

327. Hale, *Contemplations, Moral and Divine*, 201.

328. Novak and Novak, *Washington's God*, 176.

329. Quoted in Novak and Novak, *Washington's God*, 176.

330. Novak and Novak, *Washington's God*, 177.

331. Novak and Novak, *Washington's God*, 177.

332. George Washington to Landon Carter, October 27, 1777.

333. Novak and Novak, *Washington's God*, 177.

334. Novak and Novak, *Washington's God*, 179.

335. Novak and Novak, *Washington's God*, 179.

336. Aristotle, *Nicomachean Ethics*, Book III.

337. Novak and Novak, *Washington's God*, 180.

338. Novak and Novak, *Washington's God*, 177.

339. Novak and Novak, *Washington's God*, 177.

340. Novak and Novak, *Washington's God*, 124.

341. Novak and Novak, *Washington's God*, 124.

342. James Madison, "Framer's Constitution," Amendment I, Document #43, January 24, 1774.

343. James Madison, "Framer's Constitution," Amendment I, Document #43, January 24, 1774.

344. Thomas Jefferson, "Notes on the State of Virginia," Query 17, 157–61.

345. Thomas Jefferson, "Opposition to Federalism," 1810.

346. Thomas Jefferson to Richard Douglas, February 4, 1809.

347. John Adams, "Remarks at Continental Congress," September 5, 1774.

348. John Adams, "Remarks on the Militia," October 11, 1798.

349. See Article II of the 1780 *Massachusetts Constitution*.

350. James Monroe, *James Monroe Papers*.

351. George Mason, "Early Draft of the Bill of Rights," September 12, 1787.

352. Letters between Benjamin Rush and Thomas Jefferson, April–May 1803.

353. George Washington to General Committee of the United Baptists Churches of Virginia, May 10, 1789.

354. George Washington to the Quakers, October 19, 1789.

355. George Washington to Benedict Arnold, September 17, 1775.

356. Mill, *On Liberty*, 18.

357. Jellinek, *Declaration of the Rights of Man*.

358. George Washington, "Farewell Address," 1796.

359. George Washington, "First Inaugural Address," 1789.

360. George Washington to Moustier, November 1, 1790.

361. Thomas Jefferson, to Jose Correa da Sera, April 19, 1814.

362. Thomas Jefferson to Amos J. Cook, January 21, 1816.

363. Elliot, *Virginia*, 536–37.

364. Adams, "III. To the Inhabitants," para. 7.

365. Aristotle, *Ethics*.

366. De Witt Hyde, *Stoic Six Pack*.

367. Gibbon, *Rise and Fall of the Roman Empire*.

368. Aurelius, *Meditations*.

369. Aurelius, *Meditations*.

370. George Washington to Alexander Hamilton, August 28, 1788.

371. George Washington to Alexander Hamilton, August 28, 1788.

372. George Washington to Colonel Isaac C. Bassett, June 19, 1775.

373. Washington, *George Washington's Rules of Civility*.

374. Cicero, *Complete Works*.

375. Colonel William Bradford to his sister, May 15, 1778. For more on the Battle of Germantown, see: "Battle of Germantown." See also Chernow, *Washington: A Life*, 308–17.

376. Hardy, "Cato," para. 7.

377. Montgomery, "Washington, the Stoic," 19.

378. Montgomery, "Washington, the Stoic," 19.

379. Montgomery, "Washington, the Stoic," 19.

380. Chernow, *Washington: A Life*, 236.

381. Chernow, *Washington: A Life*, 236.

382. George Washington to Abigail Washington, July 16, 1775.

383. George Washington, "Address to His Officers," March 15, 1783.

384. George Washington to Henry Lamers, December 23, 1777.

385. Chernow, *Washington: A Life*, 323.

386. John Adams to Horatio Gates, March 23, 1776.

387. George Washington to George Washington Parke Custis, November 28, 1796.

Section VI

388. George Washington, "Book of Psalms," July 18, 1771.

389. George Washington, "Book of Psalms," July 18, 1771.

390. Lillback and Newcombe, *George Washington's Sacred Fire.*

391. George Washington, "Order to His Troops," May 15, 1776.

392. George Washington, "Order to His Troops," May 15, 1776.

393. Lillback and Newcombe, *George Washington's Sacred Fire.*

394. Washington, "Order to His Troops," June 17, 1776.

395. Act of Continental Congress, September 1774.

396. Ps 35:34–36 (KJV).

397. Federer, "Jacob Duché," para. 68.

398. Federer, "Jacob Duché."

399. Federer, "Jacob Duché."

400. Israel Evans, "Sermon: Presence, Sovereignty, and Compassion," Valley Forge, December 18, 1777.

401. Israel Evans, "Sermon: Presence, Sovereignty, and Compassion," Valley Forge, December 18, 1777.

402. Israel Evans, "Sermon: Presence, Sovereignty, and Compassion," Valley Forge, December 18, 1777.

403. George Washington, "Day of Thanksgiving and Prayer," October 3, 1789.

404. George Washington, "Day of Thanksgiving and Prayer," October 3, 1789.

405. George Washington, "Day of Thanksgiving and Prayer," November 26, 1789.

406. George Washington, "Day of Thanksgiving and Prayer," October 3, 1789.

407. George Washington, "Day of Thanksgiving and Prayer," October 3, 1789.

408. George Washington, "Day of Thanksgiving and Prayer," February 19, 1795.

409. George Washington, "Day of Thanksgiving and Prayer," February 19, 1795.

410. Ebenezer Bradford, "Sermon on a Day of Thanksgiving and Prayer," February 21, 1795.

411. George Washington, "Prayer Journal," October 3, 1789.

412. George Washington, "Circular Letter to the Governors," June 21, 1783. Later, we will argue that Washington was not the author of this prayer.

413. George Washington, "Prayer for Guidance," July 17, 1783.

414. Johnson, *Washington's Prayer Journal*, 122.

415. Ps 113:3 (KJV).

416. Johnson, *Washington's Prayer Journal*, 122.

417. Lillback and Newcombe, *George Washington's Sacred Fire*, 83.

418. Lillback and Newcombe, *George Washington's Sacred Fire*, 83.

419. Thompson, *In the Hands of a Good Providence*, 36.

420. Lillback and Newcombe, *George Washington's Sacred Fire*, 84.

421. Lillback and Newcombe, *George Washington's Sacred Fire*, 84.

422. Thompson, *In the Hands of a Good Providence*, 77–78.

423. Lillback and Newcombe, *George Washington's Sacred Fire*, 86.

424. Lillback and Newcombe, *George Washington's Sacred Fire*, 86.

425. Lillback and Newcombe, *George Washington's Sacred Fire*, 82.

426. Thompson, *In the Hands of a Good Providence*, 92.

427. Niemcewicz, *Life of Washington*.

428. Niemcewicz, *Life of Washington*.

429. Thompson, *In the Hands of a Good Providence*, 92.

430. General David Cobb, quoted in Thompson, *In the Hands of a Good Providence*, 92.

431. George Washington, "Letter to the Hebrew Congregation of Newport," August 18, 1790.

432. Oney Judge Staines, quoted in Dunbar, *Never Caught*, 139.

433. "Advertisement for the Capture of Oney Judge," *Philadelphia Gazette*, May 24, 1796. Washington said in the advertisement, "Ten dollars will be paid to any person who will bring her home, if taken in the city, or on board any vessel." Oney Judge Staines (1773–1848) escaped the presidential mansion in Philadelphia. Later, she relocated to New Hampshire, where she spent the rest of her life.

434. Benjamin Chase, letter to the editor, *The Liberator*, January 1, 1847; as quoted in Blassingame, *Slave Testimony*, 248–50. When Oney Judge Staines first escaped from the home of George Washington, she took passage on a vessel bound for Portsmouth, New Hampshire. When Washington found out that she had done this, he sent his nephew, Burwell Bassett Jr., to "prevail on her to return." When Bassett saw her, he used all the persuasion he could muster, but she utterly refused to return to the Washingtons. Bassett returned "with orders to take her by force." When Governor John Langdon heard of these plans, he told Oney that she must leave New Hampshire that evening. Mrs. Staines hired a carriage and horse from a local stable, and she escaped to the home of John Jack, a free black man. Jack lived in Greenland, New Hampshire, where Mrs. Staines remained for the rest of her life.

435. Novak and Novak, *Washington's God*, 121.

436. Smith, *Life, Conversion, Preaching, Travels*.

437. Novak and Novak, *Washington's God*, 121.

438. Ps 35:1 (KJV).

439. See the painting "The First Prayer in Congress" by T. H. Matteson.

440. Rhodehamel, *George Washington*, 159.

441. Rhodehamel, *George Washington*, 159.

442. Chester A. Arthur, "Oath of Office," September 20, 1881.

443. Steiner, *Religious Beliefs of Our Presidents*, 16–17.

444. Steiner, *Religious Beliefs of Our Presidents*, 16–17.

445. Steiner, *Religious Beliefs of Our Presidents*, 16–17.

446. Steiner, *Religious Beliefs of Our Presidents*, 16–17.

447. Thompson, *In the Hands of a Good Providence*, 97.

448. Thompson, *In the Hands of a Good Providence*, 97.

449. Thompson, *In the Hands of a Good Providence*, 97.

450. Thompson, *In the Hands of a Good Providence*, 97.

451. Thompson, *In the Hands of a Good Providence*, 97.

452. Thompson, *In the Hands of a Good Providence*, 97.

453. Thompson, *In the Hands of a Good Providence*, 125.

454. David Holmes, quoted in Thompson, *In the Hands of a Good Providence*, 73–74.

455. Keathley, "Praying for America."

456. Keathley, "Praying for America," para. 2.

457. Weems and Cunliffe, *Life of George Washington*, 99. See also "Isaac Potts."

458. Weems and Cunliffe, *Life of George Washington*, 100.

459. Weems and Cunliffe, *Life of George Washington*, 100.

460. Snowden, *George Washington*.

461. Thompson, *In the Hands of a Good Providence*, 98.

462. Thompson, *In the Hands of a Good Providence*, 98.

463. Thompson, *In the Hands of a Good Providence*, 98.

464. Thompson, *In the Hands of a Good Providence*, 98.

465. Thompson, *In the Hands of a Good Providence*, 98.

466. Thompson, *In the Hands of a Good Providence*, 98; Decatur and Lear, *Private Affairs of George Washington*, 199–200.

Section VII

467. Dwight, *Discourse, Delivered at New-Haven*, 10.

468. Rev. Dr. Bird Wilson, quoted in Remsburg, *Six Historic Americans*. Wilson even goes so far as to declare: "The founders of our nation were nearly all Infidels, and that of the presidents who had thus far been elected [George Washington, John Adams, Thomas Jefferson, James Madison, James Monroe, John Quincy Adams, and Andrew Jackson]—not a one had professed a belief in Christianity (Remsburg, *Six Historic Americans*, 120).

469. LaHaye, *Faith of the Founding Fathers*, 91.

470. LaHaye, *Faith of the Founding Fathers*, 105–6.

471. Martin, "Why George Washington Was Not a Deist," para. 3.

472. Lillback, *George Washington's Sacred Fire*.

473. Martin, "Why George Washington Was Not a Deist," para. 4. We may add other characteristics concerning what counts as a Christian in contemporary American life, including Biblical inerrancy and others.

474. Bays, *This Anglican Church of Ours*, 30.

475. Winiarski, *Darkness Falls in the Land*.

476. Johnson, *George Washington*, 17–25.

477. George Washington, "General Order to Troops," May 5, 1787.

478. George Washington, "Prayer Journal," May 14, 1787.

479. George Washington, "Prayer Journal," October 16, 1789.

480. George Washington, "Prayer Journal," October 16, 1789.

481. George Washington, "Prayer Journal," October 16, 1789.

482. Johnson, *George Washington*, 23.

483. Luke 14:13–14 (KJV).

484. Johnson, *George Washington*, 23.

485. Johnson, *George Washington*, 24.

486. Johnson, *George Washington*, 25.

487. Johnson, *George Washington*, 25.

488. Johnson, *George Washington*, 25.

489. Johnson, *George Washington*, 22.

490. Johnson, *George Washington*, 23.

491. Johnson, *George Washington*, 23.

492. Johnson, *George Washington*, 24. George Washington to Continental Congress, September 26, 1774.

493. Johnson, *George Washington*, 25.

494. Thomas Jefferson to James Madison, February 1, 1800.

495. Thomas Jefferson to James Madison, February 1, 1800.

496. George Washington to General Committee of the United Baptists Churches of Virginia, May 10, 1789.

497. George Washington to General Israel Putnam, October 19, 1777. General Putnam (1718–90), called "Old Put" by his men, was one

of the heroes at the Battle of Bunker Hill. In his day, there were a number of folktales told about his courage and bravery.

498. Sparks, *Writings of George Washington*, 31–34.

499. Letter from the General Assembly of the Presbyterian Church in the U.S.A to George Washington, May 26, 1789.

500. Boller, *George Washington and Religion*, 279n7.

501. John Marshall, quoted in Smith, *John Marshall*, 92.

502. Sparks, *Writings of George Washington*, 31–34.

503. Sparks, *Writings of George Washington*.

504. Sparks, *Writings of George Washington*, 33.

505. George Washington, "Christmas Day." This is a childhood poem, copied in 1745.

506. Avlon, *Washington's Farewell*, 151.

507. Avlon, *Washington's Farewell*, 151.

508. Sparks, *Writings of George Washington*, 33.

509. Sparks, *Writings of George Washington*, 33.

510. Thompson, *In the Hands of a Good Providence*, 33–34.

511. Thompson, *In the Hands of a Good Providence*, 33–34.

512. Jeff Sessions, quoted in Haselby, "What Politicians Mean," para. 1.

513. LaHaye, *Faith of our Founding Fathers*, 90.

514. LaHaye, *Faith of our Founding Fathers*, 113.

515. Lambert, *Founding Fathers and the Place of Religion*, 161.

516. Stone, "World of the Framers," 7–8.

517. Moede, "This Is a Christian Nation."

518. Moede, "This Is a Christian Nation."

519. Moede, "This Is a Christian Nation."

520. National Reform Association, "Christian Amendment," March 1864.

521. National Reform Association, "Christian Amendment," March 1864.

522. House Judiciary Committee, "Action on National Reform Association Amendment," March 1874.

523. U.S. Senate, "Proposed Amendment to U.S. Constitution," 1950.

524. Kirk Fordice, quoted in Kramnick and Moore, *Godless Constitution*, 16.

525. D. James Kennedy, "Interview on America as Christian Religion," May 19, 1776.

526. Ralph Reed quoted in Arons, *Short Route to Chaos*, 54.

527. Pat Robertson, quoted in Shorto, "How Christian Were the Founders."

528. Shorto, "How Christian Were the Founders."

529. Shorto, "How Christian Were the Founders."

530. James Robison, "Invocation," Republican National Convention, August 23, 1984, Dallas, Texas.

531. James Dobson, quoted in Dallek, Review of *Godless Constitution*.

532. See the 1842 *Rhode Island Constitution*. Although Rhode Island affirmed the U.S. Constitution on May 29, 1790, it did not have a state constitution until November of 1842.

533. See the Maryland Toleration Act of 1649. This act was passed by the Assembly of the Maryland Colony on April 21, 1649.

534. See the 1776 *Pennsylvania State Constitution*. Since that time, Pennsylvania has had four other versions of its constitution, the most recent one in 1968.

535. Thomas Jefferson to Danbury Baptists, January 1, 1802.

536. James Madison, "Letter Objecting to the Use of Government Land for Churches," 1803.

537. James Madison to Edward Livingston, July 10, 1822.

538. George Washington, "Treaty with Tripoli," 1795.

539. Noll, *Scandal of the Evangelical Mind*.

540. See Judge William Rehnquist's statement in the case of Wallace v. Jaffree, 1985.

541. See Judge Antonin Scalia's statement in *Kentucky v. ACLU*, 2005.

542. See *Everson v. Board of Education*, 1947. In this decision, the establishment clause of the First Amendment was incorporated against the states. It also ruled that the state of New Jersey was not in violation of the establishment clause.

543. *Everson v. Board of Education*, 1947.

544. Iglehart, *Theodore Roosevelt*, 307.

545. Wilson, "Bible and Progress," 238.

546. Herbert Hoover, "Radio Address to the Nation on Unemployment Relief," October 18, 1931.

547. Harry S. Truman, "Exchange of Ideas With Pope Pius XII," August 28, 1947.

548. Richard M. Nixon, "Remarks at the National Prayer Breakfast," February 1, 1972.

549. Adams, *Works of John Adams*, 46.

550. See Justice Paul Stevens's majority opinion in Lee v. Weisman (90-1014), 505 U.S. 577 (1992). Also see the op-ed by Greenhouse, "Speaking Truth to the Supreme Court."

Section VIII

551. Novak and Novak, *Washington's God*, 9.

552. Novak and Novak, *Washington's God*, 9.

553. Vicchio, *Voice From the Whirlwind*, 45–68.

554. Vicchio, *Voice From the Whirlwind*, 14–16. Plato's doctrine of creation is found in his dialogue the *Timaeus* (30a to 48). A good secondary source on Plato's understanding of creation is Vlastos, *Plato's Universe*, 26–28.

555. Vicchio, *Voice From the Whirlwind*, 15–26.

556. Vicchio, *Voice From the Whirlwind*, 69–72.

557. Vicchio, *Voice From the Whirlwind*, 30–34.

558. Vicchio, *Voice From the Whirlwind*, 104–5.

559. Vicchio, *Voice From the Whirlwind*, 126–29.

560. Vicchio, *Voice From the Whirlwind*, 129–34.

561. Vicchio, *Voice From the Whirlwind*, 14–23.

562. Vicchio, *Voice From the Whirlwind*, 14–23.

563. Vicchio, *Voice From the Whirlwind*, 14–23.

564. Chernow, *Washington: A Life*, 23–26, 74–76.

565. Flexner, *Washington, the Indispensable Man*, 212.

566. Flexner, *Washington, the Indispensable Man*, 212.

567. Chernow, *Washington: A Life*, 76.

568. Chernow, *Washington: A Life*, 76.

569. Chernow, *Washington: A Life*, 192–93.

570. Chernow, *Washington: A Life*, 100–101.

571. Chernow, *Washington: A Life*, 100–101.

572. Chernow, *Washington: A Life*, 332–33.

573. Chernow, *Washington: A Life*, 332–33.

574. Chernow, *Washington: A Life*, 332–33.

575. Jonathan Todd to his father, January 19, 1777.

576. Jonathan Todd to his father, January 19, 1777.

577. George Washington to George Clinton, February 16, 1778.

578. George Washington to George Clinton, February 16, 1778.

579. George Washington to the Delegates of New Hampshire, December 29, 1777.

580. Lieutenant William Barton to Joseph Barton, February 18, 1777.

581. Lieutenant John Blair to Joseph Barton, February 24, 1777.

582. Jones, "Prayer of Valley Forge," epigraph.

583. George Washington, Valley Forge, April 21, 1778.

584. George Washington, Valley Forge, December 12, 1777.

585. George Washington, Valley Forge, December 12, 1777.

586. Pope, *Essay on Man*, 49.

587. William Augustine Washington to George Washington, May 14, 1793.

588. George Washington to William Augustine Washington, May 20, 1793.

589. George Washington to Martha Washington, June 18, 1775.

590. George Washington to Martha Washington, April 9, 1780.

591. Thompson, *In the Hands of a Good Providence*, 116–17.

592. Thompson, *In the Hands of a Good Providence*, 116–17.

593. Thompson, *In the Hands of a Good Providence*, 115.

594. George Washington to Northern Expedition Force, September 14, 1775.

595. George Washington to Northern Expedition Force, September 14, 1775.

596. Nagy, *George Washington's Secret Spy War*, 44.

597. Nagy, *George Washington's Secret Spy War*, 44–45.

598. Novak and Novak, *Washington's God*, 86.

599. Augustine of Hippo, *Civ.* 1.21; 4.15; 5.21; 19.25.

600. See, for example, Thomas Aquinas, *Summa Theologica* 2.2.

601. "Rules For the Behavior of Officers and Soldiers," the Continental Congress,

602. George Washington to Bushrod Washington, January 15, 1783.

603. George Washington to Bushrod Washington, January 15, 1783.

604. Mark 8:22–25 (KJV).

605. Mark 8:22–25 (KJV).

606. Mandelcorn, "Chanukah Candle that Inspired George Washington," para. 1.

607. Mandelcorn, "Chanukah Candle that Inspired George Washington," para. 6.

608. Mandelcorn, "Chanukah Candle that Inspired George Washington," para. 8.

609. Mandelcorn, "Chanukah Candle that Inspired George Washington," para. 10.

610. Mandelcorn, "Chanukah Candle that Inspired George Washington," para. 13.

611. Mandelcorn, "Chanukah Candle that Inspired George Washington," paras. 14, 15.

612. Mandelcorn, "Chanukah Candle that Inspired George Washington," paras. 18–21.

Section IX

613. For more on the Rules of Civility, see the following: Moore, "Introduction to Washington's Copy"; Moore's essay also was published as

a book by Houghton-Mifflin in 1926; Toner, *Washington's Rules of Civility*; and Rasmussen and Tilton, *George Washington*, 11–13.

614. Lillback and Newcombe, *George Washington's Sacred Fire*. Lillback quotes Alexander Hamilton's wife as saying that she knelt next to and received communion with Washington on the day of his first inauguration.

615. Novak and Novak, *Washington's God*, 243–46.

616. Novak and Novak, *Washington's God*, 243–46. For more on Washington's understanding of Providence, see Mary V. Thompson's *In the Hands of a Good Providence*

617. Novak and Novak, *Washington's God*, 243–46.

618. Novak and Novak, *Washington's God*, 95–118.

619. Novak and Novak, *Washington's God*, 95–118.

620. Newton, *Principia*, 400–426.

621. Among the primary sources on deism we have consulted, there are Blount, *Oracles of Reason*; Locke, *Reasonableness of Christianity*; Clarke, *Demonstration of the Being*; Collins, *Discourse of Free Thinking*; Wolaston, *Religion of Nature Delineated*; Chubb, *Discourse Concerning Reason and Religion*; and Voltaire, *Letters Concerning the English Nation*. Important secondary sources on deism include: Orr, *English Deism*; Gay, *Deism: An Anthology*; and Waring, *Deism and Natural Religion*.

622. George Washington to Samuel Langdon, September 28, 1789.

623. George Washington to the Rev. John Rodgers, June 11, 1783.

624. Other Enlightenment thinkers—such as Voltaire and Jefferson, for example—also eschew the letters of Paul, principally because he invented ideas like Original Sin that they believed corrupted the theological message of Jesus.

625. The widow's mite narrative can be found at Mark 12:41–44, and Luke 21:1–4.

626. "Washington Bible," Martha Washington's Papers, item #51, Mount Vernon Ladies Association.

627. Although Washington wrote letters to both the Newport and the Savannah Jewish Congregations, he visited the former congregation as well, but not the latter.

628. Chernow, *Washington: A Life*, 132–33.

629. Locke, *Letter Concerning Toleration*; Nadler, *Spinoza and Toleration*; Frenchman Pierre Bayle and his article on "Toleration" are in his *Dictionary*, as are many of his other books. For more on religious toleration in the Enlightenment Era, see Dominguez, "Introduction," 1–15.

630. See Thompson, *In the Hands of a Good Providence*, 84–86.

631. The "Circular Letter," June 8, 1783; "Farewell Address," September 19, 1796; Addison, *Cato*, 1–32. Other Stoics to be found in Washington's library at Mount Vernon include Epictetus, Seneca, and Marcus Aurelius.

632. Novak and Novak, *Washington's God*, 171–72.

633. Addison, *Cato*.

634. For Washington on prayer, see Thompson, *In the Hands of a Good Providence*, 91–123.

635. For more on Washington's leadership qualities, see Rees and Spignesi, *George Washington's Leadership Lessons*; and Washington, *Washington on Leadership*.

636. Weems and Cunliffe, *Life of Washington*.

637. Atkinson, "Washington's Prayer Journal"; see Camp, *George Washington*.

638. In addition to the born-again passage in chapter 3, Nicodemus appears two other times in the Gospel of John: at 7:50–51 and 19:39–42. In the former, Nicodemus reminds the members of the Sanhedrin that a person must be heard before he is condemned. In the latter passage, Nicodemus is present at the crucifixion. There is also an apocryphal mid-fourth-century Gospel of Nicodemus that appears to be a reworking of the earlier Acts of Pilate.

639. Novak and Novak, *Washington's God*, 121.

640. See the 1796 Treaty of Tripoli. This was the first treaty signed by the United States, between Tripoli (now Libya) and the United States. The official name of the treaty was "A Treaty of Peace and Friendship Between the United States and the Bey and Subjects of Tripoli, of the Barbary Coast." It was signed by Tripoli on November 4, 1796 and on January 3, 1797 by the United States.

641. Vicchio, *Voice From the Whirlwind*, 129–53.

642. Among the New Testament narratives that exemplifies the practical approach to the problem are the leper at Galilee (Mark 8:1–4); the dead son of the widow of Nain (Luke 7:11–16); the two blind men at Capernaum (Matt 9:21–30); the blind man approaching Jericho (Luke 18:35–43); and the man born blind (John 9:1–12).

643. For more on the problem of evil, see Vicchio, *Voice From the Whirlwind*.

Bibliography

Adams, John. "III. To the Inhabitants of the Colony of Massachusetts-Bay." http://www.masshist.org/publications/adams-papers/index.php/view/PJA02d092.

———. *The Works of John Adams, Second President of the United States*, Vol. 10. Boston: Little, Brown, 1856.

Adams, Robert Merrihew. *The Laws of Virtue: Excellence in Being for the Good*. Oxford: Clarendon Press, 2009.

Addison, Joseph. *Cato*. New York: CreateSpace, 2017.

Allen, Ethan. *Reason: The Only Oracle of Man Or a Compendius System of Natural Religion*. New York: CreateSpace, 2014.

Anonymous. "Sambo Anderson." *Alexandrian Gazette*, January 18, 1876.

Arons, Stephen. *Short Route to Chaos: Conscience, Community, and the Re-constitution of American Schooling*. Boston: University of Massachusetts Press, 1997.

Atkinson, Dan. "Washington's Prayer Journal: Fact NOT Fiction." *American Creation* (blog), August 8, 2008. http://americancreation.blogspot.com/2008/08/washingtons-prayer-journal-fact-not.html.

Aurelius, Marcus. *Meditations*. New York: Penguin Classics, 1900.

Avlon, John. *Washington's Farewell: The Founding Father's Warning to Future Generations*. New York: Simon & Schuster, 2017.

"Battle of Germantown." https://www.history.com/topics/american-revolution/battle-of-germantown.

Bayle, Pierre. *An Historical and Critical Dictionary*. London: Anderset, 2015.

Bays, Patricia. *This Anglican Church of Ours*. Winfield: Wood Lake, 1995.

"Benjamin Franklin on Interfaith Engagement." *Islam and the Founding Fathers* (blog), May 14, 2013. https://islamfoundingfathers.wordpress.com/2013/05/14/benjamin-franklin-on-interfaith-engagement/

Blassingame, John W., ed. *Slave Testimony, Two Centuries of Letters, Speeches, Interviews, and Autobiographies*. Baton Rouge: Louisiana State University Press, 1977.

Blount, Charles. *The Oracles of Reason*. London: N.p., 1693.

Boller, Paul F., Jr. *George Washington and Religion*. Dallas: Southern Methodist University Press, 1963.

Boyle, Robert. *Occasional Reflections*. London: Eebo, 2010.

Bray, Gerald. *The Faith We Profess: An Exposition of the Thirty-Nine Articles*. London: Latimer Trust, 2009.

Bryan, Mark Evans. "Sliding into Monarchial Extravagance." *William and Mary Quarterly* 67.1 (January 2010) 123–44.

Burton, Robert. *The Anatomy of Melancholy*. New York: NYRB Classics, 2001.

Byrne, Peter. *Natural Religion and the Nature of Religion: The Legacy of Deism*. Routledge Library Editions: Philosophy of Religion 5. London: Routledge, 2015.

Camp, Norma C. *George Washington: Man of Prayer and Courage*. The Sowers. Boston: Baker, 1977.

Carrier, Byron. "The Widow's Mite and the Widow's Might." *Earthly Religion* (blog), January 25, 2012. https://www.earthlyreligion.com/the-widows-mite-and-the-widows-might/.

Chernow, Ron. *Washington: A Life*. New York: Penguin, 2010.

Chubb, Thomas. *A Discourse Concerning Reason and Religion*. London: Cox, 1731.

Cicero, Marcus Tullius. *The Complete Works of Cicero (106 BC–43 BC)*. Delphi Ancient Classics 22. New York: Delphi, 2014.

Clarke, Samuel. *A Demonstration of the Being and Attributes of God*. London: N.p., 1705.

Collins, Anthony. *A Discourse of Free Thinking*. London: N.p., 1713.

Conley, Caitlin. "Faith and Family: Martha Washington's Bibles." http://gwpapers. virginia.edu/faith-family-martha-washingtons-bibles/.

Coughlin, Helen, transcriber. *Colonial Churches in the Original Colony of Virginia*. Richmond: N.p., 1908.

———. "Old Pohick Church." http://genealogytrails.com/vir/fairfax/churches_ pohickchurch_truroparish.html.

Dallek, Matthew. Review of *The Godless Constitution*, by Isaac Kramnick and R. Laurence Moore. *Washington Post*, February 18, 1996. https://www.washingtonpost.com/ wp-srv/style/longterm/books/reviews/matthewdallek.htm.

Davis, Kenneth C. "America's True History of Religious Tolerance." *Smithsonian Magazine*, October 2010. https://www.smithsonianmag.com/history/americas-true-history-of-religious-tolerance-61312684/.

Decatur, Stephen, Jr., and Tobias Lear. *The Private Affairs of George Washington, from the Records and Accounts of Tobias Lear, Esquire, His Secretary*. Boston: Houghton Mifflin, 1933.

Descartes, René. *The Passions of the Soul*. Edited and translated by Stephen H. Voss. Indianapolis: Hackett, 1989.

De Witt Hyde, William. *Stoic Six Pack*. 6 vols. New York: CreateSpace, 2016.

Dickinson, Josiah Look. *The Fairfax Proprietary: The Northern Neck, the Fairfax Manors, and Beginnings of Warren County*. Front Royal: The Warren Press, 1959.

"Did George Washington Swear During the Battle of Monmouth?" *Reader's Almanac* (blog), November 18, 2010. http://blog.loa.org/2010/11/did-george-washington-swear-during.html.

Dominguez, Juan Pablo. "Introduction: Religious Toleration in the Age of Enlightenment." *History of European Ideas* 43.4 (July 4, 2016) 1–15.

Dostoyevski, Fyodor. *The Brothers Karamazov*. New York: Farrar, Straus, & Giroux, 2002.

———. *Crime and Punishment*. New York: Dover, 2001.

Dreisbach, Daniel L. "Review: Reading the Bible with the Founding Fathers." *Institute for Faith, Work, and Economics*, November 13, 2017. https://tifwe.org/review-reading-the-bible-with-the-founding-fathers/.

———. *Reading the Bible with the Founding Fathers*. Oxford: Oxford University Press, 2014.

————. "Three Letters Offering a Window into George Washington's Views on Religious Liberty." *Institute for Faith, Work, & Economics* (blog), February 16, 2015. https://tifwe.org/george-washingtons-view-on-religious-liberty/.

Dunbar, Erica Armstrong. *Never Caught*. New York: Atria, 2017.

Dwight, Timothy. *The Conquest of Canaan: A Poem in Eleven Books*. Charleston: Nabu, 2011.

————. *A Discourse, Delivered at New-Haven, Feb. 22, 1800; On the Character of George Washington, esq. at the Request of the Citizens*. New Haven: Green, 1800.

Elliot, Jonathan, ed. *Virginia*. Vol. 3 of *The Debates in the Several State Conventions of the Adoption of the Federal Constitution*. Philadelphia: Lippincoat, 1901.

Federer, Bill. "Jacob Duché Continental Congress Prayer & a Caution to 'Stand Fast as the Guardians of Liberty.'" https://selfeducatedamerican.com/2019/01/31/jacob-duche-continental-congress-prayer-a-caution-to-stand-fast-as-the-guardians-of-liberty/

Fischer, Bryan. "The U.S. Was Founded as a Christian Nation—Here's More Proof." *RenewAmerica*, June 21, 2014. http://www.renewamerica.com/columns/fischer/140621.

Flexner, James. *George Washington in the American Revolution*. Vol. 2 of *His George Washington*. Boston: Little Brown, 1968.

————. *Washington, the Indispensable Man*. Boston: Little, Brown, 1969.

Franklin, Benjamin. *Articles of Belief and Acts of Religion*. New York: Private Printing, 1966.

Frazer, Gregg L. *The Religious Beliefs of America's Founders: Reason, Revelation, and Revolution*. Lawrence: University Press of Kansas, 2014.

Gay, Peter, ed. *Deism: An Anthology*. New York: Van Nostrand, 1968.

"George Washington Inaugural Bible." http://www.stjohns1.org/portal/gwib.

Gibbon, Edward. *The Decline and Fall of the Roman Empire*. 3 vols. London: Everyman's Library, 2010.

"God in the White House." https://www.pbs.org/wgbh/americanexperience/features/godinamerica-white-house/.

Greenhouse, Linda. "Speaking Truth to the Supreme Court." *New York Times*, April 16, 2015. https://www.nytimes.com/2015/04/16/opinion/speaking-truth-to-the-supreme-court.html.

Grizzard, Frank E., Jr. *George Washington: A Biographical Companion*. Oxford: ABC-Clio, 2002.

Hale, Matthew. *Contemplations, Moral and Divine*. London: Gale Ecco, 2010.

Haselby, Sam. "What Politicians Mean When They Say the United States was Founded as a Christian Nation." *Washington Post*, July 4, 2015. https://www.washingtonpost.com/news/posteverything/wp/2017/07/04/what-politicians-mean-when-they-say-america-was-founded-as-a-christian-nation/?noredirect=on&utm_term=.25d70b61d8ad.

Hardy, Robert. "Cato." https://www.mountvernon.org/library/digitalhistory/digital-encyclopedia/article/cato.

Hayes, Kevin J. *George Washington: A Life in Books*. Oxford: Oxford University Press, 2017.

Henriques, Peter. "George Washington's Enslaved Workers." https://www.c-span.org/video/?298058-1/george-washingtons-slaves.

Herbert, Edward. *De Veritate*. Berlin: Fromman, 1966.

Hervey, James. *Meditations and Contemplations*. London: Rivington, 1752.

Hirsch, Emil G. "Jehovah." In *The Jewish Encyclopedia*, edited by Isidore Singer, 87–88. New York: Funk & Wagnalls, 1904.

"The History of Pohick Church." www.pohick.org/history.html.

Holmes, David L. *The Faiths of the Founding Fathers*. Oxford: Oxford University Press, 2006.

Iglehart, Ferdinand Cowle. *Theodore Roosevelt: The Man as I Knew Him*. New York: Christian Herald, 1919.

Israel, Jonathan. *Radical Enlightenment: Philosophy and the Making of Modernity 1650–1750*. Oxford: Oxford University Press, 2001.

"Isaac Potts." http://www.ushistory.org/valleyforge/youasked/010.htm.

Jackson, Donald, ed. *The Diaries of George Washington*. 2 vols. Charlottesville: University of Virginia Press, 1978.

Jellinek, Georg, ed. *Declaration of the Rights of Man and Citizens: A Contribution to Modern Constitutional History*. Los Angeles: HardPress, 2012.

Johnson, Samuel. *A Dictionary of the English Language: An Anthology*. New York: Penguin, 2007.

Johnson, William J. *George Washington: The Christian*. New York: Abingdon, 1919.

———. *George Washington's Prayer Journal*. New York: Christian Liberty, 1971.

Jones, Gilbert Starling. "Prayer of Valley Forge May Be Legend or Tradition or a Fact, Yet It Remains Symbolic." *Picket Post*, April 1945. http://www.ushistory.org/valleyforge/washington/prayer.html#01.

Kant, Immanuel. *Groundwork of the Metaphysics of Morals*. Cambridge: Cambridge University Press, 2012.

Keathley, Mark. "Praying for America." http://infinityfineart.com/PrayingForAmericabymarkkeathley.php.

Kilmeade, Brian. *George Washington's Secret Six: The Spy Ring that Saved America*. New York: Sentinel, 2013.

Kirk, Russell. *The Roots of American Order*. 4th ed. Wilmington: Intercollegiate Studies Institute, 2003.

Kramnick, Isaac, and R. Laurence Moore. *The Godless Constitution: A Moral Defense of the Secular State*. New York: Norton, 1997.

LaHaye, Tim F. *Faith of our Founding Fathers*. Brentwood: Wolgemunt & Hyatt, 1987.

Lambert, Frank. *The Founding Fathers and the Place of Religion in America*. Princeton: Princeton University Press, 2003.

Lear, Tobias. "The Last Illness and Death of George Washington." In *The Checkered Career of Tobias Lear*, by Raymond Brighton, 222–25. Portsmouth: Portsmouth Marine Society, 1985.

Leibniz, G. W. *Theodicy*. 1st ed. Chicago: Open Court Press, 1986.

Lengel, Edward G. *General George Washington: A Military Life*. New York: Random House, 2005.

Lillback, Peter A. "The Invisible Hand in George Washington's Leadership." *Cedarville Magazine*, July 2, 2014. https://publications.cedarville.edu/cedarvillemagazine/v2i2_summer2014/files/assets/basic-html/index.html#20.

———. "Top 10 Reasons Washington Was a Man of Prayer." *WND Exclusive*, April 19, 2014. https://www.wnd.com/2014/04/top-10-reasons-washington-was-a-man-of-prayer/.

Lillback, Peter A., and John Newcombe. *George Washington's Sacred Fire*. Bryn Mawr: Providence Forum, 2006.

Locke, John. *An Essay Concerning Human Understanding*. Indianapolis: Hackett Classics, 1996.

———. *A Letter Concerning Religious Toleration*. New York: CreateSpace, 2016.

———. *A Letter Concerning Toleration*. Edited by James H. Tully. New York: Hackett, 1983.

———. *The Reasonableness of Christianity, as Delivered in the Scriptures*. London: Churchill, 1695.

Mandelcorn, Yehuda. "The Chanukah Candle that Inspired George Washington." http://www.neveh.org/chanukah/chanwash.html.

Martin, Mark. "Why George Washington Was Not a Deist, but a Practicing Christian." *CBN News*, February 22, 2017. http://www1.cbn.com/cbnnews/us/2017/february/why-george-washington-was-not-a-deist-but-a-practicing-christian.

Marye, James. *Minutes of the Vestry Truro Parish, Virginia 1732–85*. Louisville: Gateway, 1995.

Mill, John Stuart. *On Liberty*. Dover Thrift Editions. New York: Dover, 2002.

Moede, Dewey. "'This Is a Christian Nation'—U.S. Supreme Court, 1982, Justice Brewer." https://www.fggam.org/2014/03/this-is-a-christian-nation-u-s-supreme-court-1892-justice-brewer/.

Montgomery, H. C. "Washington, the Stoic." *Classical Journal* 31.6 (Mar 1936) 371–73.

Moore, Charles. "Introduction to Washington's Copy of the Rules of Civility and Decent Behavior in Company and Conversation." In *The Papers of George Washington*. N.p., 1926.

Mouw, Richard J. *The God Who Commands*. Notre Dame: University of Notre Dame Press, 1991.

Nadler, Steven M. *Spinoza and Toleration*. Amsterdam: University of Amsterdam Press, 2010.

Nagy, John A. *George Washington's Secret Spy War: The Making of America's First Spymaster*. New York: St. Martin's, 2016.

Newton, Isaac. *Principia*. New York: CreateSpace, 2013.

———. *The Principia: Mathematical Principles of Natural Philosophy*. London: Snowball, 2010.

Niemcewicz, Julian. *A Life of Washington*. Cracow: N.p., 1803.

Noll, Mark A. *The Scandal of the Evangelical Mind*. Grand Rapids: Eerdmans, 1995.

Novak, Michael. *On Two Wings: Humble Faith and Common Sense at the American Founding*. New York: Encounter, 2003.

Novak, Michael, and Jana Novak. *Washington's God: Religion, Liberty, and the Father of our Country*. New York: Basic Books, 2006.

Orr, John. *English Deism: Its Roots and Its Fruits*. Grand Rapids: Eerdmans, 1934.

Packer, James I., and Roger T. Beckwith. *The Thirty-Nine Articles: Their Place and Use Today*. 2nd ed. London: Latimer, 2006.

Paley, William. *Principles of Morality in Politics and Philosophy*. Oxford: Oxford World Classics, 2008.

Plato. *Euthyphro*. Translated by Benjamin Jowett. New York: CreateSpace, 2012.

Plato. *Euthyphro and Clitophon*. Translated by Jacques A. Bailly. Focus Classical Commentaries. New York: Focus, 2003.

Pohick Church. Alexandria: N.p., 1845.

Pollack, Michael. "Remembering Guy Fawkes Day, Or Pope's Day." *New York Times*, October 23, 2015. https://www.nytimes.com/2015/10/25/nyregion/remembering-guy-fawkes-day-or-popes-day.html.

Pope, Alexander. *Essay on Man*. London: CreateSpace, 2013.

Rasmussen, William M. S., and Robert S. Tilton. *George Washington: The Man Behind the Myths*. Charlottesville: University of Virginia Press, 1999.

Rees, James C., and Stephen J. Spignesi. *George Washington's Leadership Lessons: What the Father of Our Country Can Teach Us about Effective Leadership and Character*. Hoboken: Wiley, 2007.

Remsburg, John E. *Six Historic Americans: Paine, Jefferson, Washington, Franklin, Lincoln, Grant, the Fathers and Saviors of Our Republic, Freethinkers*. San Bernadino: Ulan, 2012.

Rhodehamel, John. *George Washington: The Wonder of the Age*. New Haven: Yale University Press, 2017.

Robison, James. "Invocation." Presentation at the Republican National Convention, Dallas, Texas, August 23, 1984.

Rosenthal, Michael. "Is Toleration Possible in a Liberal Society?" *Digital Jewish Studies*, January 5, 2017. https://jewishstudies.washington.edu/jewish-history-and-thought/toleration-liberal-society/.

Rousseau, Jean-Jacques. *Emile*. New York: Penguin, 2007.

Sanders, Henry Arthur. *The Washington Manuscript of the Psalms*. Oxford: Palala, 2016.

Schwartz, Barry, and Kenneth Sharpe. *Practical Wisdom: The Right Way to Do the Right Thing*. New York: Riverhead, 2010.

Scott, John. *The Christian Life*. Vol. 1. London: Forgotten, 2006.

Shorto, Russell. "How Christian Were the Founders?" *New York Times*, February 11, 2011. https://www.nytimes.com/2010/02/14/magazine/14texbooks-t.html.

Slaughter, Philip. *A History of St. George's Parish in the County of Spotsylvania, and Diocese of Virginia*. Bowie: Heritage, 1998.

———. *The History of Truro Parish in Virginia*. Edited by Edward L. Goodwin. Philadelphia: Jacobs, 1907.

Smith, Adam. *The Theory of Moral Sentiments*. New York: Penguin, 2010.

———. *The Wealth of Nations*. New York: Bantam Classics, 2014.

Smith, Elias. *The Life, Conversion, Preaching, Travels, and Sufferings of Elias Smith, Vol. 1*. Portsmouth: Beck & Foster, 1816.

Smith, Jean Edward. *John Marshall: Definer of a Nation*. New York: Holt, 1996.

Snowden, N. T. "Reminiscences of George Washington." In *George Washington, Son of the Republic: His Life and Writings*, edited by Paul Gerard, 163–79. New York: Gerard, 2011.

Sparks, Jared, ed. *The Writings of George Washington*, Vol. 1. New York: Palala, 2016.

———. *The Life of George Washington*. Vol. 1. New York: Palala, 2016.

Steiner, Franklin. *The Religious Beliefs of Our Presidents: From Washington to F.D.R.* Amherst: Prometheus, 1995.

Stone, Geoffrey R. "The World of the Framers: A Christian Nation?" *University of California Law Review* 56.1 (October 2008) 7–8.

Taylor, Justin. "What the Founding Fathers Really Thought About the Bible." *The Gospel Coalition*, January 10, 2017. https://www.thegospelcoalition.org/blogs/evangelical-history/what-americas-founders-really-thought-about-the-bible/.

Thompson, Mary V. *In the Hands of a Good Providence: Religion in the Life of George Washington and His Family*. Charlottesville: University of Virginia Press, 2008.

———. "Islam at Mount Vernon." https://www.mountvernon.org/library/digitalhistory/digital-encyclopedia/article/islam-at-mount-vernon/.

Toner, J. M., ed. *Washington's Rules of Civility and Decent Behavior in Company and Conversation*. Washington, DC: Morrison, 1888.

Towles, Amor, ed. *The Rules of Civility*. New York: Penguin, 2012.

Trainer, Ted. *The Nature of Morality: An Introduction to the Subjectivist Perspective*. Avebury: Aldershot, 1991.

Vicchio, Stephen. *Jefferson's Religion*. Eugene: Wipf & Stock, 2007.

———. *The Voice from the Whirlwind: The Problem of Evil and the Modern World*. Westminster: Christian Classics, 1989.

Vicchio, Stephen, and Mary Virginia Geiger. "The Origins and Development of Anti-Catholicism." In *Perspectives on the American Catholic Church, 1789–1989*, 85–103. Westminster: Christian Classics, 1989.

Vlastos, Gregory. *Plato's Universe*. Seattle: University of Washington Press, 1979.

Volkov, Andrei I. "Dostoevsky Did Say It: A Response to David E. Cortesi." https://infidels.org/library/modern/andrei_volkov/dostoevsky.html.

Voltaire. *Letters Concerning the English Nation*. Translated by John Lockman. Dublin: Faulkner, 1733.

———. *Philosophical Dictionary*. New York: Penguin, 1984.

———. *Treatise on Tolerance*. Translated and with an introduction and notes by Desmond M. Clarke. New York: Penguin, 2017.

Waring, E. Graham. *Deism and Natural Religion: A Source Book*. London: Ungar, 1967.

"Washington at Prayer." http://www.ushistory.org/valleyforge/washington/prayer.html.

Washington, George. "George Washington Papers, Series 5, Financial Papers: General Ledger A, 1750-1772." https://www.loc.gov/item/mgw500001/.

———. *George Washington's Rules of Civility & Decent Behaviour in Company and Conversation*. New York: Applewood, 1989.

———. *Washington on Leadership: Lessons and Wisdom from the Father of Our Country*. New York: Skyhorse, 2015.

Weems, Mason L., and Marcus Cunliffe. *The Life of George Washington*. Cambridge: Belknap, 1962.

Wilson, Woodrow. "The Bible and Progress." In *The Homiletic Review: An International Monthly Magazine of Current Religious Thought, Sermonic Literature and Discussion of Practical Issues*, 62:235–38. New York: Funk & Wagnalls, 1911.

Winiarski, Douglas A. *Darkness Falls on the Land of Light: Experiencing Religious Awakenings in Eighteenth-Century New England*. Chapel Hill: University of North Carolina Press, 2017.

Wolaston, William. *The Religion of Nature Delineated*. London: Palmer, 1724.

CPSIA information can be obtained
at www.ICGtesting.com
Printed in the USA
LVHW061316140120
643575LV00028B/616